D.H. LAWRENCE
AND ATTACHMENT

D.H. LAWRENCE
AND ATTACHMENT

Ronald Granofsky

McGill-Queen's University Press
Montreal & Kingston • London • Chicago

© McGill-Queen's University Press 2022

ISBN 978-0-2280-1127-9 (cloth)
ISBN 978-0-2280-1128-6 (paper)
ISBN 978-0-2280-1281-8 (ePDF)
ISBN 978-0-2280-1282-5 (ePUB)

Legal deposit third quarter 2022
Bibliothèque nationale du Québec

Printed in Canada on acid-free paper that is 100% ancient forest free (100% post-consumer recycled), processed chlorine free

Funded by the Government of Canada / Financé par le gouvernement du Canada

Canada Council for the Arts / Conseil des arts du Canada

We acknowledge the support of the Canada Council for the Arts.

Nous remercions le Conseil des arts du Canada de son soutien.

Library and Archives Canada Cataloguing in Publication

Title: D.H. Lawrence and attachment / Ronald Granofsky.

Names: Granofsky, Ronald, 1950– author.

Description: Includes bibliographical references and index.

Identifiers: Canadiana (print) 20220165483 | Canadiana (ebook) 20220165521 | ISBN 9780228011286 (softcover) | ISBN 9780228011279 (hardcover) | ISBN 9780228012818 (PDF) | ISBN 9780228012825 (EPUB)

Subjects: LCSH: Lawrence, D. H. (David Herbert), 1885-1930 – Criticism and interpretation. | LCSH: Attachment behavior in literature. | LCSH: English literature – 20th century – History and criticism.

Classification: LCC PR6023.A93 Z644 2022 | DDC 823/.912 – dc23

This book was designed and typeset by Peggy & Co. Design in 10.5/13 Sabon.

To Amara and Emil:
you are my heart's delight,
and you always send me to the land of smiles.

CONTENTS

Acknowledgments ix

Cue Titles xi

Introduction: Equilibrium and the
Lawrentian Paradox of Attachment 3

1 Abandonment Anxiety 36

2 Gender Identification 72

3 Marriage 106

4 Class 134

5 Stories of Homecoming 159

Conclusion: The Other Side of Otherness 186

Notes 195

Works Cited 223

Index 235

ACKNOWLEDGMENTS

My thanks, first and foremost, to my wife, Birgitte, who read the entire manuscript of this book at various stages of composition and provided excellent suggestions for improvement. Her expertise in matters psychological allowed her to point out a few instances of "psychobabble" that needed attending to. My friend and colleague Michael Ross also read parts of the book in manuscript and provided invariably sensible suggestions. As always, my thanks to Michael. Thanks as well to Keith Cushman, who helped out at one point by finding a reference from his extensive Lawrence collection. Because this book was done entirely during the Covid-19 pandemic, access to libraries was impossible, but I found the Hathi Trust useful in providing electronic versions of a number of works. I am also grateful to the two anonymous publisher's readers for their numerous constructive suggestions for improvement of the manuscript, many of which I adopted. It was a pleasure to work once again with the people at McGill-Queen's University Press, in particular Philip Cercone and the copy editor Grace Rosalie Seybold. Earlier versions of some of the material in this book appeared in print as follows: the Introduction and chapter 1 include material from my article "Attachment and Autonomy in *The White Peacock*: D.H. Lawrence Read through Margaret S. Mahler," *D.H. Lawrence Studies* 14, no. 2 (2006): 185–204, by permission of the D.H. Lawrence Society in Korea; chapter 2 includes material from my article "'His Father's Dirty Digging': Recuperating the Masculine in D.H. Lawrence's *Sons and Lovers*," *Modern Fiction Studies* 55, no. 2 (2009): 242–64, by permission of Johns Hopkins University Press; chapter 3 includes material from my article "Uncanny Encounters and the Paradox of Lawrentian Attachment in *The Rainbow*," *D.H. Lawrence Review* 41, no. 2 (2016): 72–94, by permission of the Editor; and chapter 4 contains material from my book chapter "Class" in Andrew Harrison, ed., *D.H. Lawrence in Context* (Cambridge: Cambridge University Press, 2018), 173–82, by permission of Cambridge University Press.

CUE TITLES

All references are to the Cambridge Edition of the Works of D.H. Lawrence

AR	*Aaron's Rod*
BB	*The Boy in the Bush*
EME	*England, My England and Other Stories*
FLC	*The First and Second Lady Chatterley Novels*
Fox	*The Fox, The Captain's Doll, The Ladybird*
FWL	*The First "Women in Love"*
K	*Kangaroo*
1L	*The Letters of D.H. Lawrence: Volume I: September 1901–May 1913*
2L	*The Letters of D.H. Lawrence: Volume II: June 1913–October 1916*
3L	*The Letters of D.H. Lawrence: Volume III: October 1916–June 1921*
4L	*The Letters of D.H. Lawrence: Volume IV: June 1921–March 1924*
6L	*The Letters of D.H. Lawrence: Volume VI: March 1927–November 1928*
8L	*The Letters of D.H. Lawrence: Volume VIII: Previously Uncollected Letters and General Index*
LAH	*Love Among the Haystacks and Other Stories*
LCL	*Lady Chatterley's Lover and A Propos of "Lady Chatterley's Lover"*

LEA	Late Essays and Articles
LG	The Lost Girl
MEH	Movements in European History
MN	Mr Noon
PFU	Psychoanalysis and the Unconscious and Fantasia of the Unconscious
Plays	The Plays
PO	The Prussian Officer and Other Stories
Poems	The Poems
R	The Rainbow
RDP	Reflections on the Death of a Porcupine and Other Essays
SCAL	Studies in Classic American Literature
SL	Sons and Lovers
SM	St Mawr and Other Stories
STH	Study of Thomas Hardy and Other Essays
T	The Trespasser
VG	The Virgin and the Gipsy and Other Stories
VicG	The Vicar's Garden and Other Stories
WL	Women in Love
WP	The White Peacock
WWRA	The Woman Who Rode Away and Other Stories

The Cambridge Biography of D.H. Lawrence

EY	John Worthen, *D.H. Lawrence: The Early Years, 1885–1912*
TE	Mark Kinkead-Weekes, *D.H. Lawrence: Triumph to Exile, 1912–1922*
DG	David Ellis, *D.H. Lawrence: Dying Game, 1922–1930*

D.H. LAWRENCE
AND ATTACHMENT

Introduction

EQUILIBRIUM AND THE LAWRENTIAN PARADOX OF ATTACHMENT

D.H. Lawrence and Attachment Theories

There at the navel, the first rupture has taken place, the first break in continuity. There is the scar of dehiscence, scar at once of our pain and splendor of individuality. Here is the mark of our isolation in the universe, stigma and seal of our free, perfect singleness.
   D.H. Lawrence, *Psychoanalysis and the Unconscious* (*PFU* 21)

An old, partially unresolved sense of self-identity and of body boundaries, or old conflicts over separation and separateness, can be reactivated ... at any and all stages of life.
   Margaret S. Mahler, *The Psychological Birth of the Human Infant* (4–5)

D.H. Lawrence began writing fiction by thinking about literary relationships. According to Jessie Chambers, he mentioned George Eliot as a model for what he hoped to do as he turned from poetry to longer-form narrative: "'The usual plan is to take two couples and develop their relationships'" (quoted in Worthen, *EY* 137), which is exactly what he does in his first novel, *The White Peacock* (1911),[1] and then again in *Women in Love* (1920). Developing relationships, of course, entails the examination of various aspects of human attachment, and while one can certainly think of other major writers who closely explore the intricacies of attachment in one or two works – Dickens's detailed portrayal of the nuances of a dysfunctional father-daughter attachment in *Dombey and Son* (1848), for example – no writer has delved more deeply, more consistently, or more effectively into the emotional depths of attachment than Lawrence. His thinking about the roles of merger and autonomy in binary relationships and in the related struggle to create a viable selfhood anticipates by many years the ideas of attachment researchers such as W.R.D. Fairbairn, D.W. Winnicott, John Bowlby, and pioneering psychoanalyst Margaret S. Mahler. Although Bowlby was keen to claim a continuity between his ideas and Freud's (*Attachment, Volume I* 7–13 *et passim*), attachment theory can be seen as part of a more general movement in psychoanalysis, beginning with Melanie Klein, towards a pre-oedipal approach: away from Freud's emphasis on the father and toward the prior impact of mothering on the child. In tandem with this movement, recent decades have witnessed an increasing scrutiny of Lawrence's work from a pre-oedipal perspective, as Elizabeth M. Fox's useful summary in her article "A Brief History of Psychoanalytic Criticism of D.H. Lawrence" serves to show.

Attachment researchers often build on each other's studies, although there are also differences among them. Bowlby, for example, sees the role of separation less positively than does Mahler. In fact, Bowlby (in a footnote) explicitly distinguishes his use of the term from Mahler's (*Attachment, Volume II* 23n). As Paul E. Stepansky argues, Bowlby views the process of childhood development as an instinctive one that humans share with other primates. His approach is "ethological" and describes behaviour that either promotes or inhibits attachment, whereas Mahler's is psychological and views such behaviour as "external analogues to an internal process" (Stepansky xxiii). Where Bowlby would tend to see healthy attachment as a survival mechanism, a building up of the requisite emotional repertoire to deal with the inevitable separation crises that occur in life, Mahler would view it as part of a "developmental agenda" that leads to a *necessary* separation on the way to individuation (Stepansky xxii). The "separation-individuation process" (Mahler's coinage) denotes "the infant's gradual intrapsychic 'separation' from the mother and the correlative understanding of himself as a distinct individual in a world composed of other equally distinct individuals" (Stepansky xvi–xvii).

Among attachment theorists, Mahler's emphasis on separation to achieve individuation corresponds most closely to Lawrence's creative imaginings of attachment imperatives and complications. However, for Lawrence, merger and separation more closely approximate opposed needs or desires (rather than Mahler's observed behaviour) that, when in optimal balance with each other and when appropriately met at any given stage of life, provide the basis for the further development of individuation and for long-term thriving. The terms "engulfment" and "abandonment," as I use them here, denote the fears associated in Lawrence with merger and separation respectively, fears that may come into play whenever the always-fragile, "trembling" balance (as Lawrence called it) between merger and separation tendencies is lost.[2] Like Mahler's, Lawrence's ideal was a secure attachment, which may be defined simply as one that "allows the individual to simultaneously value and maintain both independence and connectedness" (West and Sheldon-Keller 81). It is a state that promotes individual freedom from a base of security. One key word for it in Lawrence's fiction is "surety," and one of a number of images suggesting it is a tree's flowers and roots vitally connected to, but growing independently away from, each other.[3] Lawrence, then, certainly knew what a secure attachment might be, but it was a goal he fell short of achieving in his own life, and it is one that no character in his writing accomplishes for more than a brief time. In *The Rainbow*, for example, Tom Brangwen's father, Alfred, and his unnamed wife are able to live "in their separate ways from one root" (R 15), but we see hardly anything of them, so that this ideal state remains untested through plot and character development. When we get to the first Brangwen whose life unfolds before us, surety seems out of reach. Tom Brangwen lacks secure attachment because he can never live up to his mother's expectations of him. In a description that seems to combine negatively the idea of surety with the image of rootedness, he comes to feel "as if his being were wrong, and his mother's conception right," and thus "he felt that the ground was never sure under his feet" (R 17, 18).[4]

Mahler's work on attachment culminated in the publication of *The Psychological Birth of the Human Infant* in 1975, rather late in her life, but it can be traced back as far as 1949 (Mahler, *Psychological Birth* ix). She was born in Hungary in 1897, practised as a pediatrician and studied psychoanalysis in Austria, then left initially for England and then, in 1938, for the United States. She studied in naturalistic, clinical settings first abnormal and then normal symbiosis and separation in child-mother relations and the various subphases of the development from the one to the other, in particular "rapprochement," where the child experiences a conflict "between his fear of losing the mother's love and his fear of being swallowed up or 'engulfed' by this same love" (Mahler, *Memoirs* 162n). She pointed to a number of crises and obstacles that could seriously compromise the normal development from symbiosis to individuation and result in attachment problems or even mental ill health.

Mahler began her major research on the course of normal attachment as a control study for her ongoing research into abnormal attachment, but eventually the control group itself became her focus. From a longitudinal study that followed thirty-eight children from birth through roughly their first three years of life, where researchers observed the children through one-way mirrors in infant and toddler rooms, Mahler and her fellow investigators concluded that the normal "separation-individuation" process that takes the child from a virtual fusion with its mother to individuality – a psychic birth or "hatching" – is composed of four overlapping stages, which, in simplified form, may be termed differentiation, practicing, rapprochement, and consolidation. Mahler further divided the crucial rapprochement stage, which we may view as the turning point *within* the overall process, into three periods: beginning, crisis, and resolution. The crisis arises at the point where the "practicing" toddler realizes for the first time that it is not the centre of the universe (*Memoirs* 149). In this connection, we must consider how far Lawrence's own and, often, his characters' development differs from the normal hatching process, a growth that takes the child in a fairly linear fashion from symbiosis to individuation and in which the child frequently (but normally less and less frequently) seeks reassuring rapprochement with the mother even while developing a sense of separate selfhood.

From her studies of abnormal attachment, Mahler knew that the problems inherent in the separation-individuation process could result in, at one extreme, a failure on the part of the child ever to achieve normal symbiosis and instead the building of a "frozen wall" between itself and its mother (a form of autism); and, at the other extreme, a "fusion ... and lack of differentiation between the self and the nonself – a complete blurring of boundaries" (*Psychological Birth* 11). In such cases of what we might call psychic stillbirth, we are dealing with mental impairment. Even during a normal developmental process the child must negotiate a tricky balance between the need for a sense of separateness and the desire for closeness while dealing with the anxieties produced by the fear of abandonment (if separation is too accelerated or the caregiving unreliable) and that of re-engulfment (if closeness is too overwhelming or the caregiver narcissistic). In short, a rough balance is the key to healthy individuation based on a secure attachment. It is a state often difficult to achieve to an optimal degree, and any achievement requires a painful struggle. Lawrence describes the navel as "the scar of dehiscence," the stigma of "the first break in continuity" between mother and child, a constant bodily reminder of the pain of separation and the "splendor of individuality."

Building on Mahler's work in her intersubjective study *The Bonds of Love* (1988), Jessica Benjamin emphasizes the importance of mutual recognition in the role attachment plays in individual development. While she accepts much of Mahler's developmental model, Benjamin offers a corrective to its positing of a "unilinear trajectory that leads from oneness to separateness, rather than a continual, dynamic, evolving balance of the two" (25). Much of Benjamin's argument is persuasive and can be enlightening in a study of Lawrence's work, which also shows such a to-and-fro dynamic within single works and in his fictional oeuvre as a whole. Her work as applied to Lawrence often yields useful negative insights in the sense that we come to realize how so many of his major fictional characters fail at mutual recognition. The dynamic movement between oneness and separateness in his work tends often to be defensive rather than creative.

As with Benjamin, the comparison between Mahler and Lawrence often brings into relief what Lawrence's characters fail to achieve. It is almost as if Lawrence provides an abnormal control group for the theorist's exploration of normal attachment development. It is perhaps also of some interest that Mahler, like Lawrence, had a very strong bond with her opposite-sex parent, in her case her father, who always opposed any thought of her marrying (she eventually did), and a very fraught relationship with her same-sex parent, whom she felt was a rejecting mother. In fact, Mahler herself traced both her youthful difficulties with members of the opposite sex and her eventual desire to study attachment back to her relationships with her parents (*Memoirs* 2–12). As suggested above, Mahler's "symbiosis" (a metaphor, for Mahler, not a biological term[5]) and "individuation" are roughly equivalent to what I ascribe to the terms "merger" and "autonomy" in discussing Lawrence's dramatization or symbolization of the process, except that for Lawrence the failure to achieve secure attachment means that the positive aspects of both are invariably tinged with negative potential. Mahler's work and that of other attachment investigators give us a vocabulary with which to better understand and appreciate Lawrence as a psychological writer intensely interested in attachment, and they provide an externally corroborating system and theory for Lawrence's intuitive insights.

One example of validation is the way Lawrence often symbolically suggests the failure to achieve or maintain attachment equilibrium by a physical loss of balance, a fall of one kind or another, as in *The White Peacock* when Annable apparently falls to his death in the quarry at a time of crisis in his life or when a drunken George Saxton keels over. In fact, the scenes in *The White Peacock* involving a loss of balance or an actual fall are quite numerous.[6] This use of somatic disequilibrium to connote a lack of emotional or psychological balance continues in

Lawrence's subsequent fiction. One thinks of Gerald Crich's dramatic collapse to death in the snow in *Women in Love* and Aaron Sisson's crumbling on the street below Rawdon Lilly's room in *Aaron's Rod* (1922) as two examples. Such symbolic representation of faltering individuation is appropriate in Mahler's terms, since a child's learning to balance itself on its two legs and walk constitutes a critical stage in separation-individuation (*Psychological Birth* 75). In *Fantasia of the Unconscious* (1922), Lawrence describes learning to walk as a twofold process that begins with "a sympathetic cleaving to the earth" and proceeds to a "voluntary rejection, the spurning, the kicking away, the exultance in power and freedom" (*PFU* 89), the equivalent in developmental terms to the emblematic significance of "the scar of dehiscence."

Mahler studied children exclusively, of course, while Lawrence explores adult feelings and relationships. However, his work contains several vivid and persuasive portrayals of childhood consciousness, his depiction of adult emotions often includes a retrospective eye to childhood experiences as foundational, and his psychology works deal centrally with children and education.[7] Mahler observed behaviour in a clinical setting while Lawrence, a brilliant untrained if sometimes eccentric psychologist, intuited general principles based on his reading and his understanding of his own conflicted process of maturation, out of which he often tended to make general pronouncements. As Judith Arcana puts it, "Lawrence was struggling in his work to understand and describe that natural process by which children separate from their mother" (139).[8] One might add that he was also struggling to understand how a child could approach an unavailable father. Obviously, the adult need for closeness is nothing like that of an infant or child while the possibilities for autonomy are far greater, but the emotional residue from early life can enormously complicate later development, especially in so ill a child and so sensitive a man as Lawrence was.

Lawrence was alert to the impact of childhood experience on adult emotional health, as evidenced, among other places, in his two psychology books, *Psychoanalysis and the Unconscious* and *Fantasia of the Unconscious*. The purpose of the former work, writes Judith Ruderman, was "to uncover the dynamics of child-consciousness that underpin adult behavior" (*Devouring* 33). Bowlby recognized that psychopathological responses attendant upon childhood separation from the mother "are the very same as are known to be active in older individuals who are still disturbed by separations that they suffered in early life" (*Attachment, Volume I* xiii). Mahler also recognized that the process of separation-individuation "reverberates throughout the life cycle. It is never finished" (*Psychological Birth* 3). More recent attachment researchers agree. Malcolm L. West and Adrienne E. Sheldon-Keller, for example, maintain that "clinical work with adults suggests strongly that the attachment styles of childhood continue into later life" (vi).[9] At the end of his excellent biography of Lawrence's early years, John Worthen suggests that the play *The Daughter-in-Law* marked the point in his life when Lawrence finally freed himself from both of his parents and from his past (*EY* 460). In some sense, the biography is the narrative of a man who liberated himself through his writing. Lawrence certainly tried to do that, but I would suggest that Worthen underplays here the extent to which the conflicts laid down by the emotions of Lawrence's early life continued to demand creative expression in his efforts to master those conflicts through the repeated imagining of characters struggling with attachment.

The key to an understanding of the persistence of childhood tendencies into adulthood from the perspective of attachment theory is the "internal working model," the concept that, early in life, we all develop an inner model of external reality and of our projected self as a tool in the service of object constancy and psychological maturation. The apparent human need for narration may have something to do with its power to hone our ability, through the reading of or listening to stories, to develop internal working models of real people as well as fictional characters. On the other side of the printed page, so to speak, there is a degree of analogy between how the internal working model functions and the way in which writers create fictional characters by passing personalities or traits from external reality through the alembic of their imagination. So it is perhaps not surprising to see a clear account of the phenomenon in Marcel Proust's *Swann's Way* (in C.K. Scott Moncrieff's translation): "But none of the feelings which the joys or misfortunes of a 'real' person arouse in us can be awakened except through a mental picture of those joys or misfortunes ... as the image was the one essential element in the complicated structure of our emotions" (91). This rather Platonic mind-model may be said to correspond to the child's mental pictures of the self and of the people who are central in the child's life, but it is one that is subject to the distortions of emotional needs. Most attachment researchers have accepted the concept that, in Bowlby's formulation, human attachments are controlled by such an internal model, which serves, in the words of Bretherton and Munholland, "to regulate, interpret, and predict both the attachment figure's and the self's attachment-related behaviour, thoughts, and feelings" (89). In the words of another attachment researcher, internal working models are "largely unconscious interpretive filters through which relationships and other social experiences are construed and self-understanding is constructed" (Thompson 267). It seems that, once firmly established in childhood, an individual's model of self and of attachment figures, according to a paraphrase of Bowlby, tends to persist "even in the face of evidence that in [any particular] case the model is not appropriate" (West and Sheldon-Keller 52). Thus childhood experiences regarding attachment are foundational. Explicitly or implicitly, patterns of relating and their attendant emotions in Lawrence's fiction quite often come from childhood, both his own childhood and the imagined ones of his characters.

There is obviously a degree of artistic shaping of reality involved whenever real-life material is turned into fiction, but the kind of counter-evidentiary persistence to which the internal working model can contribute might help to explain how Jessie Chambers could perceive as a serious, even hurtful, distortion of reality Lawrence's version of the events related in the early versions of *Sons and Lovers* (1913) (material he asked her to comment on), or at least as a misrepresentation of *her* perceived reality (Worthen, *EY* 350–6). Even Frieda, who, obviously, had not been there, felt that Lawrence had missed the point of his own fictional rendering of his early life (Kinkead-Weekes, *TE* 42–3). Lawrence seems to have been aware of some such distorting influence on one's perception of an attachment figure and is able to make conscious what is normally an unconscious filter, at least in the mind of his character. In the early, autobiographically inspired story "The Shades of Spring" (first written at the end of 1911), the Lawrence figure, John Adderley Syson, now married elsewhere, comes back to visit his former intimate, the Jessie Chambers figure, Hilda Millership.[10] He comes to realize and admit to himself that she never was, in reality, the person he had taken her for; he had, in fact, invented a version of her in his own mind: "She only wanted to keep up a correspondence with him – and he, of course, wanted it kept up, so that he could write to her, like Dante to some Beatrice who had never existed save in the man's own brain" (*PO* 110). Similarly, Aaron Sisson in *Aaron's Rod* comes to a realization that his own internalized image of himself has been a distortion: "In his mind was pinned up a nice description of himself ... this he had insisted was really himself. It was his conscious mask. Now at last, after years of struggle, he seemed suddenly to have dropped his mask on the floor, and broken it" (*AR* 163). This is not principally to say that we need to take Lawrence's fictional versions of his lived experience with a grain of salt when trying to reconstruct his life (though we probably do); the point here is rather that attachment models are useful to illuminate the emotions that motivate his fictional embodiments.

That Lawrence continued to struggle with attachment issues throughout his life and career is also evident in the repeated pattern of self-sabotage in his life and in some of his characters' actions. In "self-sabotaging interactions ... [t]here is a bondage to a mode of relating learned originally within the family that narrows the possibilities for establishing ties to others" (West and Sheldon-Keller 71). In an argument influenced by attachment theory, in particular ego-psychology, James Cowan has suggested that Lawrence's boundary-violating relationship with his mother created a lifelong desire in him for interpersonal merger that inevitably triggered a compensatory need for separation (*Self and Sexuality* 31). In addition, Lawrence's "massive disappointment" in his father's failure to provide male nurturing led to a compulsive pattern of idealization of, attempted merger with, and disappointment in other male figures in his life (*Self and Sexuality* 43). He was constantly seeking but then often subverting abnormally close relations and then viewing the inevitable rupture as a betrayal. The result was an odd state of affairs that is perhaps best explained by an internal working model that allows for both an idealization of the other when that person seems to conform to the existing model and then a demonization when fear of rejection or of abandonment is unconsciously projected onto the same person and he or she exhibits a distressing and seemingly treacherous failure to live up to the positive aspects of the model. Lawrence's touchstone for betrayal is often the biblical Judas, the extent of whose treachery Lawrence at times questions by a realization that Jesus is equally responsible: "Why did Jesus let himself be kissed? Jesus was Judas' master ... Fiendish then of Jesus to be kissed" (*K* 226).

Using repetition, even compulsive repetition, to gain mastery is an idea we find in one of the most quoted sentences in all of Lawrence's published letters. It is found in the letter written on October 1913 to his friend Arthur McLeod: "But one sheds ones [*sic*] sicknesses in books – repeats and presents again ones [*sic*] emotions, to be master of them" (*2L* 90). Most commentaries that cite this letter place the emphasis on the clause preceding the dash, but equally important is the idea of repetition in aid of mastery. That mastery was never achieved only further justifies what otherwise seems like repeated self-subversion. In fact, Lawrence's recurring self-sabotaging pattern of behaviour, hurtful as it could be to himself and to others, may well have served a positive psychic and developmental need. His father could not aid much with his childhood separation-individuation process vis-à-vis his mother because Arthur Lawrence was rendered an unavailable or unattractive model by Lawrence's "mother's active interference" (Cowan, *Self and*

Sexuality 25). As a result, on the evidence of what we know of his life, it is reasonable to suggest that Lawrence suffered a psychological injury and unconsciously sought adult relations that might help him finally to succeed in the separation process he was never properly able to complete as a child with regard to his mother and in obtaining the closeness he could never achieve with his father. In a sense, then, he compulsively if unconsciously engineered unhealthy relationships and portrayed them in his fiction without ever quite finding the right formula for the secure yet liberating attachment his childhood had denied him. It is not surprising that Lawrence in later years felt that his upbringing had been emotionally damaging, as his remarks in letters and in works such as *Fantasia of the Unconscious* suggest. Bowlby has argued that when a parent seeks security from a child rather than the other way around, as Lawrence's mother clearly did in his case, this is "almost always not only a sign of pathology in the parent but also the cause of it in the child" (quoted in Cassidy 12).

None of Lawrence's fictional characters is as pathologically attracted to fusion with another person as, for example, Emily Brontë's Heathcliff is to Catherine even after her death in *Wuthering Heights* (1847), or as merged as the telepathically gifted David and Rosalind in John Wyndham's 1955 novel *The Chrysalids*, where David feels that "[n]either of us existed any more; for a time there was a single being that was both ... a brief symbiosis, sharing all the world" (150). And, though Jack Grant in *The Boy in the Bush* (1924) is described as "marooned in his own isolation like some shipwrecked mariner" (*BB* 124), none of Lawrence's characters is quite as isolated as Daniel Defoe's shipwrecked Robinson Crusoe before he encounters Friday or as forsaken as Jean Rhys's madwoman Antoinette, locked away in the attic by the Mr Rochester character in *Wide Sargasso Sea* (1966). Nevertheless, Lawrence's profiling of various positions along what we might call the attachment continuum does run the full gamut from the regressive desire for merger to the defensive posture that Bowlby called "compulsive self-sufficiency," in which individuals "deny their need for a loving close relationship to anybody and give self-sufficiency a central place in conducting their lives" (West and Sheldon-Keller 72–3).[11]

We can see an extreme example of a Lawrentian desire for merger (albeit one that alternates with periodic withdrawals) in *The Rainbow* (1915), when the young Ursula Brangwen becomes infatuated with her class-mistress, Winifred Inger, who skillfully grooms her pupil for intimacy. For Ursula, Miss Inger's presence is like "the rays of some enriching sun, whose intoxicating heat poured straight into her veins" (*R* 312). Eventually, "[a]ll separation from her mistress was restriction from living ... The two women became intimate. Their lives suddenly seemed to fuse into one, inseparable" (*R* 316). In the early story "New Eve and Old Adam" (written in 1913), Mr Moest feels at one point that he is merging with Paula, his wife: "They clasped each other close, body to body. And the intensity of his feeling was so fierce, he felt himself going dim, fusing into something soft and plastic between her hands" (*LAH* 181). In the chapter "Gladiatorial" in *Women in Love*, Rupert Birkin and Gerald Crich engage in naked wrestling and "seemed to drive their white flesh deeper and deeper against each other, as if they would break into a oneness" (*WL* 270), the desire for fusion seemingly initiated by Birkin, whose marriage proposal to Ursula has just been rejected. The two men work themselves "into a tighter, closer oneness of struggle" so that "often, in the white, interlaced knot of violent living being that swayed silently, there was no head to be seen, only ... two bodies clinched into oneness" (*WL* 270). Once Birkin and Ursula work out their differences and are committed to each other, we get this often-quoted description of interpersonal fusion on the day before they marry: "In the new, superfine bliss, a peace superseding knowledge, there was no I and you, there was only the third, unrealized wonder, the wonder of existing not as oneself, but in a consummation of my being and of her being in a new One" (*WL* 369). It is noteworthy that two of these examples involve same-sex relations, presumably less threatening in terms of engulfment than the heterosexual fusion that might recall the mother–male child dyad, but also no doubt an expression at some level of the desire for a closeness to Lawrence's same-sex parent, his father, that he was unable to achieve in childhood. Lawrence realized that the intimacy between himself and his mother was damaging. As he writes in an often-quoted letter of 3 December 1910: "We have been like one, so sensitive to each other that we never needed words. It has been rather terrible, and has made me, in some respects, abnormal. I think this peculiar fusion of soul ... never comes twice in a life-time" (*1L* 190).

A good example from the other end of the attachment spectrum, isolation, is the alcoholic and physically wrecked George Saxton, who, at the very end of *The White Peacock*, "sat apart and obscure among us, like a condemned man" (*WP* 325). In certain moods, Rupert Birkin in *Women in Love* can be quite misanthropic: "Why bother about human relationships? ... Why form any serious connections at all?" he thinks at one point (*WL* 302). While no Robinson Crusoe, Birkin does invoke Defoe's real-life model for his islanded character, after Hermione has biffed him on the head with a paperweight, but he does so only hypothetically: "If he were on an island, like Alexander Selkirk, with only the creatures and the trees, he would be free and glad" (*WL* 108).

Sounding very much like Rupert Birkin, another Lawrence incarnation, Richard Lovatt Somers of *Kangaroo* (1923), after a war of words with Ben Cooley, "wanted so much to get out of this lit-up cloy of humanity, and the exhaust of love, and the fretfulness of desire. Why not swing away into cold separation. Why not break the bond and be single" (*K* 138). That same novel ends with a very graphic, if symbolic, scene of separation with, it is worth noting, an implicitly maternal reference. The passengers on the departing ship, including Richard and Harriet Somers, hold coloured paper streamers clutched at the other end by the people on the wharf, and as the ship sails, the streamers break like so many snapping umbilical cords "blowing away, like broken attachments, broken" (*K* 357–8). The image is similar to the one in *Aaron's Rod* that describes Aaron's feeling of isolation: "Snap, snap, snap went the bonds and ligatures which bound him to the life that had formed him, the people he had loved or liked" (*AR* 178).

The gamekeeper in *Lady Chatterley's Lover* (1928) – Parkin in the early versions, Mellors in the final iteration – is initially rather protective of his solitude; he is clearly one of Lawrence's cold isolates before he is thawed somewhat by Connie Chatterley: "He had reached the point where all he wanted on earth was to be alone ... His recoil away from the outer world was complete. His last refuge was this wood. To hide himself there!" (*LCL* 88). Even a minor character such as Michaelis in Lawrence's final novel is anti-social and happy to be an outsider: "His isolation was a necessity to him" (*LCL* 28). In the experimental and allegorical story "The Man Who Loved Islands" (1927), the protagonist, Cathcart, finds himself yearning for less and less contact with the outside world, moving from one island to another until he is completely isolated, a voluntary Crusoe, as it were. He seems to personify Lawrence's description in the 1919 version of the Whitman essay: "Some men find the highest reality in the single, separate distinctness of the soul, an even starry aloofness: a supreme isolation: an isolation reached by infinite rejection, a rejection of All, leaving the one soul alone" (*SCAL* 359–60). The man's effort initially, he believes, is to create a new paradise with a few other people. However, his reclusiveness eventually becomes extreme, and he even develops zoophobia, a disgust with his sheep and his cat. Lawrence gives us no insight into Cathcart's childhood as to the origins of his compulsive self-sufficiency, and yet, even in this story, mother-child attachment imagery subtly intrudes. We get a description of Cathcart's tiny island in comparison to the one he initially inhabited as being "like the calf of the cow" (*WWRA* 152). When Cathcart's cow is found dead at the bottom of the cliff, we can discern where this is all likely headed and perhaps where it implicitly comes from in Cathcart's childhood pattern of relating. Even more extreme is the unfinished story "The Man Who Was Through with the World," written in May 1927 (*VG* xxvii), in which Lawrence gives expression to an unqualified misanthropy. After the hermit pays a visit to the local village for food, "[a]bsence from his fellow-men did not make him love them any the more. On the contrary, they seemed more repulsive and smelly, when he came among them" (*VG* 238). Finally, Aaron Sisson in *Aaron's Rod* decides after a nasty meeting with his wife subsequent to his desertion of the family: "Henceforth, life single, not life double. He looked at the sky, and thanked the universe for the blessedness of being alone in the universe. To be alone, to be oneself, not to be driven or violated into something which is not oneself, surely it is better than anything" (*AR* 128).

The tug-of-war between dependency and autonomy is one we all face in growing up. Winnicott has discussed how an adequate balance of attachment between a child and its mother is necessary for the formation of what he calls "continuity of being which is the basis of ego strength," a sense of the developing self that is a necessary precursor to individuation in Winnicott's scheme ("Theory" 593, 594). When merged with the mother at the beginning of life, the child is dependent on her "almost magical understanding of need" (592). But eventually, if the anticipation of need persists beyond the beginnings of the child's requirement for the process of separation to begin, the child "is left with two alternatives; either being in a permanent state of regression and of being merged with the mother, or else staging a total rejection of the mother, even of the seemingly good mother" (592). Contrarily, if "maternal care is not good enough then the infant does not really come into existence in the first place: there is no continuity of being" (594). Lawrence seems to have had an inkling of Winnicott's later-formulated concept, as we see in the character Jack Callcott in *Kangaroo*, at least as Somers sees him: "What was the consecutive thread in the man's feelings? ... His friends, even his loves, were just a series of disconnected, isolated moments in his life. Somers always came again upon this gap in the other man's continuity" (*K* 59). Often in his fiction Lawrence will use the image of hollowness to suggest a personality suffering from a lack of proper attachment that results in a missing inner strength and integrity.

Growing up, Lawrence experienced these vagaries of attachment in a particularly intense way. Because of his gift of acute observation, his high emotional intelligence, and his abilities in the realm of literary embodiment, he was able to articulate the conflict as few other writers have ever done. It was the concern of his psychic life to come to terms with his own complex feelings related to his childhood and its family dynamics, and it became a central theme in his writing. While the emphasis on specific areas of attachment varies in Lawrence from work to work and over the span of his career, and while the method of dramatizing conflicts and resolutions within the attachment dynamic takes many different forms in his work, there are two constants significantly and interactively at play: equilibrium and paradox.

Equilibrium

[T]he psyche is always threatened by forces that can disturb the dynamic balance.
    Daniel J. Schneider, *D.H. Lawrence: The Artist as Psychologist* (64)

Either extreme, pure symbiosis or pure self-sufficiency, represents a loss of balance.
    Jessica Benjamin, *The Bonds of Love* (158)

"The thing overbalances to one side – I hate a toppling balance"
    D.H. Lawrence, *Sons and Lovers* (*SL* 260)

We must recover our balance to be free.
    D.H. Lawrence, "The Reality of Peace" (*RDP* 34)

Equilibrium sounds like a neutral term from physics, but it becomes an emotionally freighted concept in Lawrence's fiction because it comes to embody the struggle to attain a viable or authentic selfhood that adequately balances the opposed attractions of merger and autonomy while avoiding the perils of engulfment and abandonment that are their respective shadow dreads. Relational closeness in Lawrence is both necessary and dangerous while relational distance is both attractive and frightening. Childhood sets the pattern for what becomes, in later life, a struggle "between the drive to attain a fully individuated, autonomous state, and the nostalgic desire to fuse with another in a re-creation of the infant's identification with the mother" (Hayles 91). Mary Ainsworth has described a variant of the merger-autonomy polarity in her analogous "attachment-exploration balance." It is similar to Bowlby's concept of the "complementary yet mutually inhibiting nature of the exploratory and attachment systems" in a child, the interactions of which ideally provide security while allowing investigation of the world around the child (Cassidy 8). Lawrence knew first-hand the kind of harm a child can suffer when the normal process of individuation is thwarted, and understood the emotional residue that clings to the adult from such early injury. He realized that a balance between merger and autonomy was paramount both for the individual's own psychological well-being and for his or her relations with others, and he developed models throughout his career to explore his intuitive understanding and his own acute needs and deficits. As a result, equilibrium becomes a principle in much of his expository writing and a narrative thread in his fiction.

We see crucial examples of an imbalance in the attachment-exploration dynamic in Lawrence in "The Woman Who Rode Away" and "The Princess" (both written in 1924). They are both complex and multi-levelled stories featuring protagonists whose exploratory urge has been frustrated by an attachment to a father or fatherly husband and who finally indulge those urges with tragic results. As attachment studies suggest, exploration is needed to fully develop individuation, but it can be successful only if undertaken from a base of secure attachment. Since both the unnamed, titular woman of "The Woman Who Rode Away" and Dollie Urquhart of "The Princess" are attached to narcissistic men, they never attain such a secure base, and their explorations end very badly. Lawrence's portrayal of Dollie channels his realization of the damage done to his maturing self by his too-close attachment to a narcissistic mother. Dollie's self-centred father is a good example of Bowlby's compulsive self-sufficiency: "He was always charming, courteous, perfectly gracious in that hushed, musical voice of his. But absent. When all came to all, he just wasn't there" (*SM* 159). His emotional unavailability virtually kills his wife after three years of marriage, and the child, Dollie, grows up serving his needs and being inculcated by him with a false sense of self-sufficiency while he ends his days in occasional bouts of madness. Paul Wood, using R.D. Laing's concept of the divided self to understand Dollie, suggests that "Lawrence shows this denial of the need for emotional engagement to be the living legacy of a father almost psychotically self-sufficient" (20). Dollie feels the need for connection after her father's death and wishes to explore the wider world in a way her deficient upbringing denied her. She wants to ride up into the Rocky Mountains with the guide Romero in order to see wild animals. She gets her wish, but when she asks Romero to warm her during the frigid night and he forces her sexually, her strong, defensive attitude of self-sufficiency fuels her resistance. She realizes that "she had *willed* that it should happen to her" but really "[s]he wanted to keep herself to herself" (*SM* 188). The exploration she has yearned for is based on a self-sufficiency that is artificial rather than on a secure attachment, and, as a result, it ends in disaster with Romero killed and Dollie slightly crazed. She has not developed at all by the end: she seems to resurrect her father by marrying an elderly man, and she views Romero as having been mad.

Another interesting example of the dynamics of the attachment-exploration paradigm comes in *Mr Noon* (worked on from 1921 to 1922), Lawrence's never-finished novel that closely tracks his earliest time together with Frieda, as Mark Kinkead-Weekes details in his biography of Lawrence's middle years (*TE* 34–5). Toward the end of the work, Gilbert Noon and Johanna are setting off on one of their many treks to explore and eventually cross the Alps and arrive in northern Italy: "They set their breasts forward again towards the unknown" (*MN* 273). Unfortunately for Gilbert, part of his unknown involves an ignorance of what Johanna has been up to behind his back. For Gilbert is unaware that she has recently made love with Stanley, a new acquaintance who accompanied them on part of the journey along with his friend Terry (portraits of Harold Hobson and David Garnett, respectively). In a fit of pique, Johanna tells Gilbert of her escapade, and he forgives her, much too readily for her liking, as it turns out. Gilbert clings "to her passionately in a sudden passion of self-annihilation" (*MN* 276). They then take a wrong turn and end up mistaking the way and going in a circle back to the town of Sterzing, whence they began the journey (*MN* 278–9). Noon is bitter, as Lawrence had been, at this mistake, and there is no indication of any unconscious motive at work. However, the involuntary return to the already-known in the fiction as well as in Lawrence's life can serve symbolically to suggest one aspect of the attach-explore paradigm: a reluctant return to the security of the familiar – in this instance, in the form of a place – from exploring the unknown, in the wake of the sudden discovery of the unreliability of the person identified most with security and proxy motherhood. We might compare this symbolic retreat with Paul Morel's thoughts about his mother's suffocating influence: "sometimes he hated her, and pulled at her bondage. His life wanted to free itself of her. It was like a circle where life turned back on itself" (*SL* 389). The unreliability of caregiving removes the secure base, so to speak, and leads to a more clingy attachment, but, at the same time, that need for attachment is resented. The Sterzing episode comes rather pointedly soon after Stanley's numerous denunciations of motherhood, and his mother specifically: "men shouldn't have mothers," concludes the narrator (*MN* 256). In life, remarks Kinkead-Weekes, Frieda's infidelity "must have been a painful blow to Lawrence, who had so recently come to believe that she was committed to him at last" (*TE* 35).

Lawrence's critics have understood the importance of balance in his work from the very start. We know from Jessie Chambers – in effect, his first critic – that Lawrence consciously strove for "a sort of balance" in his debut novel, *The White Peacock*, and argued for the necessity of keeping the gamekeeper Frank Annable in the novel with an appeal to the demands of balance. In her memoir of Lawrence, Chambers quotes him as saying of Annable, "He *has* to be there. Don't you see why? He makes a sort of balance. Otherwise it's too much one thing, too much *me*" (Chambers 117). As Andrew Harrison points out, what the gamekeeper represents is not really external to Lawrence's "me." The first-person protagonist of the novel, Cyril Beardsall, and Annable represent warring aspects of Lawrence that he was trying to balance fictionally: "The truth was that Cyril's spirituality had come to seem uninteresting, and even distasteful, to Lawrence; Annable's physicality and cynicism represented another side of his nature" (*Life* 25). As Rosemary Reeves Davies expressed it quite a few years ago in an article about Lawrence's dualism and psychic division, "That there was within [Lawrence] a psychic split of a very severe kind is taken for granted by everyone who has written about him" (220). Lawrence sometimes describes a balance within a fourfold division, as in *Psychoanalysis and the Unconscious*, where he delineates "each of the four circuits to be established to perfection and yet maintained in pure equilibrium with all the others" (*PFU* 41). However, more often his categorization is dual, and he is seen as an inveterately dualistic thinker in part because of his frequent evocation of bipolar balance as an ideal in many realms of human existence.

The dualism is a function of the insights derived from Lawrence's own constant striving for balance. He generalizes a dualistic view to include the very cosmos in "The Two Principles" and his entire culture, for example, in the final version of his chapter on Hawthorne's *The Scarlet Letter* in *Studies in Classic American Literature* (1923): "It's no good. Dual we are. The cross ... We are divided against ourselves" (*SCAL* 83).[12] However, though many critics, including, notably, H.M. Daleski in his groundbreaking *The Forked Flame* (1965), have discussed Lawrence's dualism and concept of balance in some considerable detail, few, with the exception of Daniel J. Schneider and James Cowan, have bothered to examine exactly what Lawrence's concept of equilibrium means for his fiction, particularly his characterization, or where it comes from.[13] That many Lawrence characters, such as Paul Morel, Will Brangwen, and Gerald Crich, are frequently in a state of emotional turmoil can be ascribed in large part to their attempts to find an unattainable balance, a search that places them in an untenable situation of paradox as I discuss below.

Schneider names balance as the second of four ideas that Lawrence derived early in his life from the writings of "the materialists," Huxley, Darwin, Spencer, and Haeckel: "[T]he force or energy in nature, which is manifested in attraction and repulsion, always seeks a balance: the fundamental rhythm of nature is that of alternation, oscillation, or action and reaction" (*Artist* 10). Schneider reminds us that, in Lawrence's intricately built if somewhat questionable theory of the unconscious in his two psychology works, equilibrium functions as an important concept, involving as it does four centres acting along two axes: "The self develops healthily – or moves toward maximum of being – as long as all four centers exist in dynamic balance ... If permitted to function without interference, the self-regulating mechanisms of the unconscious would ensure perfect health. But in its dealings with the external world, the psyche is always threatened by forces that can disturb the dynamic balance" (*Artist* 63, 64). It is worth noting in this connection that behind Lawrence's objective-subjective and sympathetic-voluntary divisions in the psychology works, one may discern the dichotomy of merger (objective, sympathetic) versus autonomy (subjective, voluntary).

In Aldous Huxley's fictional portrayal of Lawrence in *Point Counter Point* (1928), we have one of the most memorable, if somewhat simplified, expressions of Lawrence's concept of equilibrium to be found anywhere, including in Lawrence's own writing. In chapter 34 of Huxley's novel, Mark Rampion is holding forth in his recognizably Lawrentian manner to Philip Quarles, Denis Burlap, and Maurice Spandrell about the ills of modern society and life. Because Philip's young son is ill – he will later die of meningitis – the topic of children comes up, and Rampion expresses the fear that his children will become "stuffed with knowledge" if only to spite him (402). In general, children cannot help spiting their parents, he claims, "'because the parents have probably gone too far in one direction and nature's reacting, trying to get back to the state of equilibrium.'" His own children, he predicts, will end up with "'[h]orrid little brains that do their best to suppress the accompanying hearts and bowels'" (403). What is at issue here is a kind of cultural equilibrium (or disequilibrium) – within the family, within society – mediated, it is worth noting, by nature. As Lawrence writes in *Fantasia of the Unconscious*, "We have so unduly insisted on and exaggerated the upper or spiritual or selfless mode ... that we have caused already a dangerous over-balance in the natural psyche" (*PFU* 113). Rampion goes on to set out his idea of balance within the individual by the use of a striking metaphor to describe the difficulty of attaining and preserving a certain kind of balance: "A man's a creature on a tight-rope, walking delicately, equilibrated, with mind and consciousness and spirit at one end of his balancing pole and body and instinct and all that's unconscious and earthy and mysterious at the other. Balanced. Which is damnably difficult. And the only absolute he can ever really know is the absolute of perfect balance" (408–9).

In fact, Lawrence's writing both assumes and loudly declares the desirability of balance in nearly all possible relational situations, and at times the simplicity and universality of the concept is beautifully attractive. In the *Study of Thomas Hardy* (begun in 1914; posthumously published), for example, Lawrence sets up a series of interdependent, if not exactly interchangeable, binaries – male and female, Father and Son, Law and Love, the two Wills, etc. Here, Lawrence seems more interested in the dual system itself rather than the ideal of balance, but he does discuss marriage, reconciliation, stability, the Holy Ghost, and other terms that explore the ideal state of the play of forces between the two poles. With respect to the Will-to-Motion and the Will-to-Inertia, for example, he writes: "Since there is never to be found a perfect balance or accord of the two Wills ... so must the human effort be always to recover balance, to symbolise and so to possess that which is missing." The two Wills between them "cause the whole of life, from the ebb and flow of a wave, to the stable equilibrium of the whole universe" (*STH* 59). The tragedy in Hardy's *Jude the Obscure*, Lawrence argues, "is the result of overdevelopment of one principle of human life at the expense of the other" (*STH* 121) – in other words, the consequence of disequilibrium.

By *The Crown* (first two parts published in 1915), especially in the first essay, we see that the necessity for equilibrium has become more pressing as Lawrence plays with the presence in the United Kingdom coat of arms (since the 1707 union of the formerly warring England and Scotland) of a lion and a unicorn beneath a crown: "Is not the unicorn necessary to the very existence of the lion, is not each opposite kept in stable equilibrium by the opposition of the other[?]" he asks (*RDP* 253). Equilibrium is now presented concurrently with a positive view of conflict, perhaps an unconscious rationalization under the stress of a war that Lawrence consciously if futilely opposed: "And there is no rest, no cessation from the conflict. For we are two opposites which exist by virtue of our inter-opposition. Remove the opposition and there is collapse, a sudden crumbling into universal nothingness" (*RDP* 256).[14] The essay presents the crown, the rainbow, the iris, and other images of the fragile balance – the "perfect relatedness" – achieved when two conflicting forces are in equilibrium: "The crown is upon the perfect balance of the fight, it is not the fruit of either victory" (*RDP* 262). What is remarkable, though, is that even in an expository (if tendentious) work such as *The Crown* it is possible to discern, in tell-tale traces created by Lawrence's choice of images, the connection between equilibrium as a central principle and the emotions related to the difficulty of maintaining a balance between autonomy and merger tendencies in the self and in relationships. Thus, the "sudden crumbling into universal nothingness," when opposition ceases, sounds a note of fear, an anxiety that the self will be engulfed and disappear if it does not push back, as it were. Similarly, we see extended womb imagery – often displaced onto the image of a void or vacuum – in several passages where Lawrence is ostensibly discussing the cultural and social failure of his time but where emotional factors, in particular the fear of engulfment, are also at play: "A myriad, myriad people, we roam in the belly of our era, seeking, seeking, wanting. And we seek and want deliverance. But we say we want to overcome the lion that shares with us this universal womb, the walls of which are shut, and have no window to inform us that we are in prison" (*RDP* 255).[15]

In "The Reality of Peace," the terms of balance are variously systole and diastole, dark and light, autumn and spring, tiger and lamb, death and life, love and hate, and they pertain to the entire material universe: "All is somehow adjusted in a strange, unstable equilibrium" (*RDP* 48). The essay "Love" proclaims that "all force, spiritual or physical, has its polarity" and also uses the heart's systole and diastole as a metaphor for expressing a paradoxical view of balance: "So that the coming together depends on the going apart; the systole depends on the diastole; the flow depends upon the ebb" (*RDP* 7). The rose is the symbol of perfect balance.

Lawrence's presentation of his concept of equilibrium is often couched in philosophical terms, but the idea is, at bottom, an emotional one, and it is the emotional nature of the factors lying behind Lawrence's conception of equilibrium that determines its paradoxically labile character in his writing. In *D.H. Lawrence and the Trembling Balance* (1990), Cowan shows how, in a series of essays, Lawrence works out a subtle model of "an organic equilibrium characterized as a 'trembling balance' both within the organism and between the self and the other or between the individual and the environment" (16). Such a deliberately unstable balance was meant to contrast with the fixed conception of equilibrium that science pre-eminently propounded in Lawrence's view.[16] Hayles describes Lawrence's efforts to reach "that part of the psyche which is able to hold opposites in a continuing tension without needing to resolve them" (89), a negative capability very similar to Cowan's understanding of the "trembling balance" and a perfectly good description of paradox.

As Cowan's work intimates, there are several types of equilibrium in Lawrence's work, two of which are relevant to this study. The Huxley description of a man on a tightrope alludes to a balance between mind and body, that is to say within the individual, but the balance most Lawrence readers are familiar with, mainly from Rupert Birkin's philosophical musings about "star equilibrium" in *Women in Love*, is interpersonal. Perhaps the most succinct explanation of what Lawrence means by star equilibrium is put in the mouth of Gudrun Brangwen in a rather comical scene where she is discussing Birkin's philosophy with Gerald, literally behind Birkin's back, in the rear seat of a car being driven by Birkin himself: "'He says ... that you can find an eternal equilibrium in marriage, if you accept the unison, and still leave yourself separate, don't try to fuse'" (*WL* 290). The lack of such a balance, particularly in a sexual relationship between a man and a woman, can lead to a zero-sum situation in Lawrence where what is beneficial for one partner is detrimental to the other. Daleski has called this teeter-totter state of affairs "one up, one down" (using Lawrence's phrase from his 13 March 1928 letter to Witter Bynner renouncing the leadership idea that Bynner had criticized)[17] and argued that it characterized Lawrence's leadership period in particular.[18]

Actually, we see this zero-sum problem much earlier, in the 1913 story "New Eve and Old Adam," for example, when Paula complains to her husband that he absorbs life from her but gives nothing in return: "'You make an eternal demand, and you give nothing back. You leave one empty'" (*LAH* 166). And even earlier, in Lawrence's first novel, *The White Peacock*, essentially the same problem can be seen especially in the couple relationships of Leslie and Lettie and George and Meg. At Lettie's twenty-first birthday party, the narrator, Cyril, observes that as Leslie "became more animated, more abundantly energetic, Lettie became quieter" (*WP* 114). Late in the novel, George must acknowledge to Lettie that "'[m]arriage is more of a duel than a duet. One party wins and takes the other captive, slave, servant – what you like'" (*WP* 301). In *The Trespasser* (1912), too, we see a similar winner-take-all situation in the eventually tragic relationship between Siegmund and Helena: "It was not his passion she wanted, actually. But she desired that he should want *her* madly, and that he should have all – everything. It was a wonderful night to him. It restored in him the full 'will to live.' But she felt it destroyed her. Her soul seemed blasted" (*T* 87). In Lawrence's work, there is a kind of vicious circle whereby the lack of balance in such interpersonal relations is caused by and itself causes intrapersonal imbalance.

We see the culmination of such disastrous Lawrentian disequilibrium in the Gerald-Gudrun relationship in *Women in Love* in the chapter "Snowed Up": "Sometimes it was he who seemed strongest, whilst she was almost gone, creeping near the earth like a spent wind; sometimes it was the reverse. But always it was this eternal see-saw, one destroyed that the other might exist, one ratified because the other was nulled" (*WL* 445). But even at the beginning of their sexual relationship, there is a distinct lack of balance between Gerald and Gudrun, as we see when Gerald, in the throes of an existential crisis, finds his way from the newly dug grave of his father to Gudrun's bed. Like the blighted George Saxton in Lawrence's first novel, Gerald is "like a plant whose tissue is burst from inwards by a frost" (*WL* 345), and while he finds temporary restoration in Gudrun in this scene, it is at the expense of her well-being: "He found in her an infinite relief. Into her he poured all his pent-up darkness and corrosive death, and he was whole again ... And she, subject, received him as a vessel filled with his bitter potion of death" (*WL* 344). In the novella *St Mawr* (1925), the relationship between Lou and Rico is far from being as toxic as the Gudrun-Gerald attachment; nevertheless, here too, "[a]s soon as one felt strong, the other felt ill. As soon as the ill one recovered strength, down went the one who had been well" (*SM* 24).

The Crown warns that when two people interact egotistically, "then, when a man seeks a woman, he seeks not a consummation in union, but a frictional reduction" (*RDP* 283). So in *Women in Love*, Gudrun feels "driven up against [Gerald's] perfect sleeping motion like a knife white-hot on a grindstone. There was something monstrous about him, about his juxtaposition against her" (*WL* 346). For Gerald and Gudrun, as in *The White Peacock* and so many other places in Lawrence, when the male need for fusion with a female other (and the gender distribution is almost always in that direction), or for oblivion of self, overcomes the fragile equilibrium between autonomy and merger, there is a blurring of the roles of man/child and woman/mother as the male self reverts to infantile dependency, not merely to Mahler's rapprochement stage but a full-blown regression to the symbiosis phase: "Like a child at the breast, he cleaved intensely to her, and she could not put him away" (*WL* 345). Birkin and Ursula strive for "star equilibrium" precisely because the failure to achieve interpersonal balance can be so disastrous intrapersonally.

Conversely, successful interpersonal relations are possible only if the people involved are also more or less in equilibrium intrinsically. Sometimes, for example, Lawrence will describe the lack of intrapersonal equilibrium in decidedly spatial terms. What this generally means is that a balance between inner and outer cannot be found or preserved. Metaphorical self-implosion threatens if outer pressure is not met with a solidity or an integrity from within, if the person involved, in other words, is a kind of hollow being, like Conrad's "papier-mâché Mephistopheles" in *Heart of Darkness* (1902), about whom Marlow imagines "that if I tried I could poke my forefinger through him and would find nothing inside but a little loose dirt, maybe" (29). In a study of "The Man Who Loved Islands," John Turner helpfully defines psychological hollowness in general and the Lawrentian expression of it in particular as a trait of a person who is "dedicated to the creation of a false self, and therefore always prone to the haunting sense of its own inner unreality" ("Capacity" 266). Turner adds that the problem "typically originates with a neglectful or a possessive mother who fails to create for her child the belief in a benign world where he may safely find himself" (266). We see such a hollow-man development in the life of *The White Peacock*'s George Saxton. Toward the end of the novel, George tells Cyril that "'I seem thrown off my balance'" (*WP* 288) and that, in such a state, "'[y]ou feel awful, like a vacuum, with a pressure on you, a sort of pressure of darkness, and you yourself – just nothing, a vacuum – that's what it's like – a little vacuum that's not dark, all loose in the middle of a space of darkness, that's pressing on you'" (*WP* 287–8). Another example is the desperate gambit of Anton Skrebensky in *The Rainbow* to marry quickly after Ursula has rejected him. Fairly early on in their relationship, Ursula had detected Skrebensky's hollowness: "'It seems to me ... as if you weren't anybody – as if there weren't anybody there, where you are ... You seem like nothing to me'" (*R* 289).

Once more, the Lawrentian *locus classicus* appears in *Women in Love*. There we see a hollow woman in the person of Hermione Roddice, who, in spite of her superiority in both rank and wealth, feels an insuperable vulnerability: "there was always a secret chink in her armour ... It was a lack of robust self, she had no natural sufficiency, there was a terrible void, a lack, a deficiency of being within her" (*WL* 16). More extensively explored is the similar hollowness of Gerald Crich, whose always-unstable sense of self is in danger of collapse when his dying father leaves the running of the firm to him and he has effected his own obsolescence through technological innovation. The perfect machine once set in motion, he finds, needs no mover. Here the metaphor for equilibrium-disequilibrium within the self is the bubble, a recurring symbol in the novel. A bubble is a fragile phenomenon requiring for its integrity of form a precise balance between inner and outer pressure. At the end of the chapter "The Industrial Magnate," Gerald "knew there was no equilibrium." He has bouts of sheer terror when he doubts his own reality, even (or especially) when he looks in the mirror: "His eyes were blue and keen as ever, and as firm in their sockets. Yet he was not sure that they were not blue false bubbles that would burst in a moment and leave clear annihilation" (*WL* 232). And we may compare the "clear annihilation" here with the "crumbling into universal nothingness" of *The Crown* when opposition – in other words, a balance of pressures – collapses. At the crisis, when Gerald watches his father "slowly dissolve and disappear in death," the terms of equilibrium between inner and outer are starkly in evidence: "His will held his outer life, his outer mind, his outer being unbroken and unchanged. But the pressure was too great. He would have to find something to make good the equilibrium. Something must come with him into the hollow void of death in his soul, fill it up, and so equalise the pressure within to the pressure without" (*WL* 322). Gerald's strategy to do this proves disastrous in the long run, just as Hermione's dependence on Birkin for a feeling of completeness results in his escape from attachment. What Gerald needs is a stronger sense of self-solidity, but what he seeks, in effect, is regressive fusion through a symbolic return to the womb. He can never fill the hollow of his own soul by filling Gudrun with "dark and corrosive death," so their relationship becomes mutually destructive.[19]

The approach-avoidance nature of the Lawrentian equilibrium dynamic creates a tendency toward paradox. While, as suggested above, numerous critics have observed the importance of equilibrium in his work and others have pointed to its frequently paradoxical nature, few if any have linked the two causally. The very core of his psychological make-up induces Lawrence to create narrative elements that allow him simultaneously to move toward and to protect against the fusion with an other he both desires and fears. Huxley's characterization of Lawrentian balance, although limited to the mind-body duality in the extract from *Point Counter Point* above, is quite helpful because it graphically suggests how difficult it is to achieve balance and how momentary is any achievement. The tightrope walker can never stand still and yet retain his balance; his body must make a series of tiny adjustments or he will fall off the rope. Stasis paradoxically depends upon movement, so understandably what Lawrence's fiction most often depicts is the *failure* to achieve a stable equilibrium for any length of time.

The "trembling" aspect of Lawrentian equilibrium, its essential if paradoxical instability, is one analogue to the complex psychological conflict that gives rise to it in his thinking in the first place. We might also use the swings of a pendulum as a visual metaphor to illustrate the to-and-fro movement between merger and autonomy alternatives, or we can look to W.B. Yeats for a more nuanced metaphor. In oscillating between attachment extremes, many of Lawrence's characters become caught in a kind of Yeatsian double gyre of feeling. In *A Vision*, Yeats discusses how his "instructors" granted him a vision of a double cone or vortex, basically two intersecting triangles, as a representation of hidden reality. The apex of each triangle touches the base of the other (67–79). We can use Yeats's double gyre as a visual metaphor for Lawrentian equilibrium, in which the feeling of threat from one extreme (engulfment on one side, isolation on the other) diminishes as one moves toward the narrow point of the apex. But at the same time, one is inevitably moving toward the base of, and therefore an increasing threat from, the other extreme. As Lawrence describes the near/far double bind situation in a different context: "however far you may get away from one thing, by so much do you draw near to another" (*BB* 37). Similarly but more specifically, "Love is a progression towards one goal. Therefore it is a progression away from the opposite goal" (*RDP* 8). Movement in some direction is imperative for equilibrium is never static in Lawrence, as the tightrope walker metaphor shows, but the closer one gets to merger the greater the fear of engulfment, while advancing toward autonomy proportionally increases the dread of estrangement. This aspect of Lawrentian equilibrium creates the paradox of attachment in his writing. Given his intense exploration of selfhood in the intrapsychic realm and attachment in the interpersonal, it is perhaps inevitable that Lawrence's interest in balance would involve him in a paradox. Jessica Benjamin's formulation of the relationship between the two is helpful: "Assertion and recognition constitute the poles of a delicate balance … the individual's development of a self that is aware of its distinctness from others. Yet this balance, and with it the differentiation of self and other, is difficult to sustain. In particular, the need for recognition gives rise to a paradox" (12).

We can see in condensed form how equilibrium and paradox are subtly linked in Lawrence by examining the language in a portion of one long, well-known passage of Lawrentian prose that features what James Wood calls "the distinctive, much-mocked obstructiveness of Lawrence's mature style, with its compounds … its repetitions, its massing of nouns and adjectives, its threat of tautology" (xv). It is the passage in *The Rainbow* describing Will Brangwen's ecstatic reaction to Lincoln Cathedral that so annoys Anna: "Here the stone leapt up from the plain of the earth, leapt up in a manifold, clustered desire … away from the horizontal earth through twilight and dusk … to the ecstasy, the touch, to the meeting and the consummation, the meeting, the clasp, the close embrace, the neutrality, the perfect, swooning consummation, the timeless ecstasy" (*R* 187–8). Touch, meeting, consummation, clasp, embrace, neutrality, ecstasy – which term does not belong, as they say in certain intelligence tests? The word "neutrality" seems completely out of place here. Why does Lawrence use it? What is he trying to suggest by such an apparently ill-fitting word? I would argue that the word is appropriate since one of the common meanings of "neutral" is belonging to neither of two opposites. Thus it strongly suggests balance or equilibrium.

Admittedly, much of the scene and some of the words of the portion I have quoted imply Will's desire for merger or even maternal reincorporation, but there is also a strong expression of balance in the very idea of a "twilight [that] was the very essence of life," in the keystone of the arch, in the balanced phraseology of "the very first dawn breaking, the very last sunset sinking"; the church is poised "[b]etween east and west, between dawn and sunset ... dark before germination, silenced after death," and so on (R 187). From that sense of equilibrium – the tension like a keystone keeping opposites linked but apart – it is but a small step to the state of paradox where opposites combine oxymoronically: the "jewelled gloom" of the cathedral that folds "music upon silence, light upon darkness, fecundity upon death," and where in the twilight "dawn was sunset, and the beginning and the end were one" (R 187).

The Lawrentian Paradox

> A woman, he must have a woman. And having a woman, he must be free of her.
> D.H. Lawrence, *The Rainbow* (173)

> The need for recognition entails this fundamental paradox: at the very moment of realizing our own independence, we are dependent upon another to recognize it.
> Jessica Benjamin, *The Bonds of Love* (33)

The linking of equilibrium and paradox becomes Lawrence's signature expression of the excruciatingly difficult task of negotiating the push-pull demands of the various aspects of attachment. Lawrence's sensitivity and particular childhood experiences predisposed him to perceive and to repeatedly explore the paradoxes inherent in the attachment dynamic. In very early life, for Winnicott, "the basis of the capacity to be alone is a paradox; it is the experience of being alone while someone else is present" (quoted in West and Sheldon-Keller 42), as the young child must feel secure enough by virtue of the mother's presence to tolerate her absence. In secure attachment, such a paradoxical situation eventually disappears, and the ability to be alone no longer requires the contradictory presence of another person. However, in the insecure attachments that Lawrence's characters for the most part experience, there is a failure ever to overcome the paradox, and we often see self-sabotaging behaviour as the two sides of the paradox pull in opposite directions. So for Will Brangwen and many other Lawrence characters, "[t]hose who are anxious about their relationships also engage in coercive and distrusting ways of dealing with conflict, which are likely to bring about the very outcomes they fear most" (Feeney 374).

"Paradox" literally means "contrary to received opinion," from the Greek *para* (beyond) and *doxa* (opinion), but in English it has come to denote an assertion that is self-contradictory and yet somehow true or valuable or an action that is in some way self-defeating. Lawrence is one of the most paradoxical major writers of the twentieth century: valuing otherness highly and yet at times intolerant of differences; crossing all kinds of barriers and boundaries and yet seeming to need rigid categories, including those of race and gender, to make sense of the world; prizing singleness and yet desperate for community; and in some ways "a stridently masculinist thinker" who favours aesthetics "traditionally regarded as 'feminine'" (Fernihough 5).[20]

Lawrence may have happily crossed national and more abstract frontiers all his adult life, including those of the prevailing propriety of his time, but his sense of a precarious attachment equilibrium also and paradoxically made him fastidious about certain demarcations, those of selfhood most importantly. In the early story "The Thorn in the Flesh" (1914), in fact, we see a conflation of crossing a national frontier and the demarcations of selfhood. The protagonist Bachmann, in flight from military authorities for his accidental assault on Sergeant Huber, hides out with his sweetheart, Emilie, at the home of the Baron (loosely based on Frieda's father) where she is in service, in preparation for his flight to safety across the frontier to France. But Emilie initially feels his presence as a trespass on her own boundaries. Her reserve is like a sealed border: "The girl drew away. She could not bear the intrusion ... Emilie did not want the close contact with him" (*PO* 29). Bachmann never makes it across the national frontier, but he crosses an emotional boundary with Emilie in a merger that is transforming for them both. This is one of the few instances in Lawrence where interpersonal merger works for both partners, but Bachmann's failure to cross the border (he is no doubt headed for military prison at the end) suggests symbolically an unconscious countervailing desire for an effective personal boundary. In the same letter quoted earlier about Lawrence's closeness to his mother, his "love of loves," as he calls her in a slightly later letter (*IL* 199), he vows that no one will again have the soul of him the way his mother did: "My mother had it, and nobody can have it again. Nobody can come into my very self again, and breathe me like an atmosphere" (*IL* 190–1). The need to demarcate frontiers of the self and to police them is paradoxically a function of the need for fusion.

In human attachment terms, crossing boundaries means moving towards merger with an other so that demarcations of the self disappear or at best weaken; reinforcing self-boundaries involves struggling to free oneself from the attraction of fusion and moving toward a differentiated individuation. Lawrence will often use physically delimiting objects, such as gates or fences or walls, to symbolize the boundaries of the self, which are in the process of being established or violated. For example, when an inebriated Walter Morel in *Sons and Lovers* clumsily and irritably breaks the latch of the perimeter-defining gate to his house, Lawrence is symbolically suggesting that Gertrude Morel's intolerance of her husband's drunkenness and dirtiness is a function of the threat she feels from him to her vulnerable sense of self, and that his habits unknowingly violate her precarious sense of autonomy (*SL* 31). Similarly, Tom Brangwen in *The Rainbow* is startled when Lydia Lensky first enters his home on an errand to borrow a pound of butter for the vicarage where she is the housekeeper (*R* 34). Not yet aware of local customs, the foreign woman assumes a neighbour's prerogative and barges in, thereby symbolically violating Tom's personal boundaries. Her crossing the threshold of his home unasked is an encroachment on his sense of self, a sense in which his very abode partakes.

In the short story "Rawdon's Roof," written in November 1927 (*VG* xix), the house for which the titular roof is a synecdoche represents Rawdon's sense of fragile selfhood. His preposterous determination that "'no woman shall ever sleep under my roof again – not even a female cat!'" (*VG* 89) is humorously undermined by his servant, Joe Hawken, who surreptitiously sleeps with a woman in one of the guest rooms under Rawdon's very roof, as the narrator, Joe Bradley, discovers. Like his namesake Rawdon Lilly in *Aaron's Rod*, whom Lawrence portrays self-parodically as a windbag, this Rawdon is associated with literal windbags: he studies them as musical instruments. But Rawdon is only one of three male characters who form a kind of composite Lawrence (two of them are named Joe, a coincidence upon which the plot twist depends): the cheeky working-class lad (Hawken), the middle-class man attracted to but wary of women (Rawdon), and the neutral observer who, as narrator, functions in a way analogous to a writer (Bradley). As far as Rawdon is concerned, the prohibition against female habitation has clearly much more to do with feelings of vulnerability and fragile selfhood than any proprietary sense of ownership. We get no backstory to Rawdon's determination regarding women so his motive is unclear, but if we view Bradley and Hawken as extensions or aspects of Rawdon then, symbolically speaking, when Rawdon's lover, the married Janet Drummond, arrives unexpectedly asking to sleep the night under his roof in spite of the standing injunction, we see a diminution in the composite self as Hawken is for a time nowhere to be found and Bradley hopes to make his escape. If, as in Poe's "The Fall of the House of Usher," the house functions as a symbol for the bodily/psychic self, then an encroachment under the roof represents a messing with the psyche and sense of self. The house under the eponymous roof is a metaphor for Rawdon's self, and what he fears most is the violation of his selfhood by a female presence.

Whether it involves crossing frontiers or other markers of selfhood, the paradoxical nature of Lawrence's descriptions of relationships has not gone unnoticed. James Wood writes of Lawrence's "essentialist anti-essentialism" and how, in his contradictions, he seems, rather incongruously for so lean, not to say gaunt, a figure as Lawrence was, "like a fat man ordering us to go on a diet" (xxiv). With specific reference to *The Rainbow*, Wood suggests that Lawrence is trying to enact a paradox, "a religion of the Absolute that insists on its own anti-absolutism" (xxiv). Hayles points out that Lawrence unconsciously developed "strategies of resistance ... to oppose entry into what he ostensibly sought" (86). Chris Baldick (citing Gāmini Salgādo) writes about the "self-cancelling, paradoxical, Janus-faced nature of *Women in Love*, in which each argument is shadowed by an endorsement of its incompatible opposite" (265). He also refers to Linda Ruth Williams's argument in her book *Sex in the Head: Visions of Femininity and Film in D.H. Lawrence* (1993) that film theory reveals Lawrence's self-contradiction and "how a variety of Lawrence's texts disavow what they most desire and desire what they most disavow" (Baldick 266). Similarly, Eric P. Levy notes how, in *Women in Love*, stones "frequently symbolize the act of protective withdrawal" (9) but that such retreat is self-defeating in that it "actually destroys the security it seeks" (9). Turner writes of "the paradoxical character of [Lawrence] himself, as he faced the paradoxical facts of the modern world," and of his "celebration of precisely those paradoxical experiences which belong to ambivalence" ("Capacity" 283, 286). Diane S. Bonds, in her deconstructionist book *Language and Self in D.H. Lawrence*, argues that Lawrence's conceptions of language and selfhood are interrelatedly paradoxical: "language can entangle the self in a web or, to use another of [Lawrence's] metaphors, confine the self in a prison of preexisting form. Thus language might be said both to liberate the self (from what Lawrence calls 'the unconscious' into conscious being) and to imprison it" (7). Most helpfully for the purposes of this study, in *D.H. Lawrence and the Paradoxes of Psychic Life*, Barbara Ann Schapiro argues that, in the character of Skrebensky in *The Rainbow*, we see that "[t]he empty, deficient self dreads being overwhelmed by the very power and vitality it has projected outward, onto the idealized other," so that "what the self lacks internally it craves in the external world, and thus it risks being overpowered or enslaved precisely by what it so urgently seeks" (13).

Such Lawrentian paradoxes emerge directly from the conflicting emotions pertaining to attachment and the concomitant effort to establish a balance. They encapsulate the struggle regarding interpersonal relations whereby the very thing fervently desired is at the same time dangerous and to be avoided, so that characters often seem to fight against the very relatedness they ardently seek. Alan Williamson, in discussing Lawrence's own epistolary description of the demise of William Morel in *Sons and Lovers* in terms of a fatal split loyalty between his fiancée, Gypsy Western, and his mother, between "sex" and "soul," notes that the split is also "between the need to be symbiotic with, and the need to repudiate, one and the same object" (56). Conversely, the threatening relational situation often has its tempting attraction, so that a character might be unconsciously drawn to what he or she ostensibly abhors or fears. This is the nub of the emotional incongruity that generates the Lawrentian paradox of attachment. In the quotation from *The Rainbow* in the epigraph to this section, we have one of many expressions of Lawrentian paradox related to attachment, Will Brangwen's self-defeating and contradictory need for and simultaneous dread of close attachment or merger with a woman. Earlier in the same novel, we see in the youthful explorations of Tom Brangwen into the larger world how an understandable desire to separate from his mother's influence in order to achieve a degree of autonomy can activate abandonment anxiety so that the desire becomes tinged with dread. As Mahler writes, for the child "[t]he wish to be autonomous and separate from mother, to leave her, might also mean emotionally that the mother would wish to leave him" (*Psychological Birth* 96). Tom's reaction to meeting a prostitute in his exploratory foray into the wider world turns into a seemingly incongruous encomium to the woman of the home (*R* 20), a jarring mental shift that illustrates his anxiety to maintain home connections at the same time as he pursues the unfamiliar. Even more clearly paradoxical is Tom's embrace of his wife after some years of marriage: "There was that in him which shrank from yielding to her ... opposed the mingling with her, even whilst he most desired it" (*R* 90). In Hayles's words, Lawrence is "acutely vulnerable to anxiety when subject and object begin to merge; for Lawrence, the anxiety is most apparent when he imagines a son separating from his mother" (88). When the attachment is an anxious one, the longed-for movement toward union is shadowed by the dread of engulfment, and, equally, the move away from dependency is shaded with the fear of abandonment. Such paradoxical and stressful situations, or ones analogous to them, are repeated time and again in Lawrence's writing.

In *Women in Love*, as we will see in chapter 1, Gudrun eventually finds Gerald's dependency on her as a proxy mother intolerable. Gerald Doherty suggests reasonably that "Gerald's identification of [Gudrun] as a surrogate mother" destroys her ability to see him as an "erotic object" ("Question" 31). But Gerald may be attracted to Gudrun in the first place precisely because he unconsciously detects qualities in her that remind him of his mother. He is induced to repeat his childhood emotional bond in a vain attempt to rewrite its history, a kind of repetition compulsion to deal with, if not outright maternal rejection, then the disharmony between childhood need and maternal provision. In general, the paradox of insecure attachment in childhood can be virtually paralyzing as the need for closeness is stalemated by the fear of rejection. In insecure situations, if the need for proximity to an attachment figure in the face of a perceived threat to security is met with a rebuff then the child is faced with an impossible, lose-lose situation: its need for attachment is increased because security is further threatened by the rejection, but at the same time it realizes that proximity-seeking is counterproductive to the primary goal of security because the only available means of security, i.e. attachment, will lead to further insecurity. In such cases, the more that compensatory attachment is needed the less likely it is to be successful. As Lyons-Ruth and Jacobvitz put it, in situations where a young child's attachment needs are not being met reliably, it "is faced with an unresolvable paradox ... with respect to seeking comfort from a frightened or frightening caregiver who is also the only haven of safety" (536). The same attachment investigators add that "[s]ince infants rely on their attachment figures to protect them from harm should dangers arise, fear stemming from their own caregivers places infants in an unresolvable paradox" (549).

Let us briefly look at one more illustrative example, from *Sons and Lovers*, a book I delve into more deeply in chapter 2, to see how the Lawrentian paradox of attachment works. What I have in mind is the complex, approach-avoidance relationship that Paul Morel has to each of his parents. Paul needs to identify with his father, at the very least at an unconscious level, in order to balance the powerful female identification with his mother. On the one hand, his attachment to her is crucial and immensely important in his life, as was Lawrence's attachment to his mother in his. But the attachment of Paul to Mrs Morel is also simultaneously overwhelming and precarious: overwhelming because he is a child and she demands total loyalty, and precarious because of the implicit threat of emotional sanction if her narcissistic needs are not met by his compliant attachment. Without consciously realizing it, Paul is thus led to devise strategies to both secure the attachment and protect himself from it, seemingly working at cross-purposes to his own interests no matter what he does. His connection to his father, undermined by years of maternal manipulation, is, on the other hand, almost non-existent or, at best, characterized by hostility on Paul's part, the strength of the enmity undoubtedly intensified by the buried realization that the need and the ability to connect are at odds. The link to Walter, it turns out, is both necessary and undesirable: necessary as a healthy, masculine counterweight to Gertrude, and undesirable insofar as it threatens him with the same kind of emotional isolation to which Walter has been subjected for many years. So, once again, Paul is in a paradoxical situation: needing to buttress an uncertain autonomy through an attachment that is pernicious. What works more or less for Paul and allows him to have it both ways is a bi-level campaign whereby the open, conscious, real-world identification is all with his mother while the link to his father is unconscious, symbolic, and covert. This necessity for a dual development, fairly frequently seen in his fiction, is what in large part makes Lawrence such an engaging and complex psychological writer and, moreover, such an acute critic of the buried seam of significance running through classic American literary texts.

Attachment concerns are foundational to Lawrence's work and therefore to an understanding of that work. Although Lawrence's understanding increased over time, the conflicts laid down by the relationships of his early life, most particularly the tension between the need to merge interpersonally and the desire to protect the fragile self through autonomy, continued to demand creative embodiment in his only-ever-partially successful efforts to master them through repeated creative expression. In the pages that follow, I will offer a comprehensive tracing of those efforts by means of interpretations of much of Lawrence's fictional output through the lens provided by attachment research and the paradigm of paradoxical equilibrium. Chapter 1 looks at abandonment anxiety, a constant in Lawrence's fiction but an issue most clearly seen in certain early work, *The White Peacock* and *The Trespasser*; later work, *Women in Love* and its cognate play *Touch and Go*; and, finally, Lawrence's second Australian novel, *The Boy in the Bush*, a collaboration with Mollie Skinner. The second chapter examines how gender identification is influenced by attachment complications in *Sons and Lovers* but also in the stories "The Prussian Officer" and "The Old Adam," and, finally, the first Australian novel, *Kangaroo*. Chapter 3 analyzes the theme of marriage through an attachment lens. There I will concentrate on *The Rainbow* but also look at the stories "The Overtone" and "Love Among the Haystacks." Chapter 4 is about class and how Lawrence's view of class was influenced by his relationships with both of his parents. The analysis will include various shorter works such as "Daughters of the Vicar" and "Hadrian" but also the play *The Daughter-in-Law* and the novels *The Lost Girl* and *Lady Chatterley's Lover*. The final chapter deals with stories of homecoming, a neglected theme in Lawrence's work. In this chapter I examine over a dozen shorter works in terms of how they portray mother figures and develop the theme of homecoming. The two are related in that coming home for Lawrence is often the equivalent of returning to his earliest family conflicts. The conclusion takes a fresh look at Lawrence's concept of otherness from the perspective of attachment.

This study builds upon the work of critics whose psychoanalytic approach emphasizes the importance of Lawrence's early-life struggles and utilizes a pre-oedipal model in doing so: the work of Ruderman, Schapiro, Cowan, and others. It expands upon their studies and offers a wide-ranging and comprehensive analysis of Lawrence's work from the perspective of attachment theory, encompassing almost the entire gamut of Lawrence's fiction. In doing so, it proposes a causal link between equilibrium and paradox based on emotional factors deriving from the approach-avoidance nature of the Lawrentian balance between merger and autonomy; it introduces original readings of Lawrence's works, both well-known and obscure; and, by illuminating crucial elements in that work, it reveals hidden patterns, deepens our understanding of Lawrence's characterizations, and suggests new significance to his thematic concerns such as gender identification, marriage, and class.

1

ABANDONMENT ANXIETY

Do not leave me.
> D.H. Lawrence, "Humiliation" (*Poems* 173–4)

It is a terrible thing to realise that our soul's sanity and integrity depends upon the adjustment of another individual to ourself: that if this individual, wantonly or by urgency break the adjustment and depart, the soul must bleed to death, not whole, and not quite sane.
> D.H. Lawrence, *Mr Noon* (*MN* 231)

Set off on its own, the refrain and the last line of the poem "Humiliation" is the stark plea: "Do not leave me" (*Poems* 173–4). But why the title "Humiliation"? Wherein lies the humiliation in the fear of being abandoned? Is it that being left will expose to the world the inadequacies that the speaker secretly fears have been there all along? The line appears in connection with just such a fear and a tremulous sense of selfhood. In the first stanza, we read, "Do not leave me, or I shall break" (*Poems* 173, l. 2), and a few lines further along:

> What should I be, I myself,
> "I"?
> What would it mean, this
> I?
> (*Poems* 173, ll. 8–11).

Similarly, in the poem "Wedlock," the speaker admits that "[i]f you start away from my breast, and leave me, / How suddenly I shall go down into nothing" (*Poems* 201, ll. 39–40). In Lawrence's work we see a strong connection between abandonment anxiety and a sense of inadequate selfhood that in many cases can be traced back to insecure early attachment. Even in securely bonded individuals, in the words of attachment researchers West and Sheldon-Keller, "[b]ecause security is achieved through the attachment relationship, there is a component of feared loss … But in secure relationships the fear is understood as a necessary consequence of the investment of security in another person … and is kept in bounds by the presence of a confident belief in the attachment figure's reliable availability" (81). For many of Lawrence's characters, no such belief exists, or if it does, it is a very fragile one.

The White Peacock deals with many aspects of the attachment process, and, while later works also deal with abandonment, it is in this first novel that we see most clearly Lawrence's exploration of how an insecure attachment can be plagued by the anxiety of abandonment. *The White Peacock* is also the only Lawrence novel in which we find a first-person narrator (the short stories are a different matter). The choice of focalization may be indicative of an autobiographical fidelity to Lawrence's own deep feelings during this period, if not exactly to the events of his life. The book was finalized during Lawrence's mother's terminal illness, and the publishers were able to produce an advance copy just in time for Lydia Lawrence to hold it in her hands and to hear that the dedication was to her "with love" from her son (Harrison, *Life* 53). Her departure from this world, one might say, was the ultimate, if involuntary, abandonment of a child by its mother. As Lawrence was later to write in the unfinished novel *Mr Noon*, if the individual upon whose adjustments to our needs we depend "wantonly or by urgency break the adjustment and depart, the soul must bleed to death" (*MN* 231). Certainly, Lawrence felt bereft at the loss of his mother, the one person "upon whose adjustment to [his] needs" he had indeed depended. He expressed simply his feelings in the wake of his loss in a letter to Louie Burrows, "I have died, a bit of me" (*1L* 199). As Andrew Harrison contends, on the night Lydia Lawrence died, D.H. Lawrence, by copying Greiffenhagen's "An Idyll," was thinking through how his relationship with his beloved mother "had shaped him, and how it might be transmuted into other kinds of attachment" (*Life* 54). Over time, he came to the realization that Lydia Lawrence was not, in fact, always willing to adjust to his needs but rather often, subtly, expected him to adjust to hers.

In *The White Peacock*, the interrelated approach-avoidance aspects of both merger and autonomy play themselves out in displaced and symbolic form through a series of character functions, emblematic situations, and various tropes (particularly that of rot). Nature appears in two guises overlapping, for the most part, with seasonal changes: nature as growth/abundance (spring and summer) is part of the symbolic externalization of the attractions of merger and its attendant threat of engulfment when balance is lost; nature as ripeness/rot/death (autumn and winter) is an important trope for the pull of autonomy and the fear of isolation/abandonment. The very fact that Lawrence chose to structure the work as a tragedy suggests not that decay has completely won out over growth as many readers have assumed – George as "a once healthy organism which is blighted and rots," in Michael Black's words in his Introduction (*WP* xxv) – but that the necessary balance has been lost between what the two guises of nature represent.

As others have remarked, there are numerous double figures or repeated character functions in the novel. For example, we have three father figures: Mr Saxton, Frank Annable, and the narrator's long-lost biological father;[1] but another way to view the characters is by using as a template the terms of the conflict lying behind Lawrence's conception of equilibrium. In short, many of the principal characters in *The White Peacock* suffer from an imbalance – sometimes with tragic consequences – caused by the fear of engulfment and/or abandonment, the twin dangers attendant upon the struggle to deal with the opposing attractions of merger and autonomy in the effort to achieve an attachment that feels secure and allows for exploration. Even a newly hatched chick, brought indoors by Mrs Saxton to warm up, demonstrates what can happen when the attachment-exploration balance that Mary Ainsworth describes malfunctions. The chick dies when it shows too much precocious independence and wanders into the fire (*WP* 206), a suggestive scene indicating that the urge to explore can take an individual to a dangerous place far from the security of home.

Most critics have seen the *White Peacock*'s diffident and rather effete narrator, Cyril Beardsall, as little more than a cipher.[2] In my reading, Cyril is important as a site of the emotional struggle for equilibrium, and his diffidence is part of the portrayal of his attachment crisis and failure to achieve full individuation. He is alternately beset by fears of engulfment and of abandonment. Dominated by both his mother and his sister, Cyril's voice sometimes blurs into the subjectivities of others, particularly into that of his sister, Lettie.[3] He reacts inappropriately to what he perceives to be the engulfing threats to his fragile sense of self by putting off Emily Saxton (an early Muriel/Miriam/Jessie Chambers figure with attachment issues of her own) until she tires of his standoffishness and marries someone else. Although Cyril may fear being engulfed by Emily if he commits himself to a relationship, this is largely a fear he has displaced from his connection to the two strong women of his own household. In "The Lacerated Male: Ambivalent Images of Women in *The White Peacock*," Margaret Storch succinctly expresses the approach-avoidance bind as it pertains to Cyril's experience of Emily. Storch is referring specifically to a scene in which Emily mothers the child Sam: "What is resented in Emily here is apparently the very nurturing quality that is desired" (124). This kind of paradox, in which a character seemingly reacts against his or her own apparent wishes, is the typical response in Lawrence to a loss of equilibrium, as I outlined in the Introduction. A sense of belonging and a sense of autonomy are both (and often simultaneously) enticingly attractive and frighteningly repellent for the simple reason that both are urgently needed but, at their extreme, mutually exclusive: the full attainment of one necessarily means the loss of the other in Lawrence.

For the most part, however, Cyril, Lawrence's alter ego in many ways, fears abandonment more than engulfment, a reflection, no doubt, of Lawrence's own predilections in these early, pre-Frieda years. In Mahler's terms, Cyril is a young man in a late, unresolved "rapprochement crisis," the essence of which, it bears repeating, is that the child's "wish to be autonomous and separate from mother, to leave her, might also mean emotionally that the mother would wish to leave [the child]" (*Psychological Birth* 96). Cyril's unconscious anxiety is not unreasonable, for he has, in actual fact, already experienced a form of abandonment. His father left the family when Cyril was quite young, and when Cyril views the corpse of his estranged parent early in the novel he unsurprisingly has a negative epiphany of isolation since now the relationship can never be re-established. He feels "a sense of horror, and a sense of awful littleness and loneliness among a great empty space. I felt beyond myself, as if I were a mere fleck drifting unconsciously through the dark," and he comes "back to myself" only with the renewed attachment to his mother: "I felt my mother's arm round my shoulders" (*WP* 37). Close attachment here, then, is the antidote for isolation and temporarily restores "a sort of balance" in the rapprochement crisis. Fear of abandonment wanes, but the paradoxical trouble is that, while a degree of merger is desperately needed to allay the sense of isolation, separation itself is the countervailing antidote to fear of too-close merger. Moreover, a viable sense of autonomy becomes more difficult as long as the attraction of merger prevails.

Similarly, Cyril feels isolated when Lettie gets engaged to Leslie Tempest, a turn of events that signals a further loss of an object of attachment for Cyril and one, moreover, that is proxy for his attachment to his mother (as mother and daughter have the same given name). As was the case when his father died, he has trouble consolidating any feeling of solid selfhood: "I myself seemed to have lost my substance, to have become detached from concrete things and the firm trodden pavement of everyday life" (*WP* 83). The detachment in this case has not been a voluntary one in the aid of wider exploration but rather the result of the symbolic disappearance of an auxiliary attachment figure – in other words, the prospect of an abandonment of sorts. It is also worth noting that detachment is Bowlby's third term in the sequence of observed responses in children to separation: "protest, despair, and detachment" (*Attachment, Volume II* 6).

The White Peacock is a retrospective narrative, told by Cyril after he has left his beloved valley of Nethermere. The move away forces him to attain a modicum of autonomy, but he is lonely and even more susceptible to the feeling of abandonment, an emotion that is expressed in one of his memories through the conflated image of landscape/nourishing mother that is strikingly similar to Proust's more or less contemporary image toward the end of the Combray section of *Swann's Way*. Lawrence writes: "I remember a day when the breast of the hills was heaving in a last quick waking sigh, and the blue eyes of the waters opened bright. Across the infinite skies of March great rounded masses of cloud had sailed stately all day ... adorned with resting, silken shadows like those of a full white breast ... I wished that in all the wild valley ... something would call me forth from my rooted loneliness" (*WP* 126–7).[4]

Lettie has attachment problems as well. She fears too-strong attachment, or engulfment, as she struggles for an identity separate from her mother's. Her complex relationship with George and her choice of the non-threatening Leslie rather than George as husband suggest that her struggle for individuation has been exported from the mother-child to the matrimonial realm, where she has a better chance to control the outcome. She reacts to her unconscious fear of engulfment by assertions of autonomy even where none are necessary. Her independence in this rural, early-twentieth-century community is, of course, constrained by her gender, so it never develops so far that she feels threatened by abandonment. Quite the reverse, in fact, for she is happy enough to send her husband off on business for days at a time even when he protests at her seeming lack of affection. Her years-long sporting with George's feelings for her even after she is married suggests a tangled fear of losing that attachment combined with a premonition that George's deep love would be all-engulfing. The emotional pattern has been set long before by her relationship with her mother. Leslie is much safer than George but so much less satisfying as a partner: he will never threaten engulfment, but neither will he evoke the kind of desire for merger that is meaningful to her and that she is conditioned to want from her childhood symbiosis with her mother. This deficiency is both an advantage and a deprivation. So she drifts through life unthreatened but with her passion thwarted by her own devising.

Cyril's jilted lover, Emily Saxton, in spite of her teaching position, seems to be afraid of losing her autonomy in a family where the men dominate and she functions domestically as a faint shadow of her mother. When she kills a sheep-predating dog, her actions seem grossly out of character, but they are, in fact, indicative of her unconscious struggle for equilibrium. She throttles the animal so fiercely and for so long that Cyril must recall her to herself (*WP* 67). Emily's action expresses many of the frustrations and aggressions stemming from her lack of balance. For the dog is killed in the quarry, the same location that is later the site of Annable's death by misadventure (probably an accident, possibly a murder or a suicide). Annable, the man whose motto is "be a good animal," is George's future ruined self, in effect, while the feral dog is a parody of Annable taken to the extreme of his own dubious logic, where intrapersonal equilibrium is forsaken in favour of sheer brutality. Emily's unconscious motivations, however, have as much to do with her brother as with the equilibrium between nature and culture. She has previously expressed her disgust at George's killing ways and labelled him a brute: "'There is something so loathsome about callousness and brutality ... He fills me with disgust'" (*WP* 14), and now Cyril describes how, when Emily chokes the dog, "[t]he little jerks of the brute's body were the spasms of death" (*WP* 67). Her otherwise atypical behaviour is best understood as a psychosymbolic killing of her brother George, whom we have seen kill various animals and rather callously dispatch one of the family's pet cats after it has broken a leg. Lawrence will later in his career use similar devices: the killing of an animal in *The Fox* (1923) as a proleptic prelude to a homicide and the killing of a porcupine, reluctantly undertaken at his New Mexico ranch, as the occasion for an essay-long meditation on existential themes and the orders of creation in "Reflections on the Death of a Porcupine."

It is significant that Emily explains her attack on the dog to Cyril in terms of loss of equilibrium – "'I lost my balance, and fell on him'" (*WP* 68) – as it indicates that her fear of engulfment has momentarily overridden her desire for family attachment. Emily hates the demands put upon her by the physical/masculine/animal world represented by George (and Annable). She is portrayed as someone who, except for occasional outbursts such as the bloodying of one of her students in the name of discipline, cannot let herself go physically either in dancing or in a love relationship. She must control everything mentally (at least so Cyril believes). But the only way she can strike at what she hates, apparently, is by becoming it and thereby suggesting that she is paradoxically attracted to the very thing she abominates because she must re-establish an intrapersonal equilibrium. She incongruously attacks her hated animal-killing brother, then, by killing an animal herself.[5] Emily's later careful tending of George when he is a broken man and she is happily married is an ironically symbolic atonement for her unconscious desire to kill him earlier, and suggests that she has re-established, or even established for the first time, the kind of intrinsic equilibrium that balances autonomy and merger inclinations and no longer fears engulfment or isolation.

Leslie Tempest (the emasculated male) and Annable's son Sam (whom we might call the "lacerated male" following Storch) are other figures closely associated with the fear of engulfment, while George, Cyril's father, and Annable himself are associated mostly with isolation and/or abandonment. Lawrence makes plain the connection between Cyril's father and Annable, the two symbolically most important father figures, by giving them the same first name (Frank) and using words such as "plausible" in connection with both (WP 33, 151). Cyril's father is an embodiment of isolation and dies a very lonely death early on. The eccentric Annable, too, is isolated from his community and from his own former life, and he dies when he loses his balance and falls in the quarry. His son Sam is vulnerable to re-engulfment by his mother and other female figures, so that Sam's killing of a neighbour's brood-producing doe rabbit (which then becomes the family's dinner) is at once symbolic of his struggle to maintain male autonomy (killing the mothering female) and of his resentment at the lack of proper nurturing he receives (providing the food himself).

George Saxton is the male at the centre of *The White Peacock*. By the end of the novel, he has become strongly associated with both intrapersonal disequilibrium and a lack of interpersonal balance, the failure of both his relationship with Lettie and his marriage with Meg. But it is not primarily the imbalance between nature and culture in his personality that leads to his doom, as some have argued, or even, as others have suggested, his awakening to culture in the first place.[6] George is doomed because of a complex disequilibrium that encompasses both a fear of engulfment and an overwhelming sense of abandonment consequent to his own reaction against that initial fear. In order to discuss George's imbalance, however, we must examine the portrayal of nature (landscape) in the novel, and in particular its subset, the numerous descriptions of rot.

Rot and growth are conceptual opposites: the diminution versus the augmentation of organic material. Growth is related symbolically in *The White Peacock* to a healthy connection or symbiosis in Mahler's terms, suggestive as it is of the renewed life in the vegetative and human worlds and thus of the parent-child relationship in the latter, as we have seen in the description of the landscape as nurturing breast. However, merger can easily slide over into engulfment – or so the fear is – and thus some of the more perfervid descriptions of the burgeoning natural world in this novel so full of such descriptions have an ominous symbolic overtone. One individual flower hardly matters in a field teeming with them; individuality is lost. But it is rot rather than growth that is more important for our purposes here. Early on in the novel, amidst the plethora of natural descriptions, the reader begins to perceive a pattern related to rot, waste, ruin, and decay. When Cyril's mother gets word of her husband's imminent death, for example, the autumn setting with red dahlias turning into "brown balls of rottenness" seems appropriate (*WP* 32). After an odd encounter with his father while he is still ignorant of the family connection, Cyril says that the meeting has "'made me feel a bit rotten'" (*WP* 23). The local squire lives in a "now decayed house," and his protection of his rabbits, which ravage the countryside, means that Strelley Mill and the other farms under his ownership "suffer under this gangrene" (*WP* 57, 58). And so on it goes in dozens of places.

Symbolically in this novel, while ripeness may connote a mature independence, rot suggests a failed equilibrium through an overreaction in the direction of autonomy that overshoots the mark, as it were, and leads to a feeling of isolation or abandonment. It is a blighting, a failure to thrive because the nourishment necessary for growth is cut off, either not available or rejected in an attempt to gain autonomy or in reaction to a too-strong attachment. We are never given enough information about George to be sure of the source of his need for fusion and the subsequent reaction against engulfment. However, he does feel somewhat stifled under his father's unquestioned authority on the farm, and there is one telling image that symbolically suggests father-son hostility. George points out to Cyril a sycamore tree he is fond of: "'I remember when Father broke off the leading shoot because he wanted a fine straight stick. I can remember I felt sorry'" (*WP* 223). George means this image to refer to Cyril, but since he himself is the scion or leading offshoot of his family, he may unconsciously identify with the shoot of the sycamore tree himself and feel that he has been cut off by his father from the source of nourishment. He certainly reacts strongly to his own urgent and frustrated need for Lettie. The most graphic if symbolic example of George's overreaction to his own need for attachment to a female comes in the scene where he hears of the engagement of Lettie and Leslie while he is milking a cow. As Storch has pointed out, George's harsh treatment of the cow is aggression targeted at "an obvious displacement of the comforting and nurturing quality in a woman. He strikes her so that she cowers 'like a beaten woman,' and withholds most of her milk." His behaviour reflects the emotions of an "infant overwhelmed with loss who in fantasy tears apart the maternal breast, the source of all joy and goodness" (122–3), in what is obviously a self-defeating gesture against the very source of needed nourishment. In any case, the textual indications of disequilibrium are unmistakable and include, most significantly, abandoned buildings and allusions to the biblical Samson.

There are a number of ruined or dilapidated buildings in the novel, and because they are deserted, they become an appropriate metaphor for the human fear of abandonment. When Cyril and George come upon a derelict farm and they find that, instead of the "once cultivated land," there is a clearing, Cyril's "flesh creep[s]" at the wreckage, rust, and ruin of the once-inhabited home, and George says that "'[t]his ... is what the Mill will come to'" (*WP* 60, 61). What is natural (land returning to its original state, metal rusting) is not necessarily to be prized, and it is certainly not attractive. Similarly, when Annable and Cyril meet in an old, abandoned, "mouldering" church surrounded by "decayed leaves" (*WP* 147), Annable makes an explicit connection between himself and the rotten building: "'I'm like a good house built and finished and left to tumble down again with nobody to live in it'" (*WP* 149). Annable is feeling particularly bereft this day because he has just learned that his former wife, Lady Chrystabel, has died; a few days later, Annable himself is dead. That his own funeral takes place in the early spring, with a set-piece description of burgeoning nature, serves to underscore through irony Annable's failure to attain secure attachment. He opted long ago for isolation, individual life, and social ostracization.

The reader makes a connection in the scene in the abandoned church most readily to Annable's philosophy that, as Cyril puts it in the same chapter, "all civilization was the painted fungus of rottenness" (*WP* 146). There is also a link to George's earlier fear that the Mill is bound to rot in the future, a trope for his own fear of being abandoned, as indeed he is in a sense when his family emigrates, leaving only him and Emily in England. Moreover, Annable's deterioration serves as an anticipation of George's. It is noteworthy that once Cyril has left the valley of Nethermere in Part III of the novel, he feels the nostalgic pull of its landscape, but his imagery returns us to the trope of buildings: "Since I left the valley of home I have not much feared any other loss. The hills of Nethermere had been my walls, and the sky of Nethermere my roof overhead. It seemed almost as if, at home, I might lift my hand to the ceiling of the valley ... whose sun had been all my father to me" (*WP* 260). These are the imaginary walls of a sound, sheltering building, where one's attachment is secure and the walls protective, but present behind this longing for attachment, understandable enough for someone whose father abandoned him and his entire family, is Cyril's felt lack of a protecting, nurturing parent and, consequently, his abiding fear of abandonment, a fear that George, in effect, acts out in his stead. Likewise, on a return trip in the winter to the valley when he feels his exile acutely, Cyril uses the metaphor of a house to express his sense of abandonment and doom once again: "As I trod the discarded oak-leaves and the bracken they uttered their last sharp gasps, pressed into oblivion. The wood was roofed with a wide young sobbing sound, and floored with a faint hiss like the intaking of the last breath" (*WP* 306). It is significant that what kills Annable is the tumbling down upon him of the unsafe walls of the "rotten," abandoned quarry.

Also climaxing with the ruination of a building is the story of Samson in the Book of Judges, which has relevance for a full understanding of George, whom Lettie calls "a veritable Samson!" at one point in the novel (*WP* 209). There is an allusion to Samson in *The Crown* a few years after *The White Peacock* was published that suggests the loss of social and political balance, a loss that has led to war. In both the 1915 and 1925 versions of *The Crown*, Samson becomes an image of a social failure, but no less an expression of a lack of equilibrium: "In truth, we proceed to die because the whole frame of our life is a falsity, and we know that, if we die sufficiently, the whole frame and form and edifice will collapse upon itself. But it were much better to pull it down and have a great clear space, than to have it collapse on top of us. For we shall be like Samson, buried under the ruins" (*RDP* 305).

Thus the seemingly inapt associations Lawrence creates between George and Samson are part of the pattern of symbolic fear of abandonment, which, I am arguing, is the consequence of George's overreaction to his own desire for merger. Allusions to the Samson and Delilah story, of course, are also an early hint of Lawrence's hostility to women, the most protracted of the unconscious, defensive reactions articulated in his fiction to his buried fear that his need for a satisfactory attachment will lead to engulfment because it is prompted by a desire for merger.[7] Behind Delilah in this text are other notorious women such as Eve and Salomé. However, at a deeper level, I think it is fair to say that Samson becomes an important figure indicating George's overwhelming sense of isolation and its danger, for the essence of the Samson story points to a man set apart (as required by the Nazirite code). George is in a bind because in order to deal with Lettie's rejection he must detach, but the disengagement results not in autonomy but in a feeling of abandonment against which he struggles. His heavy drinking is in clear violation of the Nazirite code as set out in Numbers 6:1–20, where the regulations pertaining to a man (or woman) who wishes to make "a vow of separation to the

Lord as a Nazirite" include abstention from all fermented drink and vinegar and from wine and anything that comes from the grapevine, including the seeds and skins of raisins. No razor may be used on a Nazirite, the hair must not be cut, and proximity to a corpse is forbidden. Samson, of course, is eventually betrayed by Delilah, who wheedles the secret of his strength out of him and then divulges the information to his enemies in return for payment. The Philistines proceed to put out his eyes and imprison him until the return of God's favour and his superhuman strength allow him to bring down the temple of Dagon upon himself and thousands of his enemies as the physical equilibrium of the building itself is destroyed.

Lawrence does not consistently parallel George's life with Samson's, but there are enough common elements to suggest that the pattern is deliberate. The similarity in the names Saxton and Samson is suggestive, as is Lawrence's choice of Sam (Sam/son of Annable) for the name of one of George's symbolic doubles. Before he ever meets Delilah, the biblical Samson marries one of the enemy, a Philistine woman from Timnah who is later killed, while George in *The White Peacock* wishes to cross class lines and marry the elegant and cultured Lettie Beardsall, who goes over to George's class enemy, the philistine Leslie Tempest, son of the colliery owner. Given the biblical prohibition on Nazirite contact with products of the vine, the chapter title "Lettie Pulls down the small gold Grapes" takes on added significance. Furthermore, not only is George a great drinker, but there is also a set-piece scene at the farm that shows him stoning and eating raisins in "The Riot of Christmas" (*WP* 92–3). In the Bible, in return for refraining from drink and from cutting his hair, Samson is given inhuman strength by God. In *The White Peacock*, there is an unusual emphasis on hair in general and particularly in connection with Lettie, but there are also two key scenes where Lettie plays with George's hair even while rejecting him as a lover or potential husband (*WP* 214, 302). In both cases, George loses all strength like a shorn Samson. The second instance is the beginning of George's precipitous decline to the point of imminent collapse at the end of the novel, where the formerly formidably strong George admits to Cyril that he is so weak that "'I couldn't team ten sheaves'" (*WP* 324), and he "sat apart and obscure among us, like a condemned man" (*WP* 325), the last words of the novel. The word *nazir*, from which Nazirite derives, means "separated" or "dedicated" (Gunn 118), so George's alienation is in keeping with the Samson story, although his apartness is hardly voluntary or sacred.

Lawrence's second novel, *The Trespasser*, also features a tragedy that is the outcome of a very deep sense of abandonment and isolation. The five-day island idyll of Helena and Siegmund at the heart of the novel is rather mawkish and overwritten, reflecting the young D.H. Lawrence struggling with the material he had received from Helen Corke about her tragic affair with H.B. Macartney and groping his way to a style that suited his gifts and his vision.[8] Lawrence himself spoke of how the first version's "purple patches glisten sicklily" (*1L* 229). But the post-idyll domestic scenes between Siegmund and his wife, Beatrice, and between Siegmund and his children look toward the precocious mastery of *Sons and Lovers* in their power, persuasiveness, and meticulous attention to domestic details. The lengthy description of Siegmund's thought processes leading up to his suicide by hanging is especially well done and convincing. Though based on a true story in Helen Corke's life, the novel was fashioned by Lawrence into his own creation. Indeed, both Corke and Lawrence viewed the finished novel as his work. Lawrence characterized it to Corke as "'a work of fiction on a frame of actual experience,' and as *his* presentation of that experience" (*T* 22), and Corke herself is on record suggesting that "much of the text of *The Trespasser* is pure Lawrence" (Corke 235). The end of the novel in particular was "Lawrence, complete Lawrence" (*T* 24).

Lawrence would have had some insights into Corke's contemporary thoughts and emotions from the writings she showed him and from their long talks together, but he was more interested in Macartney's no-longer-accessible inner life, and that is something he largely invents while passing it through the filter of his own emotions at the time of writing and rewriting.[9] In a BBC interview in July 1967, Corke called Lawrence's characterization of Siegmund "as true a conception as one mind could possibly make of another" (*T* 23), but it was also a mind revealing itself. For the convincing portrayal of Macartney's inexorable slide to suicide required a feat of sympathetic imagination at a time of turmoil for Lawrence himself. In a letter dated 21 January 1912, Lawrence wrote to Edward Garnett of the novel he was revising that "[i]t is so much oneself, one's naked self. I give myself away so much, and write what is my most palpitant, sensitive self" (*1L* 353). What exactly did Lawrence feel he was giving away about himself? His "naked," "most palpitant, sensitive" truths about himself, I would suggest, involve attachment issues, especially the always-lurking anxiety of being abandoned and the humiliation of being exposed as needy.

Between the beginning of the writing of the novel around mid-April 1910 and the final correction of proofs sent from the publisher Duckworth in May 1912, Lawrence went through a series of life crises related to "questions of relationship," as Elizabeth Mansfield, the editor of the definitive Cambridge University Press edition, puts it (*T* 13): he broke his longstanding if unofficial engagement to Jessie Chambers, watched his mother die painfully (indeed, hastened her death) and then mourned her passing, and broke off his official engagement to Louie Burrows on the pretext of finances. During this period, he also came down with pneumonia and was finding his own growing attraction to Helen Corke more and more frustratingly complicated. The novel inevitably reflects the jumbled stew of emotions Lawrence was feeling at the time: specifically those related to both sides of the abandonment coin, the guilty one who leaves (as he left Jessie and Louie) and the bereft one who is left or rebuffed (as he was by Lydia Lawrence and Helen Corke in different ways). Lawrence's mother's death had left him "derelict," as the last chapter of *Sons and Lovers* is entitled, and Lawrence recalls his raw emotions of the time through the character of Paul Morel: "'Mother!' he whimpered, 'mother!' She was the only thing that held him up, himself, amid all this. And she was gone, intermingled herself!" (*SL* 464). The description of the fictional Helena's reaction to her lover's suicide at the beginning of *The Trespasser*, before the lengthy flashback detailing the events that led up to it, could equally describe Lawrence's state after Lydia Lawrence's death: "She had received a great blow ... and she still was stunned" (*T* 45). Indeed, Neil Roberts suggests that Macartney's suicide remained traumatic territory for Corke even many years after the fact ("Writing" 26–7), as no doubt was Lawrence's mother's death for him. Added to that blow was the fact that Helen Corke had rebuffed Lawrence: "It is clear from Lawrence's letters that he sought a sexual relationship with [Helen], was repulsed (however kindly) and was bitter" (*T* 18). And Lawrence himself had painfully rejected both Jessie and Louie in turn. So although Siegmund's suicide is fashioned to look like the logical terminus of a train of thought, a careful weighing of all options in an intolerable situation, there is a strong sense of abandonment and a suggestion that the action was the result of emotional turmoil rather than rational calculation. The multiple references in the novel to mother and child trace the emotions directly back to Lawrence's most important and fraught attachment. In the character of Siegmund, Lawrence is both exploring and disguising his "most palpitant, sensitive self."

Elizabeth Mansfield speculates that the title *The Trespasser*, finally settled upon by Lawrence and his publisher after some discussion, was primarily intended to suggest "one who enters illegally the property of others, and especially the territory of love, implied by the reference to Cythera, birthplace of Aphrodite" (*T* 20).[10] I would submit that there is a further nuance to the title relevant to the theme of abandonment and attachment: the efforts to establish boundaries for the self and the violation of those very boundaries. There are no gamekeepers in *The Trespasser*, but Lawrence's recourse elsewhere in his fiction to that figure, whose job it is to find and punish trespassers, invariably coincides with an exploration of attachment issues, where the boundaries of the self are crucially relevant. In *The Trespasser*, the suicide ultimately stems from a crisis in which Helena views Siegmund as a trespasser violating her self-boundaries and repulses him, a rejection that he takes emotionally as an intolerable abandonment even though she has no intention of ending the relationship.

The abandonment anxiety comes on the heels of various scenes of merger, as is so often the case in Lawrence, since the danger of engulfment awakens the drive to autonomy. Carl Krockel's thorough examination in *The Trespasser* of the influence on its composition of the German writers Schopenhauer, Nietzsche, and Gerhart Hauptmann and the composer Wagner throws little light on the question of how Lawrence's own crises at the time play into the novel, but his characterization of the merger between the two major characters – related to Krockel's argument that Lawrence is trying to transpose Wagnerian musical technique (the *Leitmotiv*) to narrative – is well observed: "Lawrence repeats scenes, dialogue and commentary till Helena and Siegmund's characters merge with each other … [A]t times their individual traits dissolve into each other, and into the totality of the novel's *Motive*" (57).

For Siegmund, Helena is "fused in an aura of his love" (*T* 57); in a kiss "they seemed to melt and fuse together" (*T* 64); and although he feels "perfect" at times during the idyll, Siegmund's weakness seems to be an irresistible need for fusion: "In these things he recognized the great yearning, the ache outwards towards something, with which he was ordinarily burdened" (*T* 76). The typical needy Lawrentian male cannot feel whole or self-sufficient; he needs an other to complement him and strengthen his selfhood. That other is almost always a woman, and such a woman usually figures as a proxy mother. As Lawrence's character Philip says to Katharine in "The Border-Line" (1924), "'You are always real. But that's because you are a woman. A man without a woman *can't* be real'" (*WWRA* 92).[11] The sensed lack of wholeness moves the Lawrence male to seek some kind of merger but also frightens him because the very weakness that activates him toward merger makes him vulnerable to reincorporation. Siegmund's ill-considered marriage with Beatrice at the age of seventeen (Beatrice being then eighteen), as we see in his recounting of the past to Helena, reinforces the observation that his predilection in relationships is to a merger that disregards selfhood boundaries: "'she was the other half of my consciousness, I of hers'" (*T* 123). Helena is a willing participant in the fusion for the most part, but key passages suggest that she is catering to Siegmund's need rather than her own and that there is a decided element of maternal solicitousness involved as well as a revulsion at physicality.[12]

As we have seen with *The White Peacock*, the need for merger will sometimes lead a Lawrentian character paradoxically to seek more autonomy, and such a search can in turn lead to fear of abandonment as Mahler's paradox from childhood anxieties enters consciousness: the emotional logic that the child's own need to separate might imply the mother's desire to leave the child. Certainly we see in Lawrence's second novel ample evidence that the two lovers often fail to understand each other, a failure that very much includes an inability to fully comprehend the other's attachment needs: "So often, she did not take his meaning, but left him alone with his sense of tragedy ... when he tried to tell her, she balked him, leaving him inwardly, quite lonely" (*T* 58). Likewise, for Siegmund "[t]here was something in [Helena] he could never understand" (*T* 154). This sense of Siegmund as isolated or bereft is emblematized by wound imagery. He suffers a physical injury on the spur of a rock while swimming, and the wound image is reinforced when the couple comes across a carved Christ, the ultimate icon of a forsaken figure in Western culture, upon a cross in a graveyard and Siegmund identifies with him (*T* 107–8). The day after Helena's rejection, the enduring "sense of humiliation ... bled him secretly, like a wound" (*T* 144).

Helena is a very willing participant in the love affair with Siegmund, but she is described several times as self-sufficient: "Helena was something like the sea, self-sufficient and careless of the rest" (*T* 76). And, in what is clearly meant to be Siegmund's free indirect discourse, we learn that she is "sufficient to herself – she doesn't want me" (*T* 143). As in so many works by Lawrence, we have a strong woman with a clear sense of herself and a needy man unable to find his own way in life, notwithstanding the fact that in this case Siegmund is the violin master and teacher and the younger Helena his acolyte and pupil. Although each character is at times described as a child dependent upon its mother in their relationship, Siegmund's infantilism is by far the more prevalent.[13] There are half a dozen descriptions of Siegmund as a child, sometimes explicitly seeking a mother's reassurance in his relationship with Helena, but few are quite as resonant as this one: "Then, with 'Madonna' love, she clasped his head upon her shoulder, covering her hands over his hair ... All the while, delicately, she fondled and soothed him, till he was child to her Madonna" (*T* 129). It is not only Helena who wants to be in a mother-child relationship; clearly Siegmund's needs play into the dynamic: "[A]s he lay helplessly looking up at her, some other consciousness inside him murmured 'Hawwa, – Eve – Mother!' ... Without touching him, she seemed to be yearning over him like a mother. This woman ... seemed stable, immortal, not a fragile human being, but a personification of the great motherhood of woman" (*T* 103).

Lawrence notoriously generalized "that class of 'Dreaming Women,' with whom passion exhausts itself at the mouth" (*T* 64), a reference that Mansfield suggests comes from Lawrence's frustrating relationship with Helen Corke (*T* 18). The Lawrence-figure in *The Trespasser*, Cecil Byrne, who appears in the frame narrative at the beginning and end of the novel, has a counterpart in Bernard Coutts in "The Witch à la Mode," a story that also reflects the relationship between Lawrence and Corke. In this short story, we also find a Dreaming Woman, Winifred, who limits passion to a kiss: "She clipped her lips, drew them away, leaving him her throat. Already she had had enough" (*LAH* 69). And in *The Trespasser*, when Siegmund meets a man he terms his doppelgänger (*T* 115), an acquaintance from long ago named Hampson, whom Helen Corke called Lawrence's "self-portrait" (235), we get a misogynist rant about spiritual women who "'aim at suppressing the gross and animal in us'" (*T* 112). Sure enough, a good deal of the sense of rejection Siegmund experiences from Helena derives from his feelings that she is disgusted by the sexual animal in him, and the narrator at times confirms that this is exactly how she feels. At one point, in a close embrace, Helena feels that Siegmund's mouth on her throat is "something like a dog snuffing her, but with his lips. Her heart leapt away in revulsion" (*T* 64). A little later, Siegmund, feeling proud about his body, thinks, "She ought to be rejoiced at me, but she is not, she rejects me as if I were a baboon, under my clothing" (*T* 74), and Helena bathes in the sea "to clear away the soiling of the last night's passion" (*T* 76). In a key passage we examined in the Introduction as an example of the zero-sum relationship common in Lawrence's writing, we see that Helena's participation in the passion between the two of them is a sacrifice for her rather than a pleasure: "It was a wonderful night to him. It restored in him the full 'will to live.' But she felt it destroyed her" (*T* 87). The restoration of the will to live in Siegmund is very fleeting.

The crisis comes about because of disillusionment and a fear of engulfment. There is evidence that both Siegmund and Helena are vaguely aware that their love is in part based on a projection onto each other that distorts reality. In other words, there is a sudden realization that there exists a disjunction between the ideal aspect of the internal working model they project onto each other and the reality that at times seems to contradict it. When Helena experiences her "hour of disillusionment" (*T* 124) with Siegmund it proves fatal eventually. It starts when the two seem out of tune with each other, and Helena feels that all her life she has been "a destructive force" in the lives of others. She seems to see Siegmund suddenly as he really is: "His radiance was gone, his aura had ceased. She saw him a stooping man, past the buoyancy of youth ... in short, something of the 'clothed animal on end,' like the rest of men. She suffered an agony of disillusion. Was this the real Siegmund, and her own, only a projection of her soul?" (*T* 125). Siegmund's efforts to comfort her only make things worse: "She did not want his brute embrace ... The secret thud, thud of his heart, the very self of that animal in him she feared and hated, repulsed her. She struggled to escape." And it is at this point that Helena strives to assert her autonomy: "She grew frantic to be free. Stifled in that prison any longer, she would choke and go mad ... 'Let me go!' she cried ... She thrust him furiously away, with great strength" (*T* 126). Siegmund cannot understand what is going on, and Helena later regrets her reaction, but there is little doubt that Lawrence here is channelling emotions he has experienced himself, both the panic at the sense of being engulfed (her feeling) and the sense of being rejected (his emotion).

Helena's reaction, moreover, does not come completely out of the blue. While living together with Siegmund in their love cottage on the Isle of Wight, she is careful to keep a room for herself "inviolate" (*T* 72). Feeling that "Helena had rejected him" (*T* 146), Siegmund seeks merger elsewhere: like Birkin in the later novel *Women in Love* after he is attacked by Hermione with a heavy paperweight, Siegmund seeks solace in the natural world: "He found great pleasure in this feeling of intimacy with things. A very soft wind, shy as a girl, put its arms around him, and seemed to lay its cheek against his chest" (*T* 135). On the train ride home, his perception recalls that of Cyril Beardsall in *The White Peacock*; he feels a "sudden love for the earth. There, the great downs were naked like a breast leaning kindly to him. The earth is always kind: it loves us, and would foster us like a nurse" (*T* 164). Clearly for Siegmund, "a man needs a mother all his life" (*T* 179), but a surrogate will do.

Helena's brief reassertion of autonomy and Siegmund's feeling of being rejected are enough to doom him to a fatal isolation, the dark shadow of autonomy. So, when he returns home to his wife and children and finds that his isolation is complete, he cannot cope. As

Julian Moynahan observed many years ago, in Lawrence's early fiction "[a]ll of the defeated males are woefully passive and are pathologically oversensitive to feminine rebuke and resistance" (6). The rejection of Siegmund's youngest child, the five-year-old Gwen, completes the feeling of isolation so that he is like George Saxton at the end of *The White Peacock*, who, as we have seen, sits "apart and obscure among us, like a condemned man." Siegmund "felt as if he were a limb out of joint from the body of life" (*T* 201). Ironically, his way out of the intolerable feeling of abandonment is to abandon his wife and children through suicide. The self-violence in the face of failed attachment is something we see again in the figure of Gerald Crich in *Women in Love*.

We have seen how, in *The White Peacock*, George Saxton reacts violently to feeling abandoned by Lettie, and, in *The Trespasser*, how the forsaken Siegmund turns to suicide. In the character of the industrialist Gerald Crich in *Women in Love*, Lawrence creates another "lacerated male" whose abandonment anxiety leads to violence and ultimately a form of suicide. Given the significance of the wound image in *The Trespasser*, Gerald's injured hand, seen in the chapter "Water-Party," would seem to indicate in retrospect that, like Siegmund, Gerald is maimed by maternal unreliability into a permanent state of abandonment anxiety. However, when Lawrence first introduces Gerald, there is little to suggest his weakness. He is a get-up-and-go character. He describes himself as such in a conversation with Rupert Birkin in an early chapter when he mentions "making things *go*" as a defining feature of his life (*WL* 57), and others tend to view him in the same vein. In the chapter "Diver," Gudrun Brangwen says to her sister Ursula that she has never seen a man with as much *go* as Gerald, but then asks "'where does his *go* go to, what becomes of it?'" (*WL* 48). Though Gudrun's question is meant to be rhetorical, it is answered by the end of the novel: Gerald's get-up-and-go ends in a violent and self-destructive place from which he will never get up again to go anywhere. But perhaps the more interesting question we could pose is this: where does Gerald's "go" come from? What is the source of his energetic industrial reforms and of his ultimately fatal desire to "go to" Gudrun for the fulfilment of his emotional and physical needs? In fact, in Gerald's character, Lawrence brilliantly links the industrial activity to the deep-seated attachment promptings. They are mutually implicated, and much of the energy and the violence in *Women in Love* in general are connected implicitly to the dread of abandonment.

Gerald has often been seen as a portrait of sorts of Lawrence's "frenemy" John Middleton Murry, whereas it is Birkin who is the obvious Lawrence avatar in *Women in Love*.[14] The 1969 Ken Russell cinematic interpretation of the novel even has Birkin (played by Alan Bates) suggestively reciting lines from Lawrence's poem "Figs," an interpolation that indicates the then- and still-common conflation of Lawrence with his school-inspector character. James Cowan asserts flatly that "Birkin is the carrier of Lawrence's major psychic issues" (*Self and Sexuality* 39). But Gerald has more than just a touch of Lawrence in him as well. In fact, for so transparent a vehicle of Lawrentian projection, Birkin is unusually devoid of a backstory, whereas we learn a great deal about Gerald's family and even his childhood. Like several other fictional works, *Women in Love* projects the author's conflicting attachment tendencies onto two distinct characters. Birkin represents the urge toward autonomy, even solitude, the essentially defensive stance of "compulsive self-sufficiency," in the relational nexus of the novel: "why form any serious connection at all?" he thinks at one point (*WL* 302); "'I am as separate as one star from another,'" he says to Hermione at another (*WL* 103). By way of contrast, Gerald personifies the equally strong dread of abandonment and, indeed, of isolation: "'I couldn't bear to be alone. My brain would burst'" (*WL* 330), he tells Gudrun in a moment of candor.

Though often centred on Gerald, abandonment anxiety is also a rather diffuse and not always explicit dread in *Women in Love*, one that often leads to otherwise unaccountable violence. We see, for example, a pregnant Pussum, abandoned first by Halliday – "'He made me go and live with him, and now he wants to throw me over'" (*WL* 67) – and then, after one night, by Gerald, taking her bitterness out on a hanger-on of the Halliday group. She stabs "the sardonic young man" (*WL* 71) in the hand in one of several bloody scenes in the novel – an image, moreover, that finds an echo in Gerald's wounded hand later in the book. Will Brangwen's attachment issues, explored deeply in *The Rainbow* (see chapter 3), are briefly revisited in *Women in Love* when his daughter Ursula rejects him and announces her intention to sever home relations. He strikes her hard and then advances on her with the "face of a murderer" (*WL* 366). Hermione Roddice, a kind of female Gerald in her vulnerability and vacuity, attacks Birkin in a homicidal frenzy with a lapis lazuli paperweight when she feels he is about to leave their relationship. Her very need for him is an oppression that is made unbearable by his imminent departure and his seeming ability to be autonomous: "her soul writhed in the black subjugation to him, because of his power to escape" (*WL* 92). In effect, she takes control by losing it – expelling Birkin by violence rather than allowing him to abandon her – and she thereby inverts Birkin's earlier nasty comment to her that "'that loathsome little skull of yours ... ought to be cracked like a nut'" (*WL* 42). Furthermore, the assault occurs at her estate, Breadalby, which is significantly described as "[s]ilent and forsaken" (*WL* 82), and in the context of the acting out by her guests of the biblical story of Ruth, which features the extreme attachment of one woman for another.[15]

According to attachment researchers Karlen Lyons-Ruth and Deborah Jacobvitz, there is a link between violence in adult relationships and "unresolved attachment issues," which may manifest, among other things, as "intense abandonment anxiety" (545). The intolerable prospect of abandonment is an apprehension whose power derives ultimately from the childhood fear of maternal rejection and desertion. In *Women in Love*, the most significant but not sole representative of the abandoning maternal figure is Gerald's mother, Mrs Crich, whose parenting, we may surmise, has always been unreliable and extreme, sometimes smothering and sometimes indifferent. When we first meet Mrs Crich she is described as an "elderly estranged woman" (*WL* 24) who is keen to refuse a maternal role. She tells Birkin that she can hardly tell one son-in-law from the next: "'They come up to me, and call me mother. I know what they will say – "How are you mother?" I ought to say, "I am not your mother, in any sense"'" (*WL* 25). Gudrun learns from Mrs Kirk, who had nursed three of the Crich children, that her employer was a woman who, many years earlier, would not allow her young offspring to be disciplined by her and who, when Mr Crich occasionally used corporal punishment on them, would "'[pace] up and down all the while like a tiger outside [the locked door]'" (*WL* 213). That was then. Now, the narrator tells us, "[h]er children, for whom she had been so fierce in her youth ... meant scarcely anything to her" (*WL* 218). After his sister Diana has drowned, Gerald tells Birkin that his mother has altered from an over-involved, intrusive young mother to an uninvolved, indifferent older one: "'she used to be all for the children – nothing mattered ... but the children. And now, she doesn't take any more notice than if it was one of the servants'" (*WL* 203).

Mrs Crich's development from a hyper-partisan to a wholly uninterested parent – from pacing tiger to aloof house cat, so to speak – reflects in temporally extended form the subtle and complex unreliability of Lawrence's own mother, who, while apparently devoted to him, as Cowan puts it, "provided excessive mirroring at times and used him for her own selfobject needs but was unable to respond appropriately to his actual needs" (*Self and Sexuality* 44).[16] After Mr Crich has died, Christiana's bizarre response to seeing him looking youthful in death is to declare in the manner of the notoriously unmotherly Lady Macbeth that "'[i]f I thought that the children I bore would lie looking like that in death, I'd strangle them when they were infants'" (*WL* 335),[17] not exactly the kind of maternal comfort her grieving children have need of at this point. In fact, she goes on to exhort them: "'Pray for yourselves to God, for there's no help for you from your parents'" (*WL* 335). In short, unlike *Sons and Lovers*' Gertrude Morel, the narcissistic Lawrentian devouring mother *par excellence*, Mrs Crich has become the epitome of the disgorging/rejecting/abandoning mother.[18]

In Lawrence's writing, both insufficient and smothering maternal attachment lead to a failure to internalize a solid sense of self in a character, and Gerald is, indeed, one of Lawrence's hollow men, comparable to the orphan Anton Skrebensky of *The Rainbow*. His failure to develop a strong, integral selfhood has meant that he is unable to withstand the stresses and disappointments impinging upon him from the outside world: "such a strange pressure was upon him, as if the very middle of him were a vacuum, and outside were an awful tension" (*WL* 233).[19] He is also, predictably, hyper-vigilant, as we remark when Birkin, himself unseen, notices his friend at a railway station waiting for his train: "Even though he [Gerald] was reading the newspaper closely, he must keep a watchful eye on his external surroundings ... and he missed nothing" (*WL* 53). In the boat with Gudrun in "Water-Party" just before the catastrophe, Gerald is able to "[lapse] out for the first time in his life ... For he always kept such a keen attentiveness concentrated and unyielding in himself" (*WL* 178). Such habitual, largely unconscious watchfulness can only stem from a childhood extreme alertness to any symptom of attachment withdrawal by an unreliable mother and is a sure sign of a lack of basic trust. This is what Bowlby termed "anxious attachment," where the individual "has no confidence that his attachment figures will be accessible and responsive to him when he wants them to be" (*Attachment, Volume II* 213). In the words of later attachment researchers, "[t]he child learns that no pattern of response can be automatically assumed but that activation of attachment must always include watchfulness and uncertainty" (West and Sheldon-Keller, 76). And in that boat, lapsing out for the first time, the lesson Gerald learns, in effect, is that as soon as he relaxes his attention to the world around him, disaster ensues, in this case the drowning of his sister and Doctor Brindell. Much later, in the Alpine hotel room with Gudrun, Gerald's hyper-vigilance takes the form of a constant surveillance that Gudrun cannot tolerate and that he is not even aware of: "When she looked up, she saw him in the glass, standing behind her, watching unconsciously, not consciously seeing her, and yet watching" (*WL* 414). So although there may be a hint of a symbolic oedipal triangle with Gudrun and Loerke late in the novel, Gerald's extreme reaction to Gudrun's final rejection may be viewed less as jealous rage in the presence of a rival and more as a reaction to rejection by his chosen maternal surrogate. Indeed, Gudrun "knew that the fight had been between Gerald and herself, and the presence of the third party was a mere contingency" (*WL* 477).

Lawrence makes it almost too obvious in the chapter "Death and Love" that Gerald is drawn to Gudrun as a mother substitute even before the famous graveyard-to-bedroom scene. Gerald Doherty suggests that the "narrative unearths incest at the core of Gerald's erotic demand" and features "a continual substitution of the child/mother bonding for the male/female one" ("*Ars Erotica*" 144). I would only invert how Doherty relates his terms of reference: it is not that Gerald's desire for an attachment with Gudrun is an expression of an incestuous wish; rather, the symbolic incest is an expression of the need for maternal attachment. As the death of his father nears, Gerald feels "something of the terror of a destructive child" (*WL* 221). He accompanies Gudrun home after dinner at Shortlands in the wake of his mother's stinging rebuke: "'You mind *yourself*, or you'll find yourself in Queer Street ... You're hysterical, always were'" (*WL* 327). On the walk, Gerald feels reinvigorated by Gudrun's proximity as if her presence might restore his lost balance: "If he could put his arm round her, and draw her against him as they walked, he would equilibrate himself" (*WL* 328). And the imagery suggests a return to the womb: "she was the rich, lovely substance of his being. The warmth and motion of her walk suffused through him wonderfully" (*WL* 329). Gudrun herself buys into a proxy mother role, if only briefly. In the chapter "Snow," when Gerald wakes up to her smile and reflects it back to her, "[s]he remembered, that was how a baby smiled. It filled her with extraordinary radiant delight" (*WL* 419).

However, because Gerald's infantile and narcissistic needs are so great, Gudrun most often feels the union to be toxic, though, at times, thrillingly so: "The exultation in his voice was like a sweetish, poisonous drug to her ... She sipped the poison" (*WL* 329). A few days after his father's death, feeling "his own nothingness" (*WL* 337), Gerald seeks out an attachment as if his life depended on it, going in a somnambulistic state from his father's newly dug grave to the Brangwen home in Beldover and, by a kind of instinct, silently finding and entering Gudrun's bedroom. But he goes to her less as a lover and more as a child goes to its mother: "And he was a child, so soothed and restored and full of gratitude ... Mother and substance of all life she was. And he, child and man, received of her and was made whole ... as if he were bathed in the womb again" (*WL* 344). So this seemingly energetic industrialist who promotes technological progress is an emotional wreck who needs to regress childlike back to maternal security from his worldly exploits. Fatally for their relationship, however, Gudrun finds the dependency oppressive, nauseating, and exhausting. Late in the book, she thinks apropos of Gerald: "Was she his mother? Had she asked for a child, whom she must nurse through the nights, for her lover[?]" (*WL* 466). Possibly another woman with different needs of her own might have been able to give Gerald what he desired, but, then again, as I suggest in the Introduction, Gerald may be attracted to Gudrun in large part because he sees in her traits of his mother but unconsciously hopes to find in her a more reliable attachment. Thus the very privation that determines that Gudrun must be Gerald's go-to attachment object also virtually guarantees her ultimate act of abandonment.

We saw earlier that Hermione, desperate to keep Birkin from leaving her, actually drives him away in a self-defeating move to protect her fragile sense of self. Similarly, Gerald's strenuous efforts to avoid abandonment are the very thing that assures it. Like Conrad's Charles Gould in *Nostromo* (1904), Gerald has taken control of his father's mine, and, like Gould, he embraces modern technology in order to avoid the mine's abandonment. For Gerald, creating mechanical order ensures perfect repetition – *ad infinitum*, as Lawrence puts it in the character-defining chapter "The Industrial Magnate." It is a never-ending repetition that, virtually by definition, is predictable and permanent and therefore reassuringly reliable, unlike Mrs Crich's mothering. It promotes a sense of security that makes abandonment unthinkable. Thus Gerald's energetic industrial reforms serve his emotional requirements, and his compulsion for control is a function of his anxiety. This connection is made clear symbolically in the way Lawrence develops a startling identity between Gerald and the mine itself; Gerald associates his very being with the colliery. He is "afraid of some horrible collapse in himself" (*WL* 322), and, in a conversation with Gudrun, he suggests that he virtually *is* the mine on the verge of a cave-in, part of its underpinning: "'The whole of everything, and yourself included, is just on the point of caving in, and you are just holding it up with your hands … You can't stand holding the roof up with your hands, for ever'" (*WL* 325). So in emotional terms, irrational as it may sound, for the mine to be abandoned would be for Gerald himself to be forsaken. The supreme irony is that he is so successful in his modernizing task that he makes himself superfluous, much like the superannuated workers of his own firm, for whom he feels no sympathy. His "go," without which he will collapse, is no longer needed, just as his compulsive assertion of control will ensure that Gudrun must escape his mastery, as Lawrence portrays another iteration of his paradox of attachment.

Thus, like Hermione, whose need for control is expressed in a loss of control, Gerald's obsessive mastery leads to an ultimate loss of self-command. Gerald has succeeded in "his will to subjugate Matter to his own ends" (*WL* 223) in the form of the coal mine, thereby symbolically asserting control over the unreliable mother – the Latin *mater* being the etymon of the word "matter." Yet he experiences an existential crisis imaged by the "blue false bubbles" he imagines his eyes have become: he is afraid that they will "burst in a moment and leave clear annihilation" (*WL* 232). The bubble image and the word "annihilation" suggest a void at his core stemming from a childhood that also featured his accidental killing of his brother. How was Mrs Crich likely to have reacted to that event? Was there an underlying unconscious motive to the killing related to a sibling jealousy that arose out of unreliable mothering? Standing right next to Mrs Crich in "Shortlands," Birkin thinks to himself that "Gerald was Cain" (*WL* 26), the iconic model for fratricide. In the earlier story "Love Among the Haystacks" (first written in 1911, revised in 1913), there is a rivalry between two grown brothers that comes very close to fratricide, although, again, the incident in question is arguably the result of an accident.[20] It is, moreover, possible that Gerald's sudden release of Gudrun's throat, in what appeared to be the last stage of a passionate murder, as well as his earlier desperate dive to save his drowned sister are compulsively enacted attempts at a kind of displaced atonement for the killing of his brother in order to placate the abandoning mother. His deep dive into the lake certainly suggests an eventually fatal encounter with his unconscious demons, and what lies under the water, the recovery party eventually finds, is a man strangled by a woman: "Diana had her arms tight round the neck of the young man, choking him. 'She killed him,'" concludes Gerald (*WL* 189). The aborted strangling of Gudrun, then, has symbolic resonance related to Gerald's greatest fears.

By the end of *Women in Love*, Gerald Crich is no more, freezing to death in the Alpine snow when he falls over, no longer able or even willing to go anywhere. However, he is resurrected in Lawrence's play *Touch and Go*, which was completed around the end of October 1918 (*Plays* xlvi). It is not entirely clear why Lawrence reprised his characters from the novel. Possibly he felt that his story needed further development when he composed the play in October 1918 using the same central characters that appear in *Women in Love*.[21] But it is also possible that, unsettled by "tensions in the mining industry" in his home region at the time of composition (*Plays* xlv), Lawrence wished to explore the industrial conflict dramatically and simply went to characters he had already created, the Criches being based on the mine-owning Barber family of Lambclose House near Eastwood (*WL* 530). In any case, the *dramatis personae* of *Touch and Go* seem to be slightly later versions of the fictional personalities we see in the novel. Gerald Crich has become Gerald Barlow, still a colliery owner; his parents reappear as Mr and Mrs Barlow, and his sister as Winifred again. Gudrun has become Anabel Wrath, and Birkin is named Oliver Turton. The play's very title suggests a reprise of the "go" motif connected to Gerald, albeit with a different connotation.

What is remarkable about the play is that it hints strongly that familial and attachment complications rather than bread-and-butter issues are the source of the industrial violence depicted. Counter to what one might expect, the emotional cause of the violence in *Touch and Go* is no more the frustration of the demands for a living wage than the root cause of the violence depicted in *Women in Love* was the war: for Lawrence, both derive from psychological sources connected to human attachment. Industrial violence, it seems, is connected to and derives from domestic violence. Meeting Anabel/Gudrun again after a period of no contact, Gerald Barlow admits that he is angry at how their relationship ended, and it is precisely her abandonment of him that rankles: "I'm angry because you treated me – well, so impudently really – clearing out and leaving me" (*Plays* 397). That epithet – "impudent" – comes up in this same scene when Gerald adds that "I'm angry with the colliers, with Labour, for its low-down impudence" (*Plays* 397). Downing tools means abandoning one's workplace, that same workplace with which, in the novel at least, Gerald identifies on a personal, even visceral level.

Even more notable is how Lawrence connects the industrial violence to the relationship between Gerald Barlow and his mother. In one memorable scene, Mrs Barlow contemptuously mocks Gerald's attachment needs, telling him that "[y]ou only know the feeding-bottle," and equates isolation with manhood, saying that he lacks the "power to be alone" (*Plays* 401), an ability that, as we saw in the Introduction, depends on the child's trust in a mother's reliability. Mrs Barlow then becomes violent with Gerald in order to, as she says, beat some manhood into him. The stage directions read: *"suddenly advancing on him and beating him fiercely."* Shortly afterwards, she picks up a large fan and, according to the stage directions, hits him on the head with it (*Plays* 401). Having told his mother that "I am a match for you even in violence" (*Plays* 401), Gerald does become frenzied himself when, in Act III, he meets the union leader, Job Arthur Freer,[22] throwing him to the ground, kicking him, and telling him to go. When Freer replies that it is Gerald who will leave, the "go" motif takes on a threatening cast. Indeed, there is mob violence in the play's final scene directed toward Gerald, Anabel, and Oliver, where a lynching seems imminent for a time. Taken as a causal chain, the implication of the various violent scenes is that the abuse or neglect of a child by a parent leads to the development of the kind of adult who in turn both physically abuses and bullies his way through life. When that adult happens to be a "master" in an England torn by industrial strife, counter-violence on a large scale ensues.

Taking their cue from Lawrence's "Foreword to *Women in Love*," where he expresses the wish "that the bitterness of the war may be taken for granted in the characters" (*WL* 485), most readers assume that the violence in the novel is an expression of a general degradation in human relations brought about by the Great War. In his essay "Violence in *Women in Love*," Mark Kinkead-Weekes goes beyond that assumption and puts his finger on an inner hollowness and neediness, especially with respect to Hermione and Gerald, as the source of a vulnerability that can trigger violence as a defence (224, 241). He concludes that in Lawrence's novel "[v]iolence has its sources it seems both in hollowness and dependency, *and* in egotism and self-assertion" (243), but he does not explore the emotional root causes of these traits. At least in Gerald's case but also more broadly, the violence in *Women in Love* is related to a hypersensitivity to loss of attachment deriving from a persistent neediness never assuaged by reliable caregiving.

Gerald's acute sensitivity to attachment loss appears in a more covert fashion in Jack Grant, the protagonist of Lawrence's second Australian novel, *The Boy in the Bush*.[23] There are a number of superficial as well as more significant commonalities between Jack and the Gerald figure of *Women in Love*. For one thing, both Gerald and Jack are associated with the biblical Cain, the archetypal fratricidal outcast.[24] In *Women in Love*, we learn that Gerald killed his brother as a youth in some unexplained accident with a gun, and, as we have seen, Birkin thinks of him explicitly as a Cain. Jack himself feels that "[h]e was a sinner, a Cain," "born condemned," and that "[h]e belonged to a race apart, like the race of Cain" (*BB* 10, 193), a negative self-image that has been promoted in large part by a non-nurturing upbringing by aunts whose negative mirroring is burned in his memory. They called him "contrairy [*sic*]" and a "naughty little boy," "[i]nsubordinate. Untrustworthy" (*BB* 39). Unlike Gerald, Jack is a fratricide by association rather than literally, although he does kill someone. As Ruderman notes (*Devouring* 118), his killing of the brutal Easu Ellis of the Red Ellis clan evokes the Jacob-Esau sibling rivalry in Genesis, a conflict between fraternal twins that begins at birth when Jacob pulls on Esau's heel in a vain attempt to be the first born. (The name Jacob [*Ya'akov*] means "he grabbed by the heel" [*akev*].) Jacob later tricks Esau out of his primogenitary blessing from their aged and blind father, Isaac.

Lawrence clearly means to link Jack Grant to the biblical Jacob as well as to Cain. On his arrival in Australia, Jack settles in with the Jacob Ellis clan rather than their cousins, the Easu Ellises. Moreover, given Jack's bigamous ambitions late in the novel, it is relevant to note that the biblical Jacob had two wives, Leah and Rachel. Jack's blessing comes not from his parents, who fail him, he feels, in their perfunctory recognition by post of his twenty-first birthday, but in the form of a Blessing*ton*, when Hilda Blessington promises herself to him as a sort of second wife at the very end. Equally, we are clearly meant to associate Easu Ellis with the biblical Esau (and Esau is, in fact, his legal name). The hirsute and reddish Easu in *The Boy in the Bush* is even physically similar to the biblical Esau, who is born "ruddy all over like a hairy mantle" (Genesis 25:25) and who acquires the additional name Edom (red) because of his hankering after the red pottage Jacob gives him in exchange for his birthright. In Lawrence's novel, then, Jack and Easu are siblings by association, and they are rivals for a time for Monica, who gives birth to Easu's (presumed) child, Jane, but marries Jack in the end.

The link to Gerald, then, is through the motif of fratricide and the feeling of estrangement, but there are also more profound connections between Jack and Gerald in terms of deficient selfhood, abandonment anxiety, and propensity to violence. Here, I think, the comparison usefully serves to undermine the bluster regarding Jack's manhood and strength, which many readers have taken to be a self-consistent if perhaps objectionable characterization. For as we and Lawrence know, for all his vaunted mastery, Gerald is, at bottom, weak, deficient, and fragmentary, and so is Jack, in my view, albeit in a less obvious way. As we saw above, Gerald Crich feels that he is, so to speak, holding up the roof of his very selfhood with his hands and is afraid of a collapse inward like some unstable mine shaft. Similarly, when informed by Easu that Monica has had a baby and is in a relationship with Pink-eye Percy, Jack feels that "the world had caved in" on him (*BB* 274). And in his delirious wandering in the bush after his fatal encounter with Easu shortly thereafter, he feels that he "is groping in a dark, unfathomable cave, and that the walls of the cave was his own aching body," and "[h]e was stumbling as he walked. And waiting for the walls of the cave to crash in and bury him altogether" (*BB* 289). Likewise, both Gerald and Jack attempt to control aspects of the earth – Gerald in his coal works, Jack in his gold mine – and thereby symbolically to control the women they are so emotionally dependent upon. Jack sees the discovery and extraction of gold from the earth as a matter of willpower: "he must master it in the veins of the earth" (*BB* 306). Again, like Gerald, mastering the earth for Jack means controlling attachment, ultimately to the mother: earth is matter, and matter derives from *mater* (mother). For Jack the connection is more than etymological: women in general, he tells Mary, are "'not separated out of the earth. They're like black ore'" (*BB* 328).

The male swagger that partly disguises Jack's weakness is mostly attributable to Jack himself, but Lawrence at times seems to partake in the pretence as well. As David Game has written, "there appears to be much of Lawrence in Jack Grant" (*Australia* 219). Even the Cain reference links Jack to Lawrence in an indirect way, for in Lawrence's first Australian novel, *Kangaroo* (1923), the Lawrence stand-in, Richard Lovatt Somers, also sees himself as Cain when looking back on his isolation during the war years in Cornwall in the chapter "The Nightmare": "He saw himself set apart from mankind, a Cain, or worse" (*K* 249). However, perhaps because Jack's character originated in Mollie Skinner's manuscript rather than in his own experience, Lawrence is able to keep a critical distance from him, at least at times. For example, the narrator makes a comment on Jack's chronic desire simply to "get away," from he knows not what, with a typical Lawrentian statement on the double gyre of equilibrium that seems to be outside of Jack's own range of thinking: "however far you may get away from one thing, by so much do you draw near to another" (*BB* 37). More often, though, the reader sees little that Jack does not see. Through free indirect discourse, we are obliged to adopt Jack's point of view most of the time, so that we are subject to some extent to Jack's obsessions and distortions of reality without always having an objective counter to them.

When it comes to focalization in fiction, Lawrence is no Henry James, to put it mildly, and it is particularly difficult in this novel to calibrate the degree of separation at various points in the novel among Lawrence, the narrator, and Jack Grant. Lawrence developed a unique, shifting point of view in his novels after *The White Peacock* whereby, in the same novel, the narrator sometimes seems indistinguishable from the character and sometimes wholly separate and omniscient, with many shades of nuance in between. At times, Lawrence's third-person narration feels like a first-person perspective that has been converted into third person (something he actually did sometimes in revision), and often we wonder how much distance there is between the perceiving consciousness and D.H. Lawrence himself. The technique can be effective and was no doubt necessary for Lawrence to be able to inject the kind of genuine emotion into his characterizations that is a hallmark of his fiction. As David Ellis puts it, "one of his strengths as a novelist is certainly the fairly direct attribution to his protagonists of feelings of his own which in most of us go unavowed" (*DG* 138). However, if we want to determine to what extent Lawrence himself endorses his character's opinions, the slippery Lawrentian focalization can be an obstacle.

In *Kangaroo*, Somers's wife, Harriet, other characters, and even occasionally Somers himself push back strongly against the protagonist's arguments or rationales. At one point, Somers calls his own desire to save mankind "blarney" (*K* 272), and the narrator will occasionally inject comments such as "But Richard *was* wrong" or "But Somers was mistaken" (*K* 22, 42). In *The Boy in the Bush*, by comparison, there is much less in the way of opposition to Jack's way of thinking. There are some indications that Lawrence takes a more objective, even contrary, view of several of Jack's more egregious thoughts about women, gender roles, and race than some critics have assumed, but the evidence is not conclusive. As Game speculates, Lawrence's explorations in *The Boy in the Bush* may be related to his one and only separation from Frieda during their marriage while he was writing the novel (*Australia* 196), but that, nonetheless, "Jack's quest is tempered by Lawrentian irony" (195). Game recognizes the difficulties caused by the shifty point of view and pertinently asks whether the reader's sympathy is with Jack or Mary in their conflict over "The Offer to Mary," as the relevant chapter is called. On the one hand, there is "the narrator's jeering summation" of Jack's failure to achieve what he wants when Mary turns him down, an intervention that "deeply contests Jack's vision at this point." On the other hand, the offer to Mary is consistent with Jack's plans to create a community that resembles the one Lawrence dreamed of with his Rananim (Game, *Australia* 212). Indeed, "Jack wanted to make a place on earth for a few aristocrats-to-the-bone" (*BB* 308). Perhaps Lawrence is ambivalent or even confused on this point, but I believe that if we focus on Jack's emotional make-up and look at his attachment complications, we see that, while Lawrence may share some of Jack's feelings, opinions, and biases, he realizes and allows us to conclude that they come from a place of weakness and are defensive in nature. Lawrence explicitly stated that his interest in Jack was psychological, as he wrote to Mollie Skinner, "I have tried, taking your inner cue, to make a rather daring development, psychologically" (*4L* 524).

Both Game and Ruderman have written interesting analyses of particular aspects of *The Boy in the Bush*. In *D.H. Lawrence and the Devouring Mother* (1984), Ruderman sees Jack as an outlaw hero and the novel "as an important stage in the evolution of Lawrence's ideas on leadership" (115). In particular, Lawrence defines manhood here in terms of resistance to the "devouring mother" and conscripts nature into the struggle (115). Jack is hostile to women because he is afraid of them (116) and is in search of an ideal father (118). This argument is generally persuasive, but I think that Ruderman misreads Jack's character when contrasting him and his friend Tom, who is "fixated on his mother," a person he never knew (he was brought home one day as an infant by Jacob Ellis, whose son he is, presumably). Unlike Tom, writes Ruderman, Jack "does everything in his power to sever the cord between himself and his own mother," whom Ruderman suggests is one of the best parents in Lawrence's fiction (which is not saying very much) (*Devouring* 117). As I see it, Tom's fixation – or, more precisely, Jack's reaction to Tom's fixation – reflects Jack's preoccupation with his own mother, only Tom is much more conscious of his loss and open about his need: "'Who was my mother? That's what I want to know. Who was she?'" (*BB* 65). Jack can barely tolerate such naked neediness in his friend, as it threatens to bring powerfully repressed emotions to consciousness in himself. One might also argue that Jack's arrival in Australia, and specifically in the area from which his mother hails, is, at least symbolically, an attempt to get closer to her by visiting the locale of her past.[25] He craves attachment, feels abandoned, and tends to see abandonment wherever he looks. Even the lambs at Wandoo are viewed as "motherless," and Jack sees the young Ellises when he first meets them as "waifs lost in this new country" (*BB* 52), a transparent projection. "Why did these children seem so motherless and fatherless, so much on their own? – It was very much how Jack felt himself" (*BB* 54).

Ruderman picks up on Lawrence's description of Gran Ellis as a character akin to the grandmother in the fairy tale Little Red Ridinghood (*Devouring* 120; *BB* 72), almost literally a devouring mother figure like the witch in Hansel and Gretel, who promises the oral gratification denied the children by their mother but who secretly means to gratify her own oral craving by devouring them. The fairy-tale grandmother (and the witch, for that matter) can also be seen, less dramatically, as an expression of a child's experience of parental unreliability. Granny is the one who is devoured in Little Red Ridinghood, to be sure, but by taking the grandmother's place in her bed and donning her clothing, the wolf, in effect, turns Granny into a devouring mother. What big teeth, indeed. If a hungry wolf can, in effect, transform into one's grandmother, equally, one's grandmother/mother might become a voracious wolf. Certainly she would also then be a mother figure one cannot trust, just as the little boy Jack learned that he could not rely on his mother. She frequently left home to join his father abroad at his military postings while placing Jack in the care of unsympathetic and occasionally abusive proxy caregivers, the hated aunts of Jack's memory. Jack's love for his mother "could not but be intermittent" since at times she lived with him in England, but "more often she left him and went off with his father to Jamaica or some such place" (*BB* 11). Jack's mother, then, is not a devouring mother who threatens reincorporation, but rather, like the older Mrs Crich in *Women in Love*, a rejecting/abandoning mother at the other end of the attachment scale, but every bit as unreliable in the sense of prioritizing her own needs over those of her child. We do not know how far "The House of Ellis" departed from real-life events, but Lawrence seems deliberately to underscore Jack's alienation from his parents. The model for Jack, Mollie's brother, John Russell Skinner, was sent ahead to Western Australia by his family, but about a year later they joined him there and always intended to do so (*BB* xlv). No such reunion awaits Jack in the novel, and Mrs Ellis, the mother at Wandoo, is an inadequate substitute mother for Jack: she is "mother of her own children first. She felt kindly towards him. But he was another woman's son" (*BB* 49).

Game devotes three chapters wholly or in part to *The Boy in the Bush* in his 2015 study, *D.H. Lawrence's Australia*, where he places the novel within the context of his argument that Lawrence's career-long engagement with Australia had to do first and foremost with ideas of degeneration and regeneration: "Lawrence came to believe that certain indigenous races, including Australian Aborigines and Native Americans, exemplified qualities which had been lost to Europeans through industrialisation and urbanisation" (161).[26] Given his theme, Game is understandably not centrally focused on Jack Grant's psychological make-up but sees his development as "ultimately a uniquely Lawrentian expression of regeneration" (165). Game gives us a thorough and interesting take on Lawrence's evolving views of races and race relations, but to fully understand *The Boy in the Bush* and, in particular, the central figure of Jack Grant and to see that the putative rebirth is wishful thinking on Jack's or perhaps Lawrence's part, we need to delve into his psychology, and Lawrence gives us all the material we need by providing us access to Jack's interior life and his childhood.

Game's view is in line with Ruderman's suggestion that the novel is mistitled and that *The Man in the Bush* is more like it (*Devouring* 115, 123), since the novel purports to show Jack going through what amounts to a rite of passage in the bush to emerge a man, no longer a boy.[27] I would counter that Jack never actually matures much; he simply becomes less concerned over the course of the novel about concealing his true nature. Tom has it about right when, in reaction to Jack's claims of having changed fundamentally during their stint up north, he says, "'You're just the blanky same'" (*BB* 259). Jack never really outgrows his childhood narcissism, which is the product of deprivation and an upbringing that clearly fails to match his emotional needs. His later supposed authority and strength are all bluster, overcompensation, and wishful thinking. (Ruderman acknowledges that the ending is "the stuff of ... wish-fulfilment" [*Devouring* 124].) Even Jack's demonstrable charismatic attractiveness, especially to women, is only skin-deep. It has everything to do with his preternatural, almost feminine, good looks and perhaps something to do with his pugnacity, which misleadingly might seem to indicate more than mere physical strength: fighting a male kangaroo, fighting the imposing Easu, fighting Long-armed Jake at the Jamboree. As he writes to his English friend, the pugilist Pug, "Must have something to hit" (*BB* 104), and the narrator tells us that Jack "loved a fight even a long, invisible one" (*BB* 254). His appeal has nothing to do with any natural authority or genuine leadership qualities except perhaps stubbornness. In fact, Jack's puny natural authority is to Gran Ellis's formidable power what his cut-off finger is to her amputated leg: a faint echo. After her death, she becomes his touchstone, but his attempts at mastery are an assumed aping of what comes naturally to her. Jack's belief in dark gods – in some sense a spill-over from Somers's periodic preoccupation in *Kangaroo* – also signals weakness. Lawrence's references to these anti-Christian dark gods here and in other late works may have their source in Aboriginal culture (perhaps derived from Frazer's *Totemism and Exogamy*), as Game suggests (*Australia* 188–9), but, psychologically speaking, Jack's belief in them is a projection to an external authority of deep feelings and decisions he is ill-equipped to deal with given his insufficiently developed sense of self. He leaves it up to his Lord to decide if he should kill Easu and marry Monica. Of course, such a Lord will decide in favour of whatever Jack desires most, but he can pretend that the decision was made for him.

In addition, Jack is prone to delusional and paranoid thinking on occasion, especially after his two crises, the first fight with Easu and then the wandering in the bush after the later fatal encounter with his rival. Even before he fights Easu, he feels that people are out to get him: "he knew they would kill him if they found out what he really was" (*BB* 156). After the deadly confrontation with Easu, Jack wanders deliriously in the bush, suffering from loss of blood and dehydration. He thinks of

Monica: "Why had she betrayed him? Why had they all betrayed him, betrayed him and the thing he wanted from life[?]" (*BB* 287). Most significantly, after Mary rejects him and his anger builds to rage, we get one long paragraph of paranoid ravings in the first person, with no physical debility, in this instance, as a contributing factor. Everyone is out to harm him, and even Mary "would like me to be killed" because somewhere she hates him. People grudge him his very being, and it has been that way since he was born. "My aunts, my own father ... even my mother would not have tried to prevent them from destroying me" (*BB* 334). Even if we take some of these ravings metaphorically – and they are not presented that way – this is crazy stuff that suggests a serious mental disturbance.[28]

In fact, madness runs in the family and there is an implicit suggestion that it has touched Jack too. Jack's first cousin on his mother's side, John (Mad Jack) Grant, a namesake to our hero, suffers from periodic bouts of insanity. In his will, Mad Jack leaves Jack his farm, a place that, in the end, Jack is reluctant to inherit. But one wonders if he has genetically inherited the propensity to insanity instead. As Lawrence wrote elsewhere, if the individual one depends upon emotionally departs, "the soul must bleed to death, not whole, and not quite sane" (*MN* 231). While at the same farm with Jack and Mary, Jack's patron, Mr George, "thought [Jack] not normal. The boy had to be put in a category by himself, like a madman in a solitary cell" (*BB* 319), and Mary blurts out in exasperation with him, "'There's something wrong with you'" (*BB* 326). Jack's successes in the end are brought about by a fairy-tale-like fulfilment of wishes: striking gold when he is on the point of giving up his mining venture, and the arrival of Hilda Blessington, appearing out of nowhere, to accept the concubine role that Mary had rejected. Hilda and her arrival may derive in part from Lawrence's hopes for a relationship with Dorothy Brett around this time (Ellis, *DG* 156), but in the context of the novel, she seems an improbable *dea ex machina*. Without those rather unlikely plot developments, Jack appears to be on the verge of madness at the end. As it is, he has the prospect of the best of both worlds in the attachment universe: he has the security of his connection to Monica in which he has full authority to the extent of taking Hilda as his second, *de facto* wife, and he also has the unfettered autonomy to go exploring away from home. Ironically, like the wandering parents he so resented for their absence from his life, he himself, we cannot but assume, will become a nomadic and absent father to his children back home.

Both Ruderman and Game, I would say, underplay Jack's weaknesses and magnify his strengths. Ruderman accepts Jack's supposed self-sufficiency as genuine (*Devouring* 120), but, as we know from attachment studies, self-sufficiency can be a defensive pose, as I believe it is in Jack's case. At a very young age, Jack resorts to a spurious sense of autonomy in reaction to his mother's unreliability: "But [his mother] had to leave him. And he loved her, but did not dream of depending on her. He knew it as a tiny child: he would never have to depend on anybody" (*BB* 12). He also tends to rationalize his feeling of being abandoned: "His mother was far away – England was far away. He was alone there leaning on the paddock gate in Australia. After all, perhaps the very best thing was to be alone" (*BB* 137). Such ballooning bluster is definitively popped when we see the extent to which the Ellis family connection is vital to him and how extreme and paranoid Jack's reaction is when he is frustrated in his designs upon Monica and Mary. Until his arrival Down Under, he always avoided girls because of a fear of rejection, not because he is not attracted to them: "With girls and women he felt exposed to some sort of danger – as if something were going to seize him by the neck, from behind, when he wasn't looking" (*BB* 32), a far cry from any self-assurance. When he finds himself attracted to Monica "to his own surprise and disgust" (*BB* 115) and discovers that, quite against his own will, he needs her, he hates his neediness because it threatens the defence of self-sufficiency: his desire is a "shame and anguish." "He would have given anything, if this need never have come upon him" (*BB* 148). "Only when he was alone again ... did he resume the fight to recover himself from her again. To be free as he had been before ... To preserve himself intact" (*BB* 149).

Jack's habitual indifference is one of the guises of his compulsive self-sufficiency and, like Cyril Beardsall's detachment in *The White Peacock*, is akin to Bowlby's third term in the sequence of observed responses in children to separation (which, in Bowlby, unlike Mahler, is detrimental because it refers to a severance initiated by the caregiver): "protest, despair, and detachment" (*Attachment, Volume II* 6). The detachment, however, can keep at bay Jack's true anxieties for only so long: "He could go on careless and unheeding ... for a while. Then came these fits of reckoning and remembering ... His life was all unhinged. What was he driving at? What was he making for? Where was he going?" (*BB* 215). His lack of self-knowledge is as much a lack of self as it is a lack of knowledge. Sometimes his feeling of inauthenticity is overwhelming, and then he tends to project it outward, the colonial make-believe world of Australia providing a suitable target. At the church service for the strangely simultaneous deaths of Jacob and Gran Ellis, everything feels unreal to Jack, and the recourse to childhood in his thoughts is a tell-tale indication that the inauthenticity he sees around him comes from a hollowness within himself: "Was anything quite real? That was what the shadows, the people, the buildings seemed all to be asking. It was like children's games, real and not real, actual and yet unsubstantial, and the people seemed to feel as children feel" (*BB* 180).

What stands out as perhaps the most significant feature of Jack's character from the viewpoint of this study is his life-long, smouldering, and occasionally explosive anger: "He was used to feeling angry: a steady, almost blithe sort of anger. And beyond that, he had always been able to summon up an indifference to things ... retreat upon himself and insulate himself from contact" (*BB* 139). And again: as he prepares to ride off with Tom away from Wandoo to a sheep station at Geraldton, "the strange volcano of anger which slumbered at the bottom of his soul ... threw up jets of silent rage, which hardened rapidly into a black, rocky indifference ... This was his nature. He was himself vaguely aware of the unplumbed crater of silent anger which lay at the bottom of his soul" (*BB* 193).[29] His indifference, then, which can manifest as seeming self-sufficiency, is a pose in aid of temporarily dealing with feelings of rage largely through an externalizing projection – thus the appropriateness of the image of the volcano, which disgorges the raging fire within. Jack himself does not know why he deliberately provoked and humiliated Easu to the point of bringing things to a crisis between them. He has little insight into his anger and wonders at his trial "what unconscious purpose" was behind his wish to kill Easu (*BB* 297). Jack can deal with his underlying emotional turmoil through the outlet of violence, as in his fights with Easu, or by means of the defence mechanism of compulsive self-sufficiency, as in the above quotations. He oscillates between the two in the course of the novel. The former promises to achieve by force what he cannot attain by any other means, and the latter solves the problem by denying that there is one. In effect, Jack's two alternating coping strategies combine in one character the two different and ultimately futile coping styles of Gerald and Birkin in *Women in Love*.

Jack's anger, like Gerald's, originates from a chronic anxiety founded on a lack of basic trust and fear of abandonment derived from childhood experience. When Jack was only four years old, his aunts would resort to disciplining him with threats of a policeman, or they would drop him over the garden fence into the neighbouring field with threats of keeping him there all night if he did not apologize for his naughty behaviour. These are things that Jack thinks back on as he journeys to Wandoo. He also feels a kind of exultation at starting a new life in Australia, and yet, unaccountably, "somewhere in his breast and throat tears were heaving. Why? Why? He didn't know. Only he wanted to cry till he died" (*BB* 43).

Jack's profound longing for attachment becomes evident as soon as he joins the Ellis clan at Wandoo as a kind of honorary member on the strength of his mother's family's connections. Attending a benefit concert with the family on the evening of his arrival, he hears a rendition of the Scottish song "My Ain Folk" and cynically thinks "he hadn't got any 'ain folk', and he didn't want any," and yet he can hardly hold back the tears "as his heart fairly broke in him" (*BB* 34). Very soon he feels "a sort of passionate love for the family – as a savage must feel for his tribe. He felt he would never leave the family. He must always be near them, always in close physical contact with them" (*BB* 58). All of Jack's pent-up yearning for attachment becomes invested in the family: "He felt he *must* be there with the family, and then nothing else mattered" (*BB* 59). Yet he is quick to sense betrayal after years of unreliable mothering in England. Sitting at Gran's bedside as she is dying, he feels "[t]he family seemed to abandon him as they abandoned Gran" (*BB* 171). Upset later that he cannot find Monica, "[h]e hated this family and family money business" (*BB* 267).

Perhaps the best evidence that Lawrence views Jack with some distance is the character's manifest lack of self-knowledge or even of an authentic self to know in the first place. At John Grant's farmhouse after the cousin's death, when Jack and Mary look at a family photograph album, Mary notices a striking resemblance between Jack and the pictures of his mother's family, a resemblance he simply cannot see at all (*BB* 323). He is incapable of perceiving himself for who and what he is. His whole life has been an attempt to repress overwhelming and threatening feelings, and yet he can say to Mary, "'I don't care about feelings'" (*BB* 332). His denial of his dependency is so strong that he tells himself that women are the needy ones. They are incomplete fragments without men: "All women were only parts of some whole, when they were by themselves: let them be as clever as they might. They were creatures of earth, and fragments, all of them" (*BB* 332). The Lawrence who convincingly portrayed strong women and needy men in his great Brangwensaga (see chapter 3) now gives us a character who claims that women are fragmentary and need men to complete them while men are self-sufficient. It is an open question whether Lawrence here is betraying his own artistic instincts and his deepest emotional knowledge or is contesting a reaction he knows is flawed. In any case, Lawrence's deep insight into attachment quandaries and relational deficits from childhood make *The Boy in the Bush* a fascinating study in abandonment anxiety.

2

GENDER IDENTIFICATION

> I was born hating my father: as early as ever I can remember, I shivered with horror when he touched me.
> Letter to Rachel Annand Taylor, 3 December 1910 (*IL* 190)

> Lawrence's passage from mother-identified son to angry masculinist is one of the clearest and most fascinating instances in literary biography of what Jessica Benjamin has called "the Oedipal riddle" – fascinating precisely because that "riddle" was suffered through, with tortured ambivalence, over many years, not solved quickly and brutally, as it is in so many male lives.
> Alan Williamson, *Almost a Girl: Male Writers and Female Identification* (52)

> [T]he power of the liberator-father is used to defend against the engulfing mother.
> Jessica Benjamin, *The Bonds of Love* (133)

Shortly after Grace and Monica meet Jack in *The Boy in the Bush*, they remark on his "lovely eyelashes," and Monica suggests that "'[h]e'd almost do for a girl'" (*BB* 33). Another of the Ellises, Lennie, jokes to Jack that "'I'll be dressin' up in Katie's skirts n' spoonin' y' one of these bright nights'" (*BB* 86). Such gender fluidity is far from rare in Lawrence. In the short story "Tickets Please" (1919), the tram inspector John Thomas Raynor is a "fine Cock-of-the-walk" (*EME* 36) whose name (John Thomas), nickname ("Coddy"), and flirtatiousness suggest a hyper-masculinized character among a bevy of female ticket collectors during the war.[1] Nevertheless, he jocularly identifies himself as female when, with a "Ladies only" admonition, the tram girls temporarily bar him from entering the waiting room reserved for women. He replies "'That's me!' … It was one of his favourite exclamations" (*EME* 40). The key event in this story is the mob attack on John Thomas by the women as payback for his philandering ways, a scene that is loosely based on Lawrence's youthful experience while briefly working at Haywood's surgical garments factory when some of the work-girls there, considering him standoffish and superior, cornered him one day and attempted to take off his trousers (Worthen, *EY* 100–1). The autobiographical element to the scene and the story in general suggest a Lawrence who both indirectly conceded his own female identification and overcompensated to deny it, as does this statement from *Fantasia of the Unconscious*: "many young men feel so very like what they imagine a girl must feel, that hence they draw the conclusion that they must have a large share of female sex inside them. False conclusion" (*PFU* 126). In the same section of *Fantasia*, Lawrence discusses what he calls "the hermaphrodite fallacy" (*PFU* 129), whereby men begin to see themselves as half female. He insists, on the contrary, that "[a] child is either male or female ... Every single living cell is either male or female" (*PFU* 126). That there is a defensiveness to this unqualified and seemingly authoritative pronouncement is strongly suggested especially if we consider these earlier formulations regarding gender fluidity in the Hardy essay: in the act of love, "that which is mixed in me becomes pure, that which is female in me is given to the female" (*STH* 80); and "[f]or every man comprises male and female in his being, the male always struggling for predominance. A woman likewise consists in male, and female, with female predominant" (*STH* 94).

In *Aaron's Rod*, Rawdon Lilly finds Aaron lounging in bed one day and conjures up a gender confusion to describe his friend's apparent laziness: "'here you are in bed like a woman who's had a baby'" (*AR* 290). There are also several instances of cross-dressing in Lawrence's fiction, which seem to suggest female identification if not outright envy of women. Paul Morel tries on a pair of Clara's stockings in *Sons and Lovers* when he is staying overnight in her room while Clara sleeps with her mother (*SL* 381). Mr Houghton in *The Lost Girl* (1920), during his career as a designer and manufacturer of women's clothing, is rumoured to try out his creations "upon his own elegant thin person, before the privacy of his own cheval mirror" (*LG* 10). There is sometimes a fine line between a kind of solipsism and a female identification in a male character. When Paul and Clara are at the theatre, Paul's desire for her seems to turn back upon himself, as if he wants to *be* her rather than simply love her. The body he is so attracted to seems to be identified with his own: "He was Clara's white, heavy arms, her throat, her moving bosom. That seemed to be himself" (*SL* 375). Significantly, such an almost transmigratory identification seems, oddly, to leave him bereft of any identity at all: "There was no himself" (*SL* 375). It is not always easy in Lawrence to distinguish the nuances of female identification from those of an amorphous sense of self, simply because the two are implicated strongly with each other and both derive from the nature of Lawrence's primary, maternal attachment. Lawrence has a remarkable ability to strikingly dramatize psychological needs and defences, especially those related to what Schapiro calls "the deficient self" (113). Apart from his ruthless honesty, what made Lawrence such a profound psychological writer was his early-life intense – far too intense – attunement to his mother's affective life.

Lawrence often used female protagonists in his fiction and convincingly portrayed their thought processes, an ability no doubt sharpened by his closeness to his mother and his sensitivity to her moods, and later by his conversations with Frieda, during which he picked her brains for clues to a female perspective. Ursula Brangwen in *The Rainbow*, Alvina Houghton in *The Lost Girl*, and Kate Leslie in *The Plumed Serpent* (1926), just to mention the protagonists in the novels, are all major creative successes, while the characterization of Connie Chatterley in *Lady Chatterley's Lover* incorporates a persuasive portrayal of female sexuality. In the fragment "A Pure Witch," written early in 1924 but unpublished until Cambridge University Press included it in its 1995 publication of *The Woman Who Rode Away and Other Stories*, we even see a first-person female narrator whose family is close enough to Lawrence's own to suggest that she is a thinly disguised female version of himself: the family adores the mother and hates the father, a beloved older brother dies, and then the mother succumbs to cancer (*WWRA* 377). The narrator, now almost fifty years old, claims, "I was a beautiful girl" (*WWRA* 377), and recalls the time when she was nineteen and fell in love with an older Italian man named Giulio. It is a bravura performance of cross-gender identification in fiction that brings to mind Norman Mailer's characterization of Lawrence as "a man who had the soul of a beautiful, imperious, and passionate woman, yet was locked into the body of a middling male physique" (152).

Lawrence's positive female identification, derived ultimately from his strong but overwhelming bond with his mother, was not straightforward, however, because it coexisted with a denial and a sense that he lacked adequate masculine identification. As Janice Hubbard Harris puts it, "Lawrence found femaleness threatening partly because he identified strongly with it" (170). Lawrence's poem "Monologue of a Mother," told as it is from what he imagines is his mother's point of view, shows both a strong identification with her and a guilty realization that he must separate from her: the mother imagines the son as a bird with a broken wing that

> … drags and beats
> Along the fence perpetually, seeking release
> From me, from the hand of my love which creeps up, needing
> His happiness, whilst he in displeasure retreats.
>   (*Poems* 18, ll. 15–18)

The corollary to female identification in Lawrence is often a counter-attempt to bond with a man who might provide the masculine protection of a father. "[B]eware how you deny the father-quick of yourself," he writes in *Fantasia of the Unconscious*. "You may be denying the most intrinsic quick of all" (*PFU* 76). In some cases, the male-male bonding reflects a desire to substitute for the mother, as we see in *Aaron's Rod* when Lilly takes on a masculine maternal task in trying to revivify Aaron: "'I'm going to rub you as mothers do their babies whose bowels don't work'" (*AR* 96).

In the early story "A Modern Lover" (begun in late 1909), the Lawrence figure, Cyril Mersham, becomes strongly attracted to his erstwhile girlfriend's new love interest, Tom Vickers. He "noted the fine limbs, the solid, large thighs, and the thick wrists" and finds him altogether "lovable" (*LAH* 39, 40). But what becomes clear is that the attraction is associated as much with a desire to be paternally protected as it is with a sexual longing: "He rather enjoyed being taken into Tom's protection" (*LAH* 44).[2] He even fantasizes a filial relationship with him by imagining Tom in the future "with a family of children, a fine father" (*LAH* 40). The development exemplifies a pattern we often see in Lawrence's fiction: a female identification that leads to a desire for a countervailing male connection, which, in turn, appears to harken back to a child's longing for a strong, protective father figure. As Jessica Benjamin puts it, "the power of the liberator-father is used to defend against the engulfing mother" (133), but the complication in the case of Lawrence's own family is that the father was substantially devoid of power, making the filial longing forever unfulfilled. Thus the complicated gender identification, which is evident in much of his writing and enriches it, is directly related to Lawrence's earliest relationships and the attachment paradoxes they involved. His childhood situation made all the more urgent his attempt as an adult to right the identification imbalance in his writing.

That Lawrence identified at least in part with femaleness has been explored by writers as diverse as Mailer and Carol Siegel, as noted by Williamson (51–2), and as far back as Anaïs Nin in her "unprofessional study" of 1932.[3] Lawrence came by his initial female gender identification honestly, so to speak. In the words of biographer Jeffrey Meyers, "Lawrence was a weak and delicate child, who could not bear harsh criticism, rough sports or physical fights. He spent most of his time playing with girls. All his teachers and schoolmates agreed that he was girlish rather than manly" (23). The homoerotic aspects of Lawrence's writing have long been noted and seen by some as evidence of an ambivalent or bisexual orientation in Lawrence himself. For example,

Howard J. Booth argues that in *Sons and Lovers* the attraction between Paul Morel and Baxter Dawes is at least partly sexual in nature ("Later Chapters" 62 *et passim*). Whatever Paul's unacknowledged sexual desires, there is little doubt that Lawrence himself was capable of a physical attraction to men. However, the male-to-male relationships in *Sons and Lovers* and elsewhere in Lawrence are clearly associated with a yearning more for protection, security, and paternal care than for sexual relations. Both Cowan and Kinkead-Weekes consider it more likely that what this feature of his writing suggests is a struggle with gender identification: a strong tendency toward female identification, due to Lawrence's temperament and upbringing, coupled with a realization that he required a modicum of masculine identification for psychic balance. As Jan Good puts it, "[t]he deeper issue for Lawrence seems to be not simply same-sex physical desire, but rather the disposition to identify with the opposite sex," and this was a source of emotional complexity for Lawrence that presented "potential threats to personal integrity" (217).

Cowan argues that in *Women in Love*, the cancelled Prologue notwithstanding, "Birkin's wish for blood brotherhood is not disguised homoeroticism," but rather it "is a form for experiencing emotional closeness."[4] Any sexual feelings "mask a defense against the same psychic danger as his fear of being swallowed up by women" and express Lawrence's longing "for paternal nurturance" (*Self and Sexuality* 38, 39). Kinkead-Weekes acknowledges Lawrence's physical attraction to men, but, quoting a letter to Henry Savage in which Lawrence muses, "I should like to know why nearly every man that approaches greatness tends to homosexuality, whether he admits it or not" (2L 115), he argues that "it seems simple-minded to read this as a confession of Lawrence's own homosexuality" (*TE* 103). He also finds it highly unlikely that Lawrence ever had sex with the Cornish farmer William Henry Hocking, to whom he was undoubtedly attracted (*TE* 378–80). Though Jeffrey Meyers disagrees on this point and believes that there was a sexual relationship between Lawrence and Hocking (214), he also reads Cyril Beardsall's attraction to men in *The White Peacock* as "an attempt to break away from his possessive mother ... and to regain his lost father" (71). Man-to-man closeness in Lawrence's writing, then, may be an expression of several things, one of which is connected to how gender identification and attachment interact.

In the short story "The Prussian Officer" (1914), we have an interesting example of how a conflicted gender identification and attachment complications lead not only to violence but, in the end, to tragedy. An aristocratic German captain finds to his consternation that he is physically attracted to his young, lower-class orderly, Schöner. He deals awkwardly with the situation by trying to suppress his feelings and sadistically tormenting his subordinate, beating him, denying him leave to see his sweetheart, and humiliating him whenever possible. The orderly, while also attempting to suppress strong emotions of his own in reaction to the assaults, finally explodes in rage and kills his commanding officer, after which he slowly disintegrates emotionally and physically, ultimately dying in a way that foreshadows Gerald Crich's end in *Women in Love*.

A number of studies of this well-known story have cited a Lawrence letter to Edward Garnett as a gloss on its significance, either accepting Lawrence's opinion there about cruelty and soldiering or expanding and qualifying it. The letter is dated by the editor as "11? November 1912," a little more than six months before the completion of "The Prussian Officer,"[5] and reads in part: "And soldiers, being herded together, men without women, never being *satisfied* by a woman ... get their surplus sex and their frustration and dissatisfaction into their blood, and *love* cruelty. It is sex lust fermented makes atrocity" (*1L* 469).[6] As usual, Mark Kinkead-Weekes provides a level-headed reading of the story that may represent what has become the now more-or-less consensus view. While acknowledging the relevance of the letter to the story, Kinkead-Weekes suggests that "to treat the story as essentially about repressed homosexuality and sadism ... is to oversimplify" (*TE* 77). The biographer suggests that, in killing the officer, Schöner also kills something in himself, rendering his own eventual demise inevitable, just as the captain is "deathly" in repressing his feelings toward his orderly (*TE* 78). Such a reading is in keeping with Lawrence's insights about self-sabotage elsewhere, in the novella *The Fox*, for example, where Henry Grenfel's unconscious attempt to exorcize his own beastliness by killing the marauding fox merely underscores his brutality rather than eliminating it. (See chapter 1, note 5.)

Hugh Stevens agrees that "[t]his is not just a story of repressed homoeroticism spilling over into violence," nor is the violence the result of the captain not having a woman, as Lawrence's letter seems to suggest it could be (55). In fact, although Stevens does not mention this, the captain goes off for a sexual fling with a woman at one point but returns dissatisfied, his surplus sexual frustration, apparently, still very much fermenting: "It was a mockery of pleasure. He simply did not want the woman ... At the end of it, he came back in an agony of irritation, torment, and misery" (*PO* 6). Stevens mentions the captain's fixation on the orderly's scar but thinks that the key to the story lies in the bruises inflicted upon Schöner's body by the captain: "the Captain marks the soldier's flesh, inscribes the young man's flesh with authority's bruise" (55). For Stevens, therefore, "this is a story of subjection" (56). Stevens is not wrong, but, in my view, the scar is crucial to a full understanding of "The Prussian Officer," and the captain's fetishizing of the scar is very much a function of a complex gender identification.

The captain is a gentleman, "a Prussian aristocrat" about forty years old, handsome, and a great horseman. He has never married, for "no woman had ever moved him to it" (*PO* 2), and he has ruined his career prospects by excessive gambling (*PO* 2). The gambling addiction – not very unusual for a military officer of this time – is an important detail for our understanding of the captain. In a study of Lawrence's later short story "The Rocking-Horse Winner" (1926), which centrally involves gambling, Demetria DeLia argues that Lawrence understood how "acquisitiveness is often attempted compensation for an internal emptiness" that is the consequence of narcissistic mothering (136) and that "gambling masks a profound anxiety that stems from loss of love" (137). The idea that the captain is one of Lawrence's hollow men would also give credence to Stevens's contention that he has a need to make his mark on the orderly's flesh as if to insist, his inner emptiness notwithstanding, that he does exist and can make his mark somewhere or on someone if not on the larger world. In fact, his world by the end is reduced, in effect, to the relationship between him and his orderly: "This was to be man to man between them" (*PO* 14).

One aspect of the story not often dwelt upon is the symbolic father-son dynamic that it constructs. Schöner is twenty-two years old (*PO* 2) and could be the captain's son simply in terms of the age difference. Moreover, the hierarchy of military authority sets up a situation that easily recalls the power and authority of the necessarily older father in relation to the young son in family life. Military orders that must be obeyed by the subordinate soldier suggest the absolute paternal dominance over the son in many early-twentieth-century European cultures. Even the beatings the officer inflicts upon Schöner, though unusually severe, are not unlike the kind of corporal punishment that occurred in families, not least German families, of the time. In *For Your Own Good: Hidden Cruelty in Child-Rearing and the Roots of Violence* (original publication in German, 1980), Alice Miller details the emphasis on corporal punishment in popular childrearing books in the German language going back several hundred years, a prevailing cultural attitude she calls "poisonous pedagogy" (58). The emphasis was on total paternal control and absolute obedience by the child:

"Over the years a sophisticated repertory of arguments was developed to prove the necessity of corporal punishment for the child's own good ... Beatings, which are only one form of mistreatment, are *always* degrading, because the child not only is unable to defend him- or herself but is also supposed to show gratitude and respect to the parent in return" (16, 17).[7]

W.R.D. Fairbairn, one of the founders of object relations theory, studied the trauma of soldiers during the Second World War and referred to military cases in discussing the traumatic release of so-called bad objects from the unconscious (120–2). He recognized the relevance of family dynamics to the traumatic situation that military life, especially during war, can bring about. In particular, for the soldier, "every word of command is equivalent to an assault by a malevolent father" (126). Even though, at one point in the short story, in order to deal with the captain's brutality, the orderly tries to imagine "that the captain did not exist" (*PO* 10), and, at another point, that he is encountering "dream people" and is in "a blackish dream" (*PO* 11), this is not to say that the assaults on Schöner in Lawrence's story are Schöner's own fantasies but rather that the military setting may be seen as a metaphor for a hostile father-son relationship, an attachment complexity that very much engaged Lawrence.

There are obvious oedipal elements in the orderly's murder of his captain. The father figure has denied the "son" access to his sweetheart, and the "son" takes his oedipal revenge by killing the "father." After the murder, the orderly usurps the paternal position by mounting the captain's horse, an Oedipus claiming the kingdom, if not the mother, for his own, as it were. But in the process he has lost the Lawrentian equilibrium necessary for thriving and, given his profound isolation, even for survival: "Trying to get down from the horse, he fell, astonished at the pain and his lack of balance. The horse shifted uneasily. He jerked its bridle and sent it cantering jerkily away. It was his last connection with the rest of things" (*PO* 16). In this case, any possible positive attachment the younger man may have had with the older is made impossible by the captain's own deficits.

But what kind of a situation do we have from the perspective of the father figure, the captain? For one thing, there is a distinct feeling of abandonment that affects him. The orderly is due to leave his service in three months' time, and the approaching date of liberation, as much as anything else, may be the trigger to the irrational anger the Prussian officer feels and the violence he inflicts. As we saw in chapter 1, abandonment anxiety can often lead to violence. The captain "knew his servant would soon be free, and would be glad ... The captain grew madly irritable" (*PO* 4). The later isolation that Schöner finds himself in after he has attacked and killed his superior is an echo of the captain's own dread of abandonment. The captain's violation of the orderly's personal and psychological boundaries may be a clumsy attempt to deal with his abandonment anxiety through a forced and violent closeness, but what we see in the end, as I earlier discussed in the case of Gerald Barlow in *Touch and Go*, is that violence triggered by abandonment anxiety begets violence in return.

The differences in appearance, temperament, age, and class between the two men in "The Prussian Officer" might suggest Lawrence's relationship to his own father, except that the connection is distorted through inversion, the father, in this case, more cultivated than the peasant son. But the captain's lack of settled masculinity suggests Lawrence himself, especially at this stage in his life. For Schapiro, the captain "is less a castrating oedipal father than an enraged, preoedipal child who has failed to discover the reality of self or other" (62). In "The Prussian Officer," we are privy to the thoughts of both characters at various times. As Lawrence puts it in *The Virgin and the Gipsy*, "Man or woman is made up of many selves" (*VG* 66), and Jack Stewart reminds us that "Frieda saw the psychodrama between the two men [in the tale] as a projection of the split in Lawrence himself" ("Expressionism" 276). The captain's need to make the orderly aware of him personally, to break through Schöner's impersonal attendance – he "scarcely noticed the officer any more than he noticed himself" (*PO* 2) – reflects a child's need for recognition, to be seen and validated by a caregiver, more particularly, in this case, a father. As the captain's orderly, seeing to his every need, Schöner is, in effect, the caregiver.

While out on the military manoeuvres that lead to the murder, Schöner follows the figure of the captain on horseback "like a shadow" (*PO* 2), and the slow disintegration of the captain as he attempts to suppress or sublimate his powerful feelings is a foreshadowing of Schöner's later breakdown. After his most violent attack, when he brutally kicks his orderly down the stairs, the captain feels a momentary satisfaction but then "a horrible breaking down of something inside him, a whole agony of reaction" (*PO* 8). If the orderly limps with his injuries after the fall, the captain is psychologically maimed and increasingly halting in his engagement with life. It is as if the captain would like to inflict his own feeling of hollowness upon Schöner in a perverted attempt to lessen his own emptiness, and he succeeds pretty well. On the manoeuvres, Schöner feels "as if he were disembowelled, made empty, like an empty shell. He felt himself as nothing" (*PO* 11), though he also resists the annihilation and later feels that "hard there in the centre of his chest was himself, himself, firm, and not to be plucked to pieces" (*PO* 13).

If it is the case that the two characters are in some sense distorted mirror images of each other and that both represent aspects of Lawrence himself, then the captain's striking obsession with the scar on Schöner's thumb may be a symbolic example of Lawrence expressing a need to reach out for masculine identification. The deep scar becomes fetishized by the captain; he cannot keep his eyes or his mind off it: "The officer had long suffered from it, and wanted to do something to it ... He wanted to get hold of it and —. A hot flame ran in his blood" (*PO* 4). What exactly does getting hold of it mean? The captain is unsure of his manhood; he has been one "who fights with life" (*PO* 2), and he fixates on the scar because it reminds him of that lack of settled gender identification, a failing he cannot abide. In Germanic culture, fencing scars, often obtained through ritualized matches between members of the upper class in fraternities or in the military, were for generations considered emblems, even guarantors, of manhood.[8] Lawrence's preferred title for the story, "Honour and Arms," does not seem to refer to anything in particular in the plot of the story – quite the contrary, in fact. As Keith Cushman has surmised, the title may well refer to a line from an aria in Handel's oratorio "Samson" (*D.H. Lawrence at Work* 209), but that reference gets us only so far. I would suggest that the title Lawrence preferred may also relate to the German practice of duelling with swords, the *mensur* (literally "measurement"), in order to obtain a stigma of honour, the scar. The practice was indeed bound up in codes of honour and involved arms. Moreover, Lawrence's interest in German culture was far from casual. He had cousins, the Krenkows, who lived in Germany, and he and Frieda visited her family there before they were married and many times subsequently. Lawrence later devoted three chapters of his history book, *Movements in European History* (1921), to German subjects: "The Germans," "Prussia," and "The Unification of Germany." And "The Prussian Officer" is not merely incidentally about German soldiers; Lawrence specifically said that this story (along with "Vin Ordinaire") was about "German soldier life" (*2L* 26). So as hermetic as it may seem, an important strand in "The Prussian Officer" deals with a wavering gender identification that leads to a perverted expression of a desire for attachment that is dangerously distorted by the power dynamics of German military life. As we will see in the discussion of *Sons and Lovers*, in this phase of his life and career, Lawrence's attempts to balance his default female gender identification with a connection to male figures, especially older ones, are often made covertly.

A very early and clear example of how a Lawrence male protagonist reaches out unawares for masculine identification comes in the story "The Old Adam," a fiction based superficially on the family dynamics at Lawrence's lodgings in Croydon (*LAH* 233–4n). It was written in June 1911, at the same time as Lawrence was working on what eventually became *Sons and Lovers*. Somewhat in anticipation of the novel, the overall movement in "The Old Adam" from an attachment point of view is a quasi-oedipal struggle that turns into an identification with the father figure. The fight and subsequent reconciliation between Mr Thomas and the Lawrence character, Edward Severn, is similar to the development between Paul Morel and Baxter Dawes in the novel, except that Dawes is much more obviously a father figure (and a stand-in for Walter Morel) than Thomas is in the short story.

Edward Severn, twenty-seven years old, lodges with Mr and Mrs Thomas, who are loosely based on the Joneses of Croydon.[9] They have a three-year-old daughter, Mary, who dotes on Severn, and he in turn indulges her whims, including undressing her for bed, even though he is conscious of the fact that "she was growing too old for a young man to undress" (*LAH* 74). Mrs Thomas is "thirty-four years old, full-bosomed and ripe," "a good-looking woman, well made" (*LAH* 74, 77). There is a good deal of flirtatiousness between the lodger and his landlady with little Mary functioning as a proxy and rather thin buffer: "Mrs Thomas watched [Severn's] fine mouth lifted for kissing [Mary]. She leaned forward, lowering the baby, and suddenly ... she knew he was aware of her heavy woman's breasts approaching down to him" (*LAH* 74). The atmosphere between landlady and lodger is electric; indeed, they sit through a lightning storm together: "they looked at each other, till in the end they were both panting, and afraid, not of the lightning but of themselves and each other" (*LAH* 78).

Mr Thomas arrives home quite late from his legal practice to find himself shut out of the conversation. Normally "the two men were very friendly" (*LAH* 79), but in this atmosphere and with Mrs Thomas clearly annoyed with her husband for his late homecoming, Thomas studiously ignores Severn, treating him "as if he did not exist" (*LAH* 79). Eventually they get into a heated discussion about women's rights, but the crisis comes in the form of a practical task all three are to perform together. Kate, the maid, is leaving the next morning, and her heavy travelling box must be carried down a flight of stairs to be ready for transport. The two men are to co-ordinate their efforts with the trunk while Mrs Thomas lights the way with a candle. The inevitable happens: Severn slips on the stairs, and the box crashes into Mr Thomas, who bangs his head on a banister post. Believing that Severn has deliberately caused the incident, Thomas hits him in the jaw and ear, at which Severn launches at the older man's throat. The odd upshot is that the two men reconcile and develop a warm friendship that lasts Severn's entire remaining time at the lodgings, while Mrs Thomas, shocked by the consequences of her flirtation, is forever after correct and cold with Severn, "treating him as if he were a stranger" (*LAH* 86), in sharp contrast to her earlier friendliness.

The title of this story signals the official theme, which looks at what lies below the surface: the sudden giving way of a civilized veneer in the fight between the two men, as the "old Adam" erupts into the open. The violence has obvious similarities to the physical struggle between Paul and Baxter in *Sons and Lovers* as well as the strangling of the captain by his orderly in "The Prussian Officer" and Gerald's attack on Gudrun in *Women in Love*. Visiting the recovering Thomas in bed, Severn says, "'I didn't know we were such essential brutes … I thought I was so civilised'" (*LAH* 86). But far more interesting than the official theme is the way Severn's alliance shifts from Mrs to Mr Thomas. Kate's departure may be seen as a foreshadowing of the eventual expulsion of the female/motherly factor in favour of a male, father-son bonding. The Thomases are a half-generation older than Severn, and, with little Mary to care for, Mrs Thomas is very obviously a mother. The fact that Lawrence gives her the name Gertie, changed from the manuscript name, Mabel (*LAH* 234n), hints at a maternal connection in Lawrence's mind inasmuch as Gertrude Morel in the contemporary *Sons and Lovers* is so obviously based on his mother, Lydia Lawrence. The oedipal struggle that is thus set up is presented in displaced form as a fight over the catastrophe with the maid's trunk, but the unexpected male alliance, leaving the woman out of account, suggests a gesture toward masculine identification as a counterweight to a natural inclination toward female identification. For Severn's cultured demeanour has been associated with Mrs Thomas's values, as has his argument in favour of women's suffrage (in spite of her superficial taking of her husband's part in the discussion), not to mention his proxy child-minding. What this story clarifies is that the bonding of two men in Lawrence is not necessarily a function of sexual attraction but rather, as Cowan and others suggest, the expression of a need for masculine identification, often with a father figure.

Alan Williamson claims that "[n]o book has ever recorded the identificatory, as well as the oedipal, love of mother and son more passionately than *Sons and Lovers*" (52). Indeed, shortly before the novel's Paul Morel begins working at Jordan's, his plans for the future have a recognizably oedipal shape, albeit bent to a fairy-tale arc: "His ambition, as far as this world's gear went, was quietly to earn his thirty or thirty-five shillings a week, somewhere near home, and then, when his father died, have a cottage with his mother, paint and ... live happily ever after" (*SL* 114). The identification between son and mother and Paul's female identification in general is equally evident, but one must qualify its extent. Apart from his fascination with Clara's stockings, Paul's female identification, like John Thomas Raynor's, is expressed somewhat flippantly when he whistles the music-hall tune "Put me among the Girls" (*SL* 391) during a brief run-in with Baxter Dawes at work. His female identification, keyed on his mother, is complicated by several factors including the fact that Gertrude herself, who idealizes her father, identifies with men, and envies them their freedom. So Paul is not simply mother-identified; he is gender-identified with a woman who herself identifies in certain respects with the masculine world. In addition, the identification, while providing a degree of security for Paul, makes exploration of the wider world problematic. Daniel R. Schwarz writes of "Paul's bondage to his mother and the claustrophobic effects of these ties upon his emotional development" (263).

Lawrence's own attachment loyalties made any conscious masculine identification very difficult for him growing up. As Cowan has argued, "[f]or Lawrence, the rapprochement conflict of dependency versus independence could not be resolved at a phase-appropriate age, the splitting characteristic of the preoedipal period continued, and his childhood gender identity was at best unstable" (*Self and Sexuality* 23). *Sons and Lovers* records the unstable gender identification, the attachment dilemma from which it issued, and the paradox involved in the attempt to stabilize it. Judith Arcana has argued that "whatever the man Lawrence might have written or done, the character Paul Morel does not align himself with his father" (142). What such a perspective fails to recognize is the covert effort in *Sons and Lovers* to record the attempts of the son to identify with aspects of the father in parallel with the oedipal hostility and in contention with the female identification.

The novel exemplifies how the complications of attachment result in rich fiction, as Lawrence probes the multi-layered predicament of Paul Morel, his paradoxical emotional situation, and his attempts to find a viable equilibrium. Lawrence's letter to Rachel Annand Taylor of December 1910, quoted in the epigraph above, was sent shortly before his mother's death. In it Lawrence describes his parents' marriage and his own relationship to them in distinctly oedipal terms: hatred of his father "has been a kind of bond between me and my mother. We have loved each other, almost with a husband and wife love, as well as filial and maternal. We knew each other by instinct ... We have been like one, so sensitive to each other that we never needed words" (*1L* 190). Words are exactly what Lawrence used in order to obtain a more objective view of that bond and try to deal with it. The tendency to interpersonal fusion between himself and his mother that Lawrence describes in the letter is dramatized in much of his work, but it is important to recognize that it is also resisted as an imbalance. While that resistance becomes more overt as time goes on, in *Sons and Lovers* it is for the most part indirect and symbolic.[10]

The oedipal readings of *Sons and Lovers*, which Lawrence objected to, may be said to have culminated with Daniel Weiss's *Oedipus in Nottingham: D.H. Lawrence* (1962) and have since given way to a gradually formed consensus among psychologically oriented critics that the oedipal configuration, undoubtedly present, is but an interesting veneer that tends at times to obscure a much deeper and more significant pattern of pre-oedipal issues.[11] For Margaret Storch, for example, the surface oedipal pattern "conceals a fundamental antagonism towards the mother" (98), much as we have seen in "The Old Adam." As Lawrence claimed, then, the oedipal reading gets us only so far. Although, according to the Freudian paradigm, the oedipal phase is part of normal (male) childhood development, there is a sense in which there is really little reason for oedipal hostility between father and son in *Sons and Lovers*. As Cowan writes: "since the mother no longer loves her husband, the infant son [Paul], early in the oral incorporative stage, has already effectively won the oedipal rivalry with his father" (*Self and Sexuality* 21). In fact, the battle for the affection of the mother has been won even before Paul's birth, by his older brother, William, whose mantle of lover-son Paul inherits after William's untimely death, a legacy symbolized by Paul's donning of the dead William's suit with Gertrude's blessing (*SL* 297).

Now embarked on his life with Frieda after his mother's death, Lawrence begins to explore in *Sons and Lovers* how a separation from the maternal source of stifling security can be achieved in the face of the kind of abandonment anxiety that in Lawrence is always the corollary to embarking on independence. It is here that the recuperation of the masculine plays a crucial role, for healthy separation from the mother is normally accomplished through idealization of the father. As Gāmini Salgādo, has argued, the Morel sons' view of the father as an enemy in this patriarchal mining community (where husbands are routinely and not always ironically called "lord and master" by the wives) involves them in a rejection of masculine in favour of feminine values (101), and it is precisely because of that fact that the internalization of masculine values in the Morel boys is both urgent and very difficult. As Turner suggests, "[t]hroughout the novel we feel the indeterminacies of gender. Caught between his mother's dominance and his father's subjection, Paul feels insecure in his masculinity" (*Psychoanalysis* 40). Early on in the Morels' marriage, Walter had tried to assert a masculine prerogative in the upbringing of the toddler William when he cut off the boy's curls so beloved by Gertrude: "'Yer non want ter make a wench on 'im'" (*SL* 24), he says in justification. But Gertrude's enraged reaction is an effective sanction against any similar attempt in the future with the boys. "This act of masculine clumsiness was the spear through the side of her love for Morel" (*SL* 24).

A metafictional reaching out in the novel to a masculine ideal is observable in the often-noted discrepancy between the narrated and dramatized portrayals of the father, Walter Morel,[12] but there is also a covert effort by Paul Morel to identify with symbolic aspects of his father as part of an unconscious project to wrest a measure of self-integrity from the diffuseness threatened by the demands of an understandably needy mother. One effective tool used by Gertrude Morel to ensure an estrangement between Walter and the children is her moral outrage at both his dirt and his drinking, an attitude they, and Paul not least, come to share. Nevertheless, just as Rupert Birkin in *Women in Love* will argue that he needs a male companion to complement his relationship with Ursula Brangwen and, one suspects, as a counterweight to it, Paul Morel unknowingly and symbolically reaches out to his father in order to protect against the collapse of his own separate self in maternal merger. Williamson seems to think that "[b]ecause of Paul's hatred of his father, he does not experience the need to disidentify with the feminine at the age [Jessica] Benjamin tells us is culturally normal ... He seems to feel absolutely no need for distance [from his mother]" (53). But Williamson also admits that "on some level, Paul is aware of something he needs from his father" (54). It is a complicated awareness and need: Paul both identifies unconsciously with and strives to distance himself from his father's precarious familial position because countering Paul's fear of annihilative merger is his dread of the prospect of emotional ostracism. Shirley Panken agrees that Gertrude embodies for her sons a dual anxiety: "She ... emerges on the one hand as immensely self-preoccupied, withholding, and abandoning. On the other hand ... she appears guiltily oversolicitous and engulfing" (quoted in Berman 210).

Cowan and Schapiro, following Alfred Kuttner, argue that Paul Morel's inability to identify with his father lies at the heart of his developmental problems. And yet it does seem that Paul can negatively identify with his father as a fellow male in the household to the extent that he introjects the fear that he, like his father, will be emotionally abandoned by Gertrude. Her infantilization of Walter facilitates that negative identification: "'I wouldn't be such a mardy baby,'" she says to her husband when he is on the mend from an illness, and he depends on her "almost like a child" (*SL* 62). Berman suggests that "Paul's delicate health may have its sources in the same wish to elicit love and attention" (207) that, for Berman, motivates Walter's carelessness of his own health and safety, but I see this as unlikely given Walter's fate and Lawrence's own very real health problems. Walter's periodic illnesses and recovery from pit injuries, on the contrary, are occasions that surely frighten Paul: they would remind him at some level of awareness of his own need for care by his mother in the past and, given his frail constitution, likely in the future as well. Moreover, he has seen a beloved older brother fall ill and die. So although it is quite true, as Schapiro and others claim, that Paul fails to consciously identify with his father as a male model to be emulated, it is also important to note that he can and does recognize his father's palpable isolation within the family, transforming it into a fear of his own abandonment by his mother, a chronic anxiety that, together with his inability to idealize his male parent, cripples his attempts at healthy separation. As noted in the Introduction, the attachment he does have (to his mother) is both overwhelming and seemingly precarious, and the one he lacks (to his father) is both urgently needed and seemingly unacceptable, so Paul is involved in the typical if complicated Lawrentian paradox of emotion. And it is Walter's dirtiness, above all, that embodies both the attraction and the repulsion of what he represents for Paul's sense of self in *Sons and Lovers*.[13]

Kuttner contends in his 1916 Freudian book review of *Sons and Lovers* that Gertrude Morel's "whole emphasis has always been towards making Paul interested in some other occupation than his father's dirty digging" (268). He does not make much more of the term, but the image of dirty digging certainly is a suggestive one, for the associations between Walter Morel and dirt begin early in the novel and frequently recur. Walter is permanently branded by his occupation. His body, the narrator tells us, features "blue scars, like tattoo marks, where the coal-dust remained under the skin" (*SL* 235). Unfortunately for the miner, what gets under the skin of his family are his "dirty and disgusting ways," even in the case of the youngest, Arthur, once so fond of his father, who is often disgusted by him and takes to calling him a "dirty nuisance" (*SL* 141). On the day Paul is born, for example, Morel takes his after-work meal and has a rest before making the obligatory visit to see his wife and new son: "His face was black, and smeared with sweat. His singlet had dried again, soaking the dirt in. He had a dirty woollen scarf round his throat" (*SL* 43). Walter's supposedly slovenly habits gall Gertrude to an extreme degree: "The sense of his sitting in all his pit-dirt, drinking, after a long day's work, not coming home and eating and washing, but sitting getting drunk on an empty stomach, made Mrs Morel unable to bear herself" (*SL* 85). And after he does come home from the pub, Walter typically eats and then sleeps at the table with a "dirty and inflamed" face (*SL* 87).

The emotional freighting of dirt with so much disgust, a very powerful affect, is a bit odd in the context of the culture described in *Sons and Lovers* because *all* of the miners emerge from the pit coal-blackened every working day of their lives; the dirt is a function of their livelihood. As Paul Delany has pointed out, there were no proper washing facilities at the East Midland mines at this time (158). The importation of coal dust into the home would, of course, be a constant and threatening reminder to Gertrude of the possibility that her sons will follow their father into the pit. But, more than that, for Gertrude the dirt (and Walter's drinking) represents everything that she struggles against emotionally and has been conditioned to repress. Indeed, that the cause of her disgust relates to unhealed injuries to her own sense of self is indicated by the phrase "unable to bear *herself*" when she thinks of Walter drinking at the pub unwashed. If we consider Gertrude in the child's position for a moment, it is plausible to suggest that aspects of Walter's behaviour that upset her relate to her own emotional deficits: the withholding of money, for example, might be an echo for her of her father's withholding of affection.[14] But for Paul, his father's dirty ways become an unacknowledged source of symbolic autonomy in his struggle to deal with his too-close attachment to his mother. The unconscious attraction is tinged with the fear, however, that autonomy might lead to abandonment just as his father's flaunting of his dirtiness and drinking in order to assert himself has merely led to his isolation through Gertrude's narcissistic regulation of emotion in the family.

In one iconic scene of the novel, Gertrude is entertaining Mr Heaton, the clergyman, whose presence invokes the memory of Gertrude's long-ago lost love, John Field, when Walter arrives home. Walter declines to give Heaton his hand to shake because "'ther's too much pick-haft and shovel dirt on it'" (*SL* 46). He then ostentatiously places his arms "black with coal dust" on the white tablecloth his wife has laid out for the distinguished if frequent visitor, graphically, as it were, marking his territory. Here dirt and the colour black are class indicators differentiating the clergyman and miner and vividly portraying Gertrude's anguished and self-defined class entrapment. For her, apparently, a cultivated Heaton (or Field) is preferable to an uncouth Morel, whose name is evocative of the moldy fungus that thrives in darkness and dirt. Dirt and black are, furthermore, emblematic here of the two senior Morels working at cross-purposes (most tragically in their parenting): Gertrude trying to keep a clean and tidy home fit for visits by the likes of Mr Heaton and Walter bringing his pit dirt home as an entitlement and measure of his labour. Moreover, the coal that "was drawn to the surface by donkeys" (*SL* 9) in the little gin pits we read about in the novel's first paragraph is a symbol of hidden things brought to light, most significantly the anger that Paul shares with his father but, unlike him, usually tries to repress.[15]

Order and cleanliness are the two most prominent domestic virtues that Gertrude's puritan morality has imported into her marriage and inculcated in her children as imperatives. Walter's drinking and dirtiness and her inability to tolerate them doom the marriage, then, and lead inevitably to his isolation in the maternally dominated Morel household. Anthropologist Mary Douglas's explanation of the significance of dirt is helpful in understanding Gertrude's reaction to it even in a cultural context where it is normal: "[D]irt is essentially disorder. There is no such thing as absolute dirt: it exists in the eye of the beholder. If we shun dirt, it is not because of craven fear, still less dread or holy terror. Nor do our ideas about disease account for the range of our behaviour in cleaning or avoiding dirt. Dirt offends against order. Eliminating it is not a negative movement, but a positive effort to organise the environment" (2). For Gertrude, indeed, order and cleanliness are psychologically equivalent, and both are necessary to maintain her sense of self. Just as he sullies the cleanliness of the house with his pit dirt, Walter also upsets its order, sometimes literally, when he is intoxicated. For example, he comes home one night nearly drunk and "in passing, he lurched against the dresser, setting the tins rattling, and clutched at the white pot knobs for support" (*SL* 52). In interpersonal relations, an extreme order implies a need for uniformity and control and an intolerance for deviation that ultimately bespeaks deep anxiety. Gertrude's demand for order and aversion to dirt and drunkenness within her realm, the home, grows out of her need to demarcate her selfhood and replicate it as far as possible in her children because her own sense of diminished selfhood demands both boundaries (from her husband and from "inferiors" in Bestwood) and aggrandizement (from her children). Gertrude's reaction to dirt is, then, related to her need to solidify an otherwise precarious sense of self and can be understood in the context of the symbolic and social significance Douglas discusses: it is bound up in "a total structure of thought whose key-stone, boundaries, margins and internal lines are held in relation by rituals of separation" (41).[16]

In Gertrude's mind, then, dirt takes on the symbolic significance of a threat to her internalized sense of a vulnerable self in need of boundaries, a sense that has its external analogues in rooms, in the house itself (where she presides but which is not hers, as Walter makes clear), even in the perimeter-defining gate, the latch of which Walter breaks in his drunken clumsiness. The children's needs are different, but any overt divergence from the prescribed order threatens maternal sanction. This is Paul's dilemma as he reaches out to integrate a masculine component into his sense of identity.

The masculine identification by indirect means obviates the need for a conscious alliance between Paul and his father that might provoke a maternal repudiation. Delany writes that "Morel tries to bring his dirt and his own passion into the closed circle of mother and children, and is driven to the outer edge of family life for his pains" (163). However, what we see in several key scenes is a subtextual recuperation of the dirty, drunken father figure into the circle that has otherwise excluded it. For example, when Paul hears of his winning first prize in a painting competition, he is "washing in the scullery" (*SL* 295) while his returning father is smeared in the ubiquitous black coal dust (*SL* 296–7). Lawrence is obviously counterpointing the two men, one clean and the other dirty, particularly concerning the affections of Gertrude. Yet the narrator uses a mining metaphor that recalls Walter's job – as he puts it to Mr Heaton, "'drivin' a pick into 'ard rock all day'" (*SL* 47) – to describe Paul's intellectual progress in the extension to this scene: "He had shovelled away all the beliefs that would hamper him, had cleared the ground, and come more or less to the bedrock of belief" (*SL* 298). It is precisely his artistic and, more broadly, his intellectual abilities that will keep Paul away from shovelling and driving a pick into hard rock. His artistic labour does not sully Paul's hands as the digging and clearing in his father's pit stall would, and yet the otherwise strikingly incongruous metaphor seems to suggest that Paul yearns for the dirt his mother has taught him is disgusting, something we also see in other crucial scenes.

Schapiro claims that, for all that the mother figure in Lawrence's writing may seem to embody in the son's unconscious a reincorporative threat to the vulnerable self, "[b]eneath the fantasy of the dominating, devouring mother is the experience of a wounded, fragile mother whose impaired subjectivity is vital to an understanding of Lawrence's imaginative world" (18). In *Sons and Lovers* it is the perceived *weakness* of the mother that, for Schapiro, creates in the child/protagonist the inability to resolve the crises of selfhood. The hostility to mothers in Lawrence's fiction, she argues, emerges "less in response to the mother's real power or strength than as a reaction to her impaired state, to her emotional calcification and psychic fragility" (106). I agree with Schapiro to the extent that we need to see Gertrude Morel, especially the Gertrude of the first three chapters of *Sons and Lovers*, as embodying a "thwarted subjectivity" linked explicitly by the text to her gender position in a patriarchal culture, a situation Lawrence portrays with a sympathy that bespeaks his only partially acknowledged gender identification.

Peter Balbert perhaps overstates the case to a degree when he suggests that Gertrude is frustrated "that she was not born male" and suffers from a "sexual envy of the state of manhood itself" and not merely "a socially conditioned envy of class, caste or business opportunity" (*Phallic* 21–2), but certainly her resentment of her husband's relative freedom is palpable, and her treatment of her male children derives in part from her unacknowledged design to thwart their masculine prerogative and retain their identification with her, thus enhancing her own otherwise fragile sense of self. They become sons and lovers, then, for reasons that have more to do with gender roles and selfhood than with sexuality per se. That such female resentment of male freedom and privilege is fairly common in Lawrence's fiction suggests, again, his attunement to his mother's frustrations and his identification with her. The women in "Tickets, Please" and Mabel in "The Horse-Dealer's Daughter" (written as "The Miracle" in 1916; revised and published in 1922) come to mind, while Mrs Morel's youthfully defiant comment to John Field that "'[i]f *I* were a man, nothing would stop me'" (*SL* 16) is echoed in Gudrun Brangwen's more plaintive remark to her sister Ursula, "'God, what it is to be a man … [t]he freedom, the liberty, the mobility!'" in the chapter "Diver" in *Women in Love* (*WL* 47).

For Paul in particular, the problem is that Gertrude's "narcissistically impaired state" helps create a feeling in him of "insubstantiality or hollowness" (Schapiro 94). Where her own hollowness is filled both literally and emotionally by the fetus she carries when she is pregnant with Paul, that creature, once externalized through the birth process, continues to be the object of her need for fulfilment, thus the applicability of the "devouring mother" archetype, where "devouring" means a failure to accept the authentic otherness of her son and to mirror him positively, ignoring his independent needs, because he must fill her inner void. "Devouring" from his point of view means that he senses her neediness through long practice at sensitivity to her moods – the statement "The boy was attentive to her" says it all (*SL* 99) – an attunement that prevents him from uninhibited self-expression and pursuit of his own life imperatives. As Schapiro writes, Lawrence was clear-eyed enough to realize that "another person can never complete or fill the void in the self" (96), but many of his characters at this stage of his writing are far from reflecting that same realization.

From Paul's perspective, over-identification with and idealization of the mother because of the early abnormally strong bond lead to a weakened sense of his own self and to a narcissistic rage unconsciously directed at the mother and usually powerfully repressed. The rage is triggered by the frustration of the need to be recognized as an authentic self in his own right, but, according to Schapiro's reading, it can never be expressed except indirectly because of the fear that such a powerful emotion will destroy the mother. In Lawrence's own case, his criticism of his mother found direct expression only after her death. Likewise, the positive view of the father in *Sons and Lovers* finds back channels of expression. As many observers have noted, Paul's conflict and then friendship with Baxter Dawes serves as a kind of substitute for and a chance to symbolically mend his ties with his father.[17] In fact, the two older men are linked by the text through the dirt motif: when Paul meets Baxter Dawes, we learn that the man's "speech was dirty with a kind of rottenness" (224). He is described in one scene as wearing "old clothes, the trousers were torn at the knee, and the handkerchief tied round his throat was dirty" (*SL* 406). Clara tells Paul that she felt degraded in her marriage with Baxter, "'[a]nd he seemed dirty'" (*SL* 318), thus reinforcing for Paul the link to Walter Morel and between Clara and his mother. Clara's separation from Baxter echoes the withheld affection in the Morels' marriage; moreover, when Paul chides her for her treatment of Baxter he is indirectly criticizing his mother.

Schapiro reads the famous lily scene – where, after a violent quarrel, a pregnant Gertrude is locked out of the house by a drunken Walter – as one where Gertrude herself performs the role of the "maternally rebuffed and bereft child" (100), and her deep inhaling of the flowers' scent is "an attempt to access a hidden, repressed sensuality or bodily vitality" (100). I see this scene somewhat differently in the context of the pervasive dust/dirt and drink motifs found elsewhere in the book. The immediate trigger to Walter's rage and determination to oust Gertrude from the house in this scene is her comment "'The house is filthy with you'" (*SL* 33), and the flowers, of whose scent Gertrude "drank a deep draught" (*SL* 34), are relatable to Walter, whose presence at their first meeting Gertrude experienced as a warmth, "as if she had drunk wine" (*SL* 18). However, the flowers represent only part of Walter. The pollen dust of the flowers is a golden colour, in contrast to the black coal dust Walter is forever tramping into the house, and would not be classified as dirt by Gertrude, while the drinking in of the flower scent echoes and contrasts with Walter's beer-swilling habits. Gertrude has just had a violent conflict with her husband, and while locked outside, she obsessively goes over the details of their fight again and again in her mind, "certain phrases, certain moments coming each time like a brand red hot, down on her soul" (*SL* 33–4). She is preoccupied here with her husband, then, and the phallic connotation of the long-stemmed lilies reinforces the idea that this is a strengthening of Gertrude's defences in an intolerable situation with respect to her husband.

In essence, I think, Gertrude here has split off the good, attractive Walter of their early relationship, her inner working model of the idealized husband, and associated *that* Walter with the pollinating flowers (she is, after all, pregnant with his child). According to Daniel Dervin, Mrs Morel here experiences "something on the order of a second impregnation, or pollination, by means of purely natural elements" (*"Strange Sapience"* 129). The positive feelings for this Walter will henceforth be projected onto the boys, and this hiving off is a necessary first step in the creation of the idealized male, the male of benign dirt (outside, golden) and drink (non-alcoholic) – the yellow pollen, the imbibed scent of flowers – and one who is, moreover, related through the flowers to John Field of blessed memory. These are lilies of the field, so to speak. The unfortunate consequence of the splitting of Walter's image is that it leaves him as a gross caricature because he has become the repository of only negative traits, and it is this caricature, in effect, that Lawrence later regretted as a distortion of the reality of his father.[18] The caricature Walter may exist in Lawrence's mind and in the minds of Mrs Morel and her children, but few readers have shared this simplified view of the character.

In the much-discussed incidents of the doll-burning and the bread-baking, I would suggest an alternative to both the conventional interpretation of the scenes and Schapiro's modern psychoanalytic reading. In the first, when Paul is still fairly young he accidentally breaks his sister Annie's doll. He deals with the situation by conducting a disturbing ritual of sacrifice that involves burning the doll, and then "he poked among the embers with a stick, fished out the arms and legs, all blackened, and smashed them under stones" (*SL* 83). For many readers, the doll here is a stand-in for Mrs Morel, and Paul's actions allow him to play out his feelings of rage toward his mother in a safe way. Schapiro, citing Winnicott, argues that the sacrifice is, rather, in the service of the child's need to see the object of his attack actually survive because that survival will serve to build up the child's own emerging sense of self through the discovery of what Lawrence came to call "otherness" – that is to say, the realization that the object is not fully subject to the self, even to the self's explosive rage, and is therefore separate from that self. But, of course, the doll does not survive, and this failure is an emblem of Paul's greatest fear regarding his mother: her vulnerability to "the child's ruthless self-assertion" (Schapiro 108), which assertion thereby becomes taboo.

The other scene comes later in Paul's life, when he is tending baking loaves of bread for his absent mother and is visited by both Miriam and the much more sexually forward Beatrice. Again a burning takes place, this time the accidental scorching of the loaves. Schapiro cites Storch's interpretation of this scene as symbolizing Paul's unconscious wish for his mother to die (the burnt loaves are wrapped in a kind of shroud), but Schapiro suggests, again, that what we have here may indeed be a death wish, but one attendant upon a vulnerable and not a powerful mother. Like the doll, the burnt loaves fail to survive, and for Schapiro they represent a fear more than a wish that the mother cannot endure the aggressive assertion of the self (109–10).

What I would like to point out about both scenes is the oblique presence of the neglected figure of the father. Tending loaves of bread and "playing" with a doll, of course, suggest Paul's female identification once again, albeit in a way that hints at a certain rebelliousness against it since the doll is destroyed and the bread burnt; but the doll's blackened arms harken back to Walter's habitual position after work with coal-blackened, weary arms assertively placed on the table. As he says to the visiting clergyman, "'When a man's been drivin' a pick into 'ard rock all day, Mister Heaton, his arms is that tired, 'e doesn't know what to do with 'em'" (*SL* 47). Schapiro suggests that the final line of the doll episode, which indicates that, at least for Annie, Paul "seemed to hate the doll so intensely, because he had broken it" (*SL* 83), is an indication of Paul's fear of his own destructive potential and the vulnerability of his mother (107), but a very similar turn of phrase is used by Lawrence to describe Walter's feelings after having hit his wife with the corner of a drawer: "He dreaded his wife. Having hurt her, he hated her" (*SL* 57). So the phrase may, in fact, suggest a connection between father and son. Daniel Dervin goes so far as to suggest that Paul's destruction of the doll "resembles in a childish way the other acts of violence previously carried out in the novel by Morel" and that it intimates an "acted-out identification with the sexual father" ("Play" 86). Similarly, in the loaves scene, there is an oblique reference to Walter in that Paul's inattentiveness has carbonized some of the bread, in effect, into "charcoal" (*SL* 244), the very stuff of his father's occupation. In Lawrence's contemporaneous play, *A Collier's Friday Night* (written in 1909 but first published in 1934), which enacts much of the same atmosphere as *Sons and Lovers* and some of the same episodes, a similar bread-burning takes place, and there too the connection to coal is evident. The Paul character, called Ernest here, takes a knife to cut away the burnt crust, looking at which he declares: "By Jove, there *is* a lot! It's like a sort of fine coke" (*Plays* 38). In this play, too, the Walter figure, Mr Lambert, complains to his wife that she is teaching their children to hate him: "You make me like dirt for 'em: you set 'em against me," he says (*Plays* 51).

When we come to Paul's relationship with Clara Dawes, what is most interesting to note is not so much how the connection inevitably replicates some aspects of Paul's maternal bond but rather, again, how Walter is obliquely imported into the complex psychic mix. It is true, of course, that his relationship with Clara is helpful to Paul because it allows him to work out his vexed relations with his mother at one remove. Williamson goes so far as to suggest that "[t]he intense physicality of their relationship gives Paul a way of reliving the experiences of infancy ... that lie at the root of the whole problem of individuation and merging" (63). Clara's resemblance to Mrs Morel in terms of a desire for class advancement is dramatized memorably when she insists that she and Paul "dress" for the theatre. Baxter sneeringly refers to Paul's get-up as "'a bob-tailed evening suit, on the lardy-da,'" clearly a class-tinged comment. Dawes is registering a protest at Clara's class aspirations since they are a rejection of him, but in the symbolic scheme of the novel Paul's reluctant agreement to don the formalwear is an agreement, in effect, to reject the father's class for the mother's aspirant social position.

While Paul may go along with both Clara and his mother in repudiation of Dawes/Walter, his reconciliation with Dawes and rejection of Clara finally suggest that he realizes at some level that he must align himself with aspects of his father's world. Though he and Baxter are "confirmed enemies" at this point, Paul notices a "peculiar feeling of intimacy" (*SL* 386) between them, and, even in the vicious fight itself, "[i]t was the other man's mouth [Paul] was dying to get at," almost as if he were longing for a kiss (*SL* 409–10). Clara's feminism and resentment of men pique Paul as well because they are similar to his mother's attitude, and, insofar as the uncouth Baxter resembles Walter, Paul is, of course, re-enacting his own family's dynamic, oedipal and otherwise, in his involvement with this pair. Even his trying-on of Clara's stockings (a striking scene cut by Edward Garnett, the publisher's reader, for the original publication) suggests not only a confusion in terms of gender identification, as I suggested earlier, but also a need for Paul to assume the child's position in his relationship with Clara. It is a "dressing up" typical of a child's emulation of its mother.

In another notable episode, Paul leads Clara down a declivity towards the river alternately making love to her and interrogating her about her relationship with Baxter. Clara's "shoes and skirt bottom" become covered in mud (*SL* 354), which Paul assiduously cleans away before they return to work in order to restore her to respectability. Given Clara's resemblance to Gertrude and given what we have seen of the significance of the motif of dirt in this novel, this mucking-up of Clara by Paul is very suggestive and analogous to the blackening of the doll and the bread. If Clara is in some ways a stand-in for Gertrude in Paul's unconscious, and her marriage to Baxter, as Miriam says to Paul, is "'something like your mother and father'" (*SL* 361), then what Paul is doing, in effect, is subjecting his mother to Walter's dirt and squalor in order to bring about a symbolic reunion between the Morels that will allow him to idealize both, just as he brings about an actual one between the Daweses. Weiss claims that Paul lapses into his father's dialect with Clara in the mud scene in order to debase the relationship and place himself "on terms of equality with his father" (108). But the sullying must remain covert, unconscious; Paul cleans Clara's dress because Clara must return to her immaculate self before she returns to public life. Thus, even as Walter Morel is exiled emotionally by his family, Paul's need to mitigate the unhealthy degree of attachment to his mother leads to a yearning for his "dirty digging" and what it represents of autonomy.

This strand of subtextual recuperation of the masculine throughout *Sons and Lovers* may also be responsible in part for the intuitive sympathy readers have always had for Walter. The wisdom of the writing is in its subtle reaching-out to Walter Morel even as he is shunned by his family, because at the deepest level Lawrence recognized his own and the fictional Paul's need for "narcissistic repair" in Schapiro's term, or what I would call a selfhood that seeks a viable position between merger and autonomy, and, in this case, between a natural predilection for female identification and a need to balance that with a male modelling. Storch has noted that when Paul feeds his mother the morphia that ends her suffering and her life, his inversion of the power-dynamic of their relationship is underscored by his use of milk, the basis and symbol of the early mother-child bond, for the fatal potion (106–7). He feeds her as she had fed him, but he kills her while she gave him life. Furthermore, it is an overdose of medicine that Paul puts in the milk, as if to suggest symbolically the toxic nature of his mother's maternal role when offered in too large a dose, as it indeed was. What has not often been noted is that shortly after Mrs Morel's death, Paul's father becomes the nurturer, offering milk to his son, and Paul accepts the offering: "'Sithee – I made thee a drop o' hot milk. Get it down thee, it's cold enough for owt.' Paul drank it" (*SL* 444).

The model of covert recuperation of the masculine we have seen in *Sons and Lovers* is repeated with variations in other work. In the poems "Man and Bat" and "Snake," for example, we see how the speaker goes through a process of rejecting aspects of the eponymous animal because of features that are relatable to Walter Morel (and, by extension, Lawrence's own father), only to find a way to identify with the creature and embrace aspects of it in the end.[19] In the first poem, the bat is termed "disgusting" (*Poems* 296, l. II), said to be in an "impure haste" (*Poems* 296, l. 27), to "[squat] there like something unclean" (*Poems* 299, l. III), to be "obscene" (*Poems* 299, l. 112). This is mid-morning in Florence, and the speaker eventually realizes that the normally nocturnal animal is more afraid of the bright light outside than of the frenzied human inside:

> He *could* not go out;
> I also realized ...
> He could not plunge into the daylight that streamed at the window.
> It was asking too much of his nature.
>   (*Poems* 297, ll. 59–64)

This is the beginning of an identification or at least sympathy with the abhorred creature that finally allows the speaker to imagine what he needs to do in order to solve the problem both for himself and for the bat. By the end of the poem, the identification has become so complete that, in spite of a measure of irony, the speaker, now in the evening, has assumed a batty identity, in effect becoming one with the bat as it looks down upon him, the speaker, sitting on the terrace. He speaks for the animal:

> *There he sits, the long loud one!*
> *But I am greater than he ...*
> *I escaped him ...*
>   (*Poems* 300, ll. 153–5)

What we are seeing here, in abstract terms, is very similar to the internalization of a part object related to the father that in *Sons and Lovers* finally allows Paul Morel to accomplish a limited identification with his rejected father and thereby achieve a measure of psychic independence from his much-loved but, in terms of selfhood, boundary-violating mother. Walter Morel is no nocturnal being, but he has done his work in the dark of the colliery pit since the age of ten. And because of that he prefers the dark to the light, as we learn at the end of a famously sympathetic description of the miner's solitary early-morning habits when he would sit "down to an hour of joy" at breakfast (*SL* 37): "He preferred to keep the blinds down and the candle lit, even when it was daylight. It was the habit of the mine" (*SL* 38). Like the bat to the speaker of the poem, Morel, in the second chapter of the novel, is to the visiting clergyman, Mr Heaton, "a sort of strange beast" (*SL* 48), and to his family, again like the bat, he is unclean, impure, and disgusting. Just as the speaker of the poem finally realizes that he must not ask the bat to go against its own nature, the narrator of *Sons and Lovers* suggests that the tragedy in the Morels' marriage stems in part from their very different natures and from what Mrs Morel asks of her husband. She "could not be content with the little [Walter] might be, she would have him the much that he ought to be. So, in seeking to make him nobler than he could be, she destroyed him" (*SL* 25). I doubt that Lawrence had his father or even his character Walter Morel in mind when he wrote this poem, although his choice of the bat as a poetic subject may owe something to emotional residue related to Arthur Lawrence.

In "Snake," a slightly different scenario plays out, but a similar pattern of identification is central. Here the speaker, now living in Sicily, is initially annoyed at finding the snake at his water trough, yet at the same time he feels rather honoured by the visit. Instead of terms of othering such as those used to initially distance the speaker from the bat in the previous poem, here the speaker attempts to lessen the strangeness of the reptile with domesticating similes such as the comparison to drinking cattle (*Poems* 303, ll. 16–17). Long before writing this poem but after *Sons and Lovers*, Lawrence would say of the snake in the essay "The Reality of Peace" that it represents something natural inside us that we do not want to recognize: "Shall I kill him with sticks the moment he lifts his flattened head on my sight?" In answering in the negative, Lawrence argues, "let the serpent of living corruption take his place among us honourably" (*RDP* 37). The surface conflict in this well-known and often-anthologized poem is between what the speaker calls "[t]he voice of my education" (*Poems* 303, l. 22), which enjoins him to kill the snake because it is venomous, and his own sense that such an act would be a violation of some undefined kinship between him and the snake. It is only when the snake turns to retreat back into the fissure in the earth wall whence it emerged that something in the speaker – surely *not* the voice of his education primarily but something much deeper – prompts him to throw a log at the snake, fortunately doing no damage. What has led to the violence is not the assumed venomous nature of the snake but rather the speaker's "horror, a sort of protest against his withdrawing into that horrid black hole, / Deliberately going into the blackness" (*Poems* 304, ll. 52–3), a description that can be and has been interpreted sexually and misogynistically but equally lends itself to a sense of a child's protest against a father abandoning it to enter the darkness of the pit, the "horrid black hole," while the voice of education is the mother's egging him on to hostility, even violence, toward the father. In *Sons and Lovers*, Walter Morel justifies himself to Mr Heaton as "'a man as has been down the black hole all day'" (*SL* 47).

In fact, in *Sons and Lovers*, Walter Morel is described in the decidedly serpentine terms of venom and hissing in the scene where he comes home to find his wife and son just parting from a passionate embrace and he almost comes to blows with Paul: "'At your mischief again?' he said, venomously ... '– Ussha!!' hissed the father, swiping round with a great stroke" (*SL* 252, 253). The snake of the poem, somewhat like the emasculated Mr Morel, is likened to "a king in exile, uncrowned in the underworld," and the speaker, like Paul or perhaps the older Lawrence himself, has "something to expiate" for his unjustified hostility (*Poems* 305, ll. 69, 73), an expiation, one might argue, that began when the venom was administered to Mrs Morel by her son in a putative act of mercy killing by poisoning.

The obvious phallic symbolism of the snake makes it a representation of the kind of masculinity that Lawrence's writing frequently attempts to recuperate. Furthermore, the phallicism here looks forward to the extreme, almost cultish, phallicism of Lawrence's later writing, be it the rod in *Aaron's Rod* (which the biblical Aaron turned into a serpent in front of the pharaoh), the snake symbolism of *The Plumed Serpent*, the erection in the "phallic" second half of the novella *The Escaped Cock* (1929) (originally called "The Risen Lord"),[20] or Mellors's address to his penis in *Lady Chatterley's Lover*, all of which suggest what might be termed an emotional synecdoche whereby Lawrence came to identify, as Cowan has argued, the part object, the phallus, "with the idealization he could not invest in the whole object, his father" (*Self and Sexuality* 24). This use of a masculine part object was crucial to the development of a sense of "autonomous selfhood ... independent of the relationship with the mother" (Cowan, *Self and Sexuality* 25). In *Sons and Lovers*, dirt plays a similar role as introjected part object that allows Paul to develop without conscious intention a degree of identification with his otherwise rejected father and thereby attempt to achieve at least some independent selfhood. In fact, the way Walter's dirt is described in the novel makes it clear that it is not only a superficial covering that is washed away every evening: he is permanently branded by his occupation; it has become part of him. His body, as we have seen, features "blue scars, like tattoo marks, where the coal-dust remained under the skin" (*SL* 235). This makes the dirt, like the phallus, available as a partial father substitute. In Lawrence's self-described "naughty" book, *Lady Chatterley's Lover*,[21] the full embrace of idealized masculinity and all its associations with obscenity, phallic potency, and preference for working-class values is achieved.

In the highly autobiographical *Kangaroo*, published ten years after *Sons and Lovers*, we see a D.H. Lawrence stand-in, still ambivalent about his gender identification, coming to a country where the men, at least on the surface, strike the newcomer as manly and entrenched in a culture of mateship that would seem to offer the masculine identification he longs for. As portrayed in the novel, that culture becomes a testing ground and an opportunity for the Lawrence surrogate, Richard Lovatt Somers, to clarify his own relationship to masculinity even as he thinks he is intellectually and physically exploring the Australian landscape, spirit of place, culture, and politics. As the narrator tells us: "Poor Richard Lovatt wearied himself to death struggling with the problem of himself, and calling it Australia" (*K* 28). In Scott Brewster's words, we can read the novel "as boomeranging inescapably between maternal and masculine symbolic space" (217–18). Because Somers for a time is attracted to a leader with fascist leanings, it is apposite to refer to Jessica Benjamin's observation that such a fascination is due to "the frustration of identificatory love" with a father and "the absence of paternal nurturance" (146).[22] What Somers learns and, presumably, Lawrence discovers in writing the novel is that the attraction to male purposive activity is emotional in nature rather than intellectual or ideological. It promises "pure male activity ... [that would be] womanless, beyond woman" (*K* 96). The attraction is a function of his uncertain gender identification, but, contrary to his feeling that masculine identification can be a refuge from maternal merger, it ends up paradoxically escorting him back to a kind of merger that, far from providing protection to the vulnerable self, seems downright threatening.

Matthew J. Kochis rightly points to facial hair as a key signifier of masculinity in *Kangaroo* (6–7). Indeed, Somers so frequently comments (mostly through the narrator's free indirect discourse) on his own bearded face in contrast to the clean-shaven Australian men, particularly Jack Callcott, that the reader begins to suspect that he is defensively protesting his masculinity a little too much. In fact, Somers is quite sensitive about his masculinity all the way through the text. Kochis points to the "Nightmare" chapter, a flashback to the war years Lawrence and Frieda (Somers and Harriet) spent in Cornwall, and to the periodic compulsory summonses to be examined for military fitness, as the most obvious connection between beards and masculinity in the novel since, in "The Nightmare," Somers's beard is explicitly seen as part of his masculine identity (Kochis 7). This is so, however, only in a negative sense of a masking of doubts about that very masculinity. We know from a letter Lawrence wrote in October 1914 to Catherine Carswell (Catherine Jackson as she was then) shortly after growing his beard that he considered the hairy covering to be just that, a cover for what almost seems to be an Adamic, postlapsarian shame: "I think I look hideous, but it is so warm and complete, and such a clothing to ones [sic] nakedness, that I like it and shall keep it" (2L 226). Far from a sign of potent masculinity, then, Lawrence's beard and Somers's thoughts on unshaven men are markers of doubt and a weakness that must be compensated for.

Somers's lack of confident gender identification is something he both realizes and denies, and when he is not aware of his confusion himself, the narrator reminds us of it. When Jack calls him a "sort of queen bee to a hive" he is taken aback (K 95). Yet, when contemplating his own feeling of "black devilishness," "[h]e really felt like a woman who is with child by a corrosive fiend" (K 164). After the riot at the Labour meeting, Somers, sick to his stomach, feels "as he imagined a woman might feel after her first child, as if something had been ripped out of him" (K 316). When repudiating the dying Kangaroo in hospital, Somers "spoke very gently, like a woman" (K 336). The uncertain gender identification leads not only to an ultimately abandoned attempt to engage in the (male) world of Australian politics but also to a projection of his feelings of hollowness that are attendant upon a rickety sense of self and originate in a lack of secure attachment. Australia's relatively void geographical middle serves as a handy emblem of such a feeling, which becomes magnified to take in the entire culture. We see expressions such as "vacancy," "without any core or pith of meaning," and "absence of any inner meaning" (K 27) applied to the country upon the arrival of Richard and Harriet. As the transplanted Cornishman Jaz tells Somers, "'Go into the middle of Australia and see how empty it is. You can't face emptiness long. You have to come back and do something to keep from being frightened at your own emptiness and everything else's emptiness'" (K 204). Likewise, the perception of a degree of inauthenticity in Australian colonial life is, in part, an expression of Somers's own self-doubts. He sees Sydney as "a London without being London ... made in five minutes, a substitute for the real thing ... as margarine is a substitute for butter" (K 20). Because Somers becomes closest to Jack Callcott among his Australian acquaintances,

Jack, venal as he is, becomes the repository of doubtful characterizations of a wanting personality. On the one hand, Somers sees Jack, unlike himself, as "the consciously manly man" (*K* 38) and feels that Jack looks at him scornfully at times, with "the contempt of the confident he-man for the shifty she-man" (*K* 291). On the other hand, Jack's manliness cannot, must not, be more than superficial for Somers because it would otherwise threaten his own identity. So there is a hollowness and inauthenticity, Somers feels, even to Jack's masculinity, and he is able to laugh at Jack's manliness, "knowing it didn't go right through. It takes more than 'manliness' to make a man" (*K* 38).

Throughout the novel, Somers remains ambivalent toward the masculine association on offer through mateship or political engagement with other men, an ambivalence that comes to resemble the emotional double gyre regarding merger and autonomy that twists so many other Lawrence characters into paradoxical pretzels. Somers trembles with emotion when Jack tells him "'you're one of us'" and offers mateship (*K* 46), and "[h]e vibrated helplessly in some sort of troubled response" (*K* 47). At the same time, he is already beginning to feel the futility of the effort: "Somers himself had never felt more alone and far off" (*K* 47). There is no doubt that the mateship and political engagement that Jack offers Somers are intrinsically associated with masculinity, almost a test of masculinity. He pointedly asks Somers: "'you'd answer me man to man, wouldn't you? ... You'd treat everything I say with common honour, as between man and man?'" (*K* 57). However, in a significant reversal of a key scene in *Women in Love* and with very similar wording, as others have also noted, Somers refuses the offer of the kind of blood brotherhood that an earlier Lawrence avatar, Rupert Birkin, himself offered to Gerald Crich.[23] Somers's ambivalence is palpable: "What was offered, he wanted so much ... And yet he felt he couldn't. Not quite. Something stopped him" (*K* 105). That "something" turns out to be the fear of fusion, engulfment, perhaps losing himself in the stronger personality: "this mingling, this intimacy, this truly beautiful love, he found his soul just set against it" (*K* 107). So what Lawrence-Birkin fervently desires and puts forward as an offer in the earlier novel, Lawrence-Somers finds he cannot accept when proposed to him in this later work. The contradiction is in keeping with the Lawrentian paradox whereby characters will repudiate the very thing they long for and have striven for as they near its accomplishment because, willy-nilly, that proximity raises the spectre of its negative shadow: a fusion of either the Dante/Beatrice or the David/Jonathan type threatens a loss of self. In this case, the longing and the repudiation are years apart and incarnated in two separate characters, but they are there nevertheless.

Jack's embrace of Somers, both physical and metaphorical (*K* 57, 92), looks forward to the much more significant embrace of Ben Cooley, aka Kangaroo, the leader of the Diggers, a political and cultural movement based on malcontented former military men. The character Kangaroo is mostly convincing as a political figure in the plot of the story, but, as Bruce Steele puts it, he comes across at times as "almost an allegorical figure, for elements in Lawrence's internal debate" (*K* xxxiii), and, as Roberts suggests, he can sound very much like D.H. Lawrence (*Travel* 66). What is most interesting about him, though, is his androgynous status as a parent figure, combining elements of fatherly and motherly attributes. Fiona Becket discusses the "masculine maternal" and "the idea of androgynous fatherhood" in Lawrence without reference to *Kangaroo* (262), but the figure of Ben Cooley seems to embody just such a concept. It would seem that the masculine maternal appears occasionally in Lawrence's work in the search for an alternative to maternal security that cannot quite embrace the full-blown paternal. Thus we have, for example, the scene where Cyril in *The White Peacock* comes across two lark chicks nestling against each other, and he feels that "[i]n my heart of hearts, I longed for someone to nestle against, someone who would come between me and the coldness and the wetness" (*WP* 220). This description is closely followed by the scene where George rubs Cyril dry after swimming, thus fulfilling Cyril's wish by banishing the cold and wet, like a male mother performing her maternal duties after a child's bath. For George, in Cyril's mind, it is "as if I were a child, or rather, a woman he loved and did not fear" (*WP* 222) so that gender fluidity interacts with homoeroticism. From Cyril's point of view, George is performing a maternal task.

In *Kangaroo*, it does seem somewhat odd and not very convincing that an aspiring political leader who has fantasies of staging a *coup d'état* through violent means should place love at the centre of his ideology. The awkward collocation is a result of Lawrence's fictional plotting coming under the influence of his partially unacknowledged attachment desires and dreads. On the one hand, Kangaroo promises the fatherly embrace that will embody the masculine identification Somers-Lawrence longs for as a counterweight to the maternal embrace of his wife (whom he conflates with his mother in a dream [*K* 96]): "'Man needs a quiet, gentle father who uses his authority in the name of living life,'" Kangaroo tells Somers, and the Australian people are his children (*K* 113, 131). For Jack, Kangaroo is a father figure as well. When

Kangaroo takes power, Jack thinks, he will be "'a boss like a fat father who gets up first in the morning'" (K 187). Whatever else it might be, Somers's fantasy of a dark god who enters from below (K 176), his justification for male priority in marriage, is also linked to the need for fatherly/masculine identification. For, as I will argue in chapter 4, there is a strong association between darkness and descent (as well as warmth) and the positive aspects that Arthur Lawrence represented for his son.

On the other hand, however, Kangaroo is himself maternal. In his company, "[y]ou felt you were cuddled cosily, like a child, on his breast ... and that your feet were nestling on his ample, beautiful 'tummy'" (K 118). This marsupial, it seems, is a female member of the species with a pouch, as Kangaroo himself puts it, "'to carry young Australia in'" (K 120). It turns out, as Ruderman has written, that Kangaroo "is just a 'devouring mother' in men's clothing" (*Devouring* 111). But even as a father figure, his support is highly conditional in Somers's case; in fact, he is an unreliable father who threatens to eliminate his "son" if the son proves recalcitrant: "'I could have you killed,'" Kangaroo says to Somers when he senses him resisting his blandishments (K 209). Perhaps because of the questionable nature of Kangaroo's love, Somers's thoughts turn briefly to his mother in the next chapter of the novel, "The Nightmare," when he thinks of the friend (based on Dollie Radford) who, at some risk to herself, allowed him and Harriet to stay briefly at her place in London after the expulsion from Cornwall: "She was a little delicate lady who reminded Somers of his mother" (K 247).

It is easy to see why Lawrence's American agent of the time, Robert Mountsier, objected to the chapter describing Somers's and Lawrence's wartime experience in Cornwall as "not integral to the book" (K xxxix), but the "Nightmare" chapter does help to explain why Somers ultimately decides that he cannot be part of any mass movement in Australia. For the very kind of intrusive and constant surveillance he was subjected to in Cornwall and described in that chapter is what he experiences in a more muted form in Australia. Somers is watched from the very opening scene of *Kangaroo*. He is questioned repeatedly, almost interrogated at times, and he is threatened several times and generally mistrusted. By the end, Jack tells him he is no better than a spy (K 291), exactly what he was suspected of being in Cornwall. The violence of the chapter "A Row in Town" would also undoubtedly recall the dark and violent time of the war for Somers. It becomes impossible, then, for Somers to be part of the masculine activity on offer. The last opportunity, with Willie Struthers's socialist Labour movement, has its attractions and would recall for Somers his father's allegiance, but Struthers, like Kangaroo, unaccountably bases his otherwise hard-headed ideology on love. Since both Kangaroo and Struthers offer love and a form of merging, it is natural for Somers to equate what they represent with the love merger from which he is trying to escape to begin with. The equilibrium of attachment at the centre of so many of Lawrence's works remains elusive here. In the end, as much as Somers desires a viable masculine identification, the prospect that, at least in the Australian context, it would require the same kind of merger he has been attracted to and resisting from his earliest days, pushes him toward the other end of the attachment spectrum where coldness and wetness are welcome: "He wanted to be cold, cold, and alone like a single fish" (*K* 125).

3

MARRIAGE

"There's very little else, on earth, but marriage ... You can save your soul seven times over ... but your soul goes gnawin', gnawin', gnawin', and it says there's something it must have ... *If* we've got to be angels ... and if there is no such thing as a man nor a woman amongst them, then it seems to me as a married couple makes *one* angel."
    D.H. Lawrence, *The Rainbow* (R 128–9)

[W]hy on earth urge people to marry in Tolstoyan spiritual rapture, when, as far as marriage goes, spirits, like angels, *n'ont pas de quoi* [do not have the means].
    D.H. Lawrence, *Mr Noon* (MN 146)

Awful! That's what you call being married! What's to be done about it? Ridiculous, to know it all and not do anything about it!
    D.H. Lawrence, "Two Blue Birds" (*WWRA* 10)

Outside of the practitioners of the novel of manners, few fiction writers in English are as engaged in their work on the subject of marriage as D.H. Lawrence. Simply put, for Lawrence, "marriage was the central relationship," as Michael Squires asserts (173). But Lawrence's exploration of marriage is a far cry from the novel of manners' portrayal and implicit critique of the intersection of wedlock with material interests and structures of power, class, and gender. His artistic attention on marriage is focused instead on the emotional states of the characters involved and the way they relate to each other: their attachments and motivations, both conscious and deeply unconscious. In effect, Lawrence embeds an illustration of the contrast between his view of the significance of marriage and that of the typical novel of manners in his short story "Daughters of the Vicar" (1914).[1] The authorial intention to focus on that contrast is evident in the original title of the story, "Two Marriages," for here we have two sisters, Mary and Louisa Lindley, whose views on the implications of the matrimonial state are dramatically opposed to one another. The tale features a dilemma similar to the one often faced by Jane Austen's characters: to marry for love or for material comfort. Mary is like a character from an Austen novel who has wandered onto the pages of the wrong story. She chooses to accept the offer of marriage from the very unimpressive and rather repulsive but undeniably respectable clergyman Mr Massey in a plot turn that easily recalls Charlotte Lucas embracing the marriage proposal of Mr Collins in *Pride and Prejudice* (1813) "solely from the pure and disinterested desire of an establishment" (163), after Elizabeth Bennett's vehement rejection of him even in the face of the reality that she may never receive another offer. (Austen's words drip with irony: "disinterested," indeed.) Louisa, on the other hand, is a character who, like Lawrence's "lost girl," Alvina Houghton, like Connie Chatterley, and like other female characters in Lawrence when faced with a similar choice, opts for passion, even when, as in this case, significant considerations militate against that decision. As these last examples suggest, instead of portraying two women making differing choices, as Austen does, Lawrence will often set up a marriage or mating dilemma where one woman considers offers from, or life choices with, two or more unalike men the better to highlight the Lawrentian theme. Alvina Houghton, for example, goes through a number of more or less eligible suitors before finally settling on the socially inferior and unsuitable but attractive Italian Ciccio. Lettie Beardsall in *The White Peacock* chooses more like a Charlotte Lucas or Mary Lindley than a Louisa Lindley by opting for the prosperous Leslie Tempest as a marriage partner over the more physically alluring George Saxton, with unhappy consequences for everyone involved.

Lawrence is interested in his characters' choice in the context of social and class pressures, but he is even more engaged in their motivations, which often turn out to have deeply hidden roots that go back to earliest childhood. As attachment researchers Cindy Hazan and Debra Zeifman write, "[t]he evidence indicates that attachment needs persist from the cradle to the grave. And, just as Bowlby surmised, in adulthood such needs are satisfied by pair bonds" (352). Indeed, what we see play out in many of Lawrence's marriage narratives is a dynamic that derives either obviously or implicitly from the interactions of the mother-child attachment, but the needs are far from always being satisfied, and the dynamic can be destructive. For example, both Gerald Crich and Gudrun Brangwen in *Women in Love*, according to Eric P. Levy, can conceive of love "only from the perspective of the child whom love bullied or deprived." "For each of them, the ultimate purpose of love is to transfer to the other the sense of rejection and exclusion that exposure to love can bring, just as it did in childhood" (15). Examples of the connection between the earliest bond and adult pair-bonding in Lawrence's writing are many, an obvious and extended treatment of the idea coming in *Sons and Lovers*, where Paul Morel struggles in his romantic entanglements to satisfy conflicting attachment imperatives involving his mother and potential mates. In the early tale "Goose Fair" (1910), at the end of the relationship between Lois and Jack, the two characters seem to become mother and son: "She was his conscience-keeper ... And he walked at her side like a boy who has to be punished before he can be exonerated" (*PO* 142). Colonel Hale in "Glad Ghosts" (1926) realizes, regarding his deceased first wife, who was eight years older than himself, that "'I suppose she mothered me, in a way.'" Encountering her ghost in a church is comforting to him: "'She had her arms round me, and I was like a child at peace'" (*WWRA* 190, 191). In "The Blue Moccasins" (1928), Lina McLeod is twenty-three years older than the man she marries, Percy Barlow, who seems to be looking for a maternal substitute: "he disliked his step-mother ... [and] feared his father," while she sees "[t]he orphan in him" (*VG* 166). In several stories, women tell their future husbands straight out that they are old enough to be their mothers (which is not always strictly true) and then proceed to marry them anyway.

As with so much else related to attachment in Lawrence, we see a shift in emphasis over time with respect to his attitude to marriage, as the three epigraphs above serve to suggest.[2] While Tom Brangwen may be drunk when he makes his speech about marriage at his stepdaughter's wedding in *The Rainbow*, and while he may confuse earthly and heavenly points of reference, there is little doubt that his creator shares his character's overwhelmingly positive view of marriage at this point in time. James Wood observes that "marriage [is], for Lawrence, the emblem of fulfilment, and indeed of the eternal and infinite" (xx). But if this is so, it is most true of early Lawrence.[3] Certainly in *Women in Love* we can still read that for Birkin "[t]his marriage with [Ursula] was his resurrection and his life" (*WL* 369). However, by the unfinished *Mr Noon* (worked on sporadically in 1921 and 1922), the angel of marriage has become a contradiction in terms, and a marriage of "spiritual union" is seen as a "perversion" (*MN* 226). In that same novel, the narrator opines, "This angel business, this spirit nonsense! Even spirits, such as really exist, are potent sensual entities" (*MN* 189). No doubt the vehemence of the dismissal of the spiritual here is a function of the extent to which Lawrence once subscribed to it. By mid-1926, at least in the story "Two Blue Birds," which is loosely based on the relations of Compton Mackenzie and his wife, the angel's wings are beginning to look suspiciously like those of an albatross wrapped around a neck. Mr and Mrs Gee are "sincerely attached" to one another and "eternally married," yet cannot possibly live together (*WWRA* 5).

Sometimes Lawrence will show the deleterious effects on marriage prospects of a father-daughter attachment rather than that of a mother-son, but the dynamic is very similar. Brought up by a narcissistic father, Dollie Urquhart in "The Princess" turns her thoughts to marriage after her father's death in a misguided attempt to replace him: "She thought that *marriage*, in the blank abstract, was the thing she ought to *do*" (*SM* 166). In "The Woman Who Rode Away," the eponymous woman marries a father figure, a man who is twenty years older than she is and who sees her as "some peculiar secret vein of ore in his mines" (*WWRA* 41). Her arrested development leads to the long-delayed but irresistible urge to explore, like a child first setting out to find independence. The effort, like Dollie's, ends tragically since exploration and the attainment of individuation can be successful only when they are based on a secure attachment.

Often in Lawrence's writing there is an overt debate or conversation about marriage, again, at times, involving two sisters, as in Austen's *Sense and Sensibility* and *Pride and Prejudice*. For example, the scene at the beginning of *Women in Love* has such a conversation, and the novel also features a later chapter entitled "Marriage or Not," where the male equivalent of the discussion takes place between the quasi-blood-brothers Rupert Birkin and Gerald Crich. In that opening scene, the two Brangwen sisters, Ursula and Gudrun, discuss marriage before they go out to gawk at an actual wedding that is underway at the local church. In a dialogue that echoes the one in *Women in Love*, the two sisters Lucille and Yvette talk about love and marriage early on in *The Virgin and the Gipsy* (written in 1926) (*VG* 9–10). And the story "In Love" (1927) opens with the sisters Hester and Henrietta considering the prospect of marriage with some skepticism. Hester is engaged to Joe but finds that being engaged to marry brings out artificial expectations in a suitor and an awkward attempt to live up to being "in love," while the younger Henrietta, "mercifully unengaged," "had not the faintest intention of jeopardising her peace of mind by accepting any sort of fatal ring" (*WWRA* 138).

As for Lawrence's male characters, in *The Rainbow*, for example, they long for marriage as fervently as any Jane Austen debutante, although for emotional/attachment reasons rather than material and social ones. Their very lives, certainly their emotional well-being, seem to depend upon it. In the case of the novel's Anton Skrebensky, in fact, "[f]or him it was life or death" regarding the fulfilment of his desire to marry Ursula (*R* 410). Even so conventionally minded a character as Skrebensky, then, is able at times to see the deeper meaning in marriage beyond the social and material, though he is cognizant of those aspects as well. When he first suggests marriage to Ursula, he worries that "[i]f she were his social wife, if she were part of that complication of dead reality, then what had his under-life to do with her? One's social wife was almost a material symbol. Whereas now she was something more vivid to him than anything in conventional life could be" (R 419).[4] At this point, far from being "fatal," a wedding ring is positively charged with significance. In fact, *The Rainbow*, at one stage during its composition, was entitled "The Wedding Ring." It begins with "How Tom Brangwen Married a Polish Lady" and features a subsequent chapter "Wedding at the Marsh."

Over time, as his own marriage with Frieda begins to fray, Lawrence's depiction of the significance of marriage changes, and decoupling begins to look more and more attractive. In *Aaron's Rod*, in a paragraph that uses an extended metaphor of marriage as a religious sacrament, Lawrence writes that a woman in marriage "is driven mad by the endless meal of the marriage sacrament, poisoned by the sacred communion which was her goal and her soul's ambition" (AR 165–6). In *Kangaroo*, in a chapter entitled "Harriet and Lovatt at Sea in Marriage," the "at sea" descriptor is less a characterization of the state of the Somers' marriage than it is an indication of Richard's desire to be the unassailable captain of the good ship Somers, as Lawrence works in the nautical metaphor throughout the chapter. Unfortunately for Somers, the Harriet crew is rather mutinous. Somers is attracted to his neighbour Victoria Callcott in part because she seems to provide a positive mirroring not always available from the recalcitrant Harriet: "Queer, thought Somers, this girl at once sees perhaps the most real me, and most women take me for something I am not at all. Queer to be recognised at once, as if one were of the same family" (K 33). Continuing Lawrence's evolving views, Mrs Witt and her daughter, Lou, debate the merits and demerits of marriage in *St Mawr*, with both mother and daughter expressing various degrees of cynicism and disillusionment. Like the groom Lewis, who tells the similarly named Lou that "'I'm not by nature a marrying man'" (SM 122), Lou tells herself "'I am not a marrying woman'" (SM 139). The view of marriage or even mere coupling turns even more negative in works such as "Rawdon's Roof," although there without the substitutive role that landscape seems to play to some extent in *Kangaroo*, in *St Mawr*, and elsewhere in Lawrence, where nature appears to be capable of inspiring the kind of attachment that would normally be interpersonal or even conjugal.

For Hayles (referencing Evelyn Keller), Mother Nature in Western culture is an "objectification of the archetypal female" (87–8), and what we see in Lawrence is that the caregiving and compensatory role of landscape is a tendency that goes back as far as his first novel, *The White Peacock*, where the landscape stands in at times for maternal attachment, as we saw in chapter 1, but it becomes more pronounced in later work (especially once Lawrence arrives in New Mexico). In the "Burns Novel" fragments, probably written in late 1912 (*LAH* xxxvii–xxxviii), when Jack Haseldine and Mary Renshaw first embrace and kiss, the conflation of woman and landscape in Jack's mind, in what is perhaps the single most vivid description in the entire truncated work, is an amplification of his feelings of wonder and pleasure: "The whole secret of the night and the stars was in these soft, smooth grooves and mounds and hollows. It was her face! ... And it was the darkness he was kissing, discovering. It was the night he had his mouth upon" (*LAH* 209). Less positively, in *Women in Love*, after nearly being killed by his erstwhile lover, Hermione Roddice, Rupert Birkin thinks of his naked romp with the vegetable world as a kind of wedlock: "This was his place, his marriage place" (*WL* 108). Lawrence always had a hyper-sensitive appreciation for the beauty of landscape, but when it takes on the role of symbolic maternal provider or marriage partner there is an intersection going on with emotional attachment issues that suggests something amiss. In *Mr Noon*, Gilbert, whose "spooning" with Emmie has ended rather badly, seeks solace in "plant-histology" and, in his family's wood yard, lovingly runs "his finger over a heavy-grained oak surface ... to him it was an exquisite pleasure, vibrating in his veins like music, to realise the flexible but grandly-based rhythm in the morphological structure of the tree, right from the root-tip through the sound trunk, right out to a leaf-tip" (*MN* 34). In Part II of the same novel, Lawrence sketches Gilbert's transport of happiness with Johanna at Kloster Schaeftlarn in Germany and effusively describes the paradisal landscape around them (*MN* 199–200), to which somehow Johanna becomes assimilated: she "wore a smoke-blue gauze dress and a white hat, and was like the landscape" (*MN* 201). Retrospectively at least, Lawrence seems to be expressing misgivings here about the married state even in the throes of his earliest, most passionate time with Frieda prior to the outbreak of war. In the wake of a cavalcade of soldiers coming past, Gilbert feels "the deep longing, and the far-off desire to be with men, with men alone ... to be away from woman, beyond her" (*MN* 209).

Landscape is not always solace for a failed relationship or in sync with a character's happiness; it (or whatever it is that motivates the attraction to it) is sometimes the cause of breakdown. The short story "The Overtone," likely written in the spring of 1924 (*SM* xxi), features a fusion of wife and landscape, at least in the mind of the protagonist, Will Renshaw. Renshaw sees his wife, Edith, pantheistically: she "was everything – moon, vapour of trees, trickling water and drift of perfume – it was all his wife" (*SM* 7). Ominously, he feels that "[h]e had married her, and there was nothing more to own. He owned her"

(*SM* 7). His overwhelming need for merger and his failure to consider Edith's self-boundaries destroy the marriage at its core even though it appears to persist amicably on the surface. Will had asked Edith to make love one night *en plein air*, up on a hill, and she had refused. His one desire is "to give himself, clean and clear, into this night, this time. Of which she was all, she was everything" (*SM* 9). Everything and therefore nothing, one might argue. Her refusal results in his unconsciously hating her "as if she had kept him out of the promised land that was justly his" (*SM* 9).[5] Regardless of the view of marriage itself, what does not change in Lawrence is marriage's deep connection to early-life attachment complications. Even Cathcart, the protagonist of "The Man Who Loved Islands," dramatizes in negative form an aspect of the strong emotions related to attachment as he detaches from the wife and child he has almost accidentally acquired and from everyone else as he moves to the third island.

Lawrence's great piece of marriage fiction is *The Rainbow*, but he deals with the subject in novel, novella, play, and short story form throughout his career, from the satisfactory spouse-hunting of the brothers in "Love Among the Haystacks" to the dysfunctional and sometimes violent relationship of Mr and Mrs Morel in *Sons and Lovers* to the sexless marriage of Basil and Daphne in *The Ladybird* (1923) to the repressive marital relations Connie Chatterley shares with Clifford in *Lady Chatterley's Lover*.[6] Hazan and Zeifman's investigation of pair-bond attachments suggests that "the factors found to exert the greatest influence on the selection of pair-bond partners are ... similar to those used by infants in 'choosing' among potential attachment figures" (342). They also remind us that the etymology of the word "familiar" is the Latin *familia* (family) and that similarity or familiarity is a key factor in attraction and mate choice (342), something evident in Somers's attraction to Victoria Callcott as described above. This is especially true in the case of Lawrence, whose abnormally close relationship with his mother made his contemplation of a marriage partner so intensely problematic until he met Frieda Weekley.

Lawrence had a hard time figuring out whom to marry and whether to marry at all. On the evidence of his letters, his essays, and his autobiographical fictionalizing of the situation in *Sons and Lovers*, his mother-attachment is what stood in the way. In discussing the core idea behind *Sons and Lovers* in a letter to Edward Garnett, Lawrence explains that when the boys in the fictional family "come to manhood, they can't love, because their mother is the strongest power in their lives, and holds them" (*1L* 477). In *Psychoanalysis and the Unconscious*, similarly, Lawrence, writing in the third person but undoubtedly with his own background in mind, sketches the following scenario: "a man finds it impossible to realize himself in marriage. He recognizes the fact that his emotional, even passional, regard for his mother is deeper than it ever could be for a wife" (*PFU* 13). In *Fantasia of the Unconscious*, Lawrence writes of a woman unfulfilled in marriage, devoting her love to her son instead in such a way that it "is poison to her boy" (*PFU* 148). Later in the same work, in a discussion of dreams, he mentions the mother-image that derives from a situation where "the mother ... arrests [the son] from finding his proper fulfilment on the sensual plane" (*PFU* 181).[7] When Gerald's Crich's father dies in *Women in Love* and Gerald walks in a trance-like state from a solitary visit at the paternal grave to Gudrun's bedroom, we may be seeing in displaced form a retrospectively guilt-stricken Lawrence contemplating his over-hasty engagement to Louie Burrows so very close in time to his mother's death: death and love, as the chapter title proclaims, without explicitly suggesting that the latter is possible only because of the former.[8] In the end, of course, Lawrence married a woman in Frieda Weekley who was very different from Lydia Lawrence, but her status as a mother and the age difference between them (Frieda being six years older than Lawrence) may have had an appeal not totally unconnected to his maternal bond. There is, then, some irony in Worthen's suggestion that when Lawrence met Frieda he was in a sense recapitulating his mother's initial fascination with his father: "he found himself like Lydia Beardsall attracted to Arthur Lawrence back in 1874; drawn to the exciting, sensual and highly unsuitable partner who, because of their utter difference, offered the promise of freedom" (*EY* 381).

The short story "Love Among the Haystacks," begun in late 1911 (*LAH* xxx), about a year after Lydia Lawrence's death, is a significant early attempt by Lawrence to explore the connection between childhood attachment and marriage, and, like *The Rainbow*, which can be seen as its elaboration in some ways, it explores the role of familiarity and unfamiliarity in pair bonding. Two brothers in the Wookey family, Geoffrey and Maurice, are far from possessing a good fortune but are, nevertheless, each in want of a wife. The two men, in their early twenties, are "fiercely shy of women," and their mother, who never actually appears in the story, figures prominently in their reticence: "until this hay harvest, the whole feminine sex had been represented by their mother, in presence of any other women they were dumb louts" (*LAH* 89).[9] The Wookey mother is described in terms that look forward to aspects of Gertrude Morel. She is "proud," speaks "pure English," and is not native to the place she lives in. She has made it clear that she snobbishly considers the "common girls" of the district beneath her family. "So the two young men had grown up virgin but tormented" (*LAH* 89). What is different about this hay harvest is the presence at the neighbouring vicarage of the alluring governess Paula Jablonowsky. At first, the two brothers become almost deadly rivals for Paula's affections. She comes from Germany but is of Polish descent and speaks halting English, and it is her foreignness above all that seems to attract both brothers, perhaps because, in her literal outlandishness, she seems to be beyond the remit of the maternal sanction on local girls. Geoffrey thinks: "For Paula was strange, foreign, different from the ordinary girls: the rousing, feminine quality seemed in her concentrated, brighter, more fascinating than in anyone he had known" (*LAH* 109–10). It turns out, though, that Geoffrey and Paula are not suited to each other in the least, and, in the end, Lawrence provides a different and more suitable mate for Geoffrey in order to bring about an almost fairy-tale ending.

There are interesting differences between Geoffrey, the older brother, and Maurice, one year younger. (There is a third brother, Henry, who is senior to Geoffrey, but his role in the story is minor.) Perhaps because of his status as the middle brother in birth order, Geoffrey seems to suffer from insecure attachment and has trouble believing in his own worthiness, a common result of insecure or unreliable attachment in childhood. He exemplifies Lawrence's pronouncement in the Hardy study: "Let a man walk alone on the face of the earth, and he feels himself like a loose speck blown at random. Let him have a woman to whom he belongs, and he will feel as though he had a wall to back up against" (*STH* 58). Indeed, Geoffrey feels that "[h]e *must* have something firm to back up to, or he would go mad. He was so lonely, he who above all needed the support of sympathy" (*LAH* 94). For "he was a man who could not bear to stand alone, he was too much afraid of the vast confusion of life surrounding him, in which he was helpless" (*LAH* 103). As a result, like a child seeking the safety of a caregiver in the face of danger, he needs the security of the familiar even as he is fascinated by the foreign in Paula. And Lawrence gives him what he needs in the figure of the tramp's wife, whom Lawrence names Lydia, thereby, in effect, transferring his own feeling of familiarity with the name to his character. Like the portrayal of the Wookey mother, the first description of the "rather small, and finely made" Lydia Bredon might be a superficial portrait of Lydia Lawrence (or Gertrude Morel): "save for the look of bitterness and aloofness … [s]he gave an impression of cleanness, of precision and directness" (*LAH* 101).

Beyond the transferred familiarity from author to fictional character, there is also an intrinsic and immediate feeling of relatedness between Geoffrey and the woman. When Geoffrey first encounters her, he at once senses that "[t]here was a sort of kinship between them. Both were at odds with the world" (*LAH* 102), wording that calls to mind the kinship aspect of pair-bonding postulated in some attachment studies: "Others who are similar can seem like family members and may be especially appealing partners for kin relationships" (Hazan and Zeifman 342). For her part, Lydia feels that Geoffrey "seemed to understand her" (*LAH* 102). Although Geoffrey is the first to encounter Paula and believes that he "would have loved her wildly" (*LAH* 110), Lydia is a far better match for him given his attachment needs. When one night he finds her surreptitiously entering the Wookey shed, it seems almost to be a magical fulfilment of his just-thought wish that "if only some woman would come and take him for what he was worth, though he was such a stumbler and showed to such disadvantage" (*LAH* 110). He senses that she is just what he needs as a buttress to his own inadequacies: "having her, he felt he could bruise the lips of the scornful, and pass on erect, unabateable. With her to complete him, to form the core of him, he was firm and whole" (*LAH* 117). The fact that Lydia is already married does not seem to pose an insuperable barrier to their plans; in fact, it may be an added, unconscious attraction for Geoffrey insofar as she is a maternal proxy. (She had a child who died in infancy.) However, her marital status is certainly inconvenient and is one more element in Geoffrey's anxiety about being able to make the relationship permanent. His insecurity makes him fear that she will leave him: "Brooding rather bitterly, he told himself she'd forsake him ... 'I bet I s'll niver see you again'" (*LAH* 118).[10]

It is no wonder that Paula Jablonowsky prefers the more outgoing and carefree Maurice to the brooding, anxious Geoffrey. For whatever reason, Maurice comes across as a much more secure person, and with him Lawrence portrays the attraction of exploring the unfamiliar that is so important in establishing a sense of individuation. He is much more at home in his own skin than his brother is, and, in fact, marvels at that skin and his own naked body when he washes himself in the darkness at a water trough (*LAH* 105). But his exuberance and tendency to needle his brother about Paula are both insensitive and dangerous. This needle in the haystack almost costs him his life when Geoffrey angrily pushes him and he falls to the ground from atop a very high stack. Maurice also seems to be less risk-averse than Geoffrey, and, at Paula's behest, furiously and dangerously rides with her bareback on his mare in the dark of the night. Unlike his brother, who cannot stand alone in the world, Maurice "was very much excited ... at finding himself alone" (*LAH* 104), while awaiting Paula's arrival from the vicarage, though he is also "almost afraid." Furthermore, he has greater self-esteem than Geoffrey and feels "that he was worthy, having a sense of his own wonder" (*LAH* 105). Nor is Maurice terrified of Paula leaving him as Geoffrey is later on of losing Lydia. When he and Paula quarrel over her baseless accusation that he pretended the ladder had fallen off the haystack and that they would therefore have to remain on the stack together all night (unknown to them, in fact, Geoffrey has repositioned the ladder a short time before), he wisely lets events unfold as they will, allowing her to fume while denying any trickery. Like his brother, Maurice has found the proper partner for himself – "[o]ne felt instinctively that they were mated" (*LAH* 96) – but his life does not seem to depend on marrying her the way Geoffrey's does on pairing with Lydia. So what we see, in effect, in "Love Among the Haystacks" is a splitting between the two brothers of what is elsewhere in Lawrence often portrayed within one character: the paradoxical and ambivalent struggle for meaningful attachment and the conflict between the urge to explore and the need for security, the allure of the unfamiliar versus the safety of the familiar.

The story has many elements that recur in *The Rainbow*, especially in the first generation of the novel: the way the characters are startled at times of potentially life-changing events, the protagonists' air of expectancy, the male feeling of incompleteness and fear of abandonment, and, most particularly, the figure of the foreign woman working in the vicarage, Paula Jablonowsky. Her posting, foreign background, and Polish ancestry all recur in the figure of *The Rainbow*'s Lydia Lensky. The past lives of the two women are very different, but they have similar narratological and thematic functions. In *The Rainbow*, as well, as we will see, Lawrence continues probing the role of familiarity in pair-bond attachments, but instead of splitting the respective attractions of the familiar and the unfamiliar between two characters, he combines them in the concept of the uncanny. He discovers the intense connection in romantic attachments between the familiar and the unfamiliar and what they can represent of a character's attachment quandary. His use of the uncanny in the novel gives him a tool to explore those developments in each generation in a way that does justice to the complexity of the emotions involved.

The exploration of the familiar and the unfamiliar in *The Rainbow* begins in the prelusive section that describes in quasi-biblical language the generations of mostly unnamed Brangwens leading up to our first protagonist, Tom.[11] The family chronicle proper begins with Part II of the first chapter within the context of the "trespass" and "invasion" of a canal, colliery, and railway, all built in rapid succession around the year 1840.[12] The Brangwens are at first "astonished" by the unfamiliar sights and sounds, but they soon enough become inured to the presence of the once-disturbing but "now familiar" canal embankment, while the initially "startling" run of the winding engines of the colliery becomes a "narcotic to the brain," and the "shrill" train whistle actually creates "fearsome pleasure" in its signalling "the far-off come near and imminent" (R 14). The terms Lawrence uses in this sensitive recounting of the human reaction and adaptation to momentous change echo linguistically and conceptually throughout the book. In fact, the adaptive strategies briefly depicted here come to act as metaphors for crucial attachment issues that Lawrence explores in each generation by using uncanny encounters. In key scenes featuring the uncanny, the foreign, distant, and strange signify both the desire to explore the unknown in the movement from symbiosis to individuation (using Mahler's terms) and the concomitant fear of emotional distance and estrangement. Domesticating the foreign, bringing the far-off near, and familiarizing the strange become tropes for the need for renewed security and the psychological means of coping with the emotional complexities of attachment anxieties. In short, we see the Lawrentian equilibrium of attachment play itself out, often in paradoxical form.

I use the word "uncanny" here in the Freudian sense of *unheimlich*, the simultaneously strange and familiar. According to Hugh Haughton, Freud's short work "The Uncanny" (1919) is a very strange essay "about a particularly intense experience of strangeness" (xlii). But the point here is that it is also, significantly and paradoxically, about familiarity. Freud asserts that the word *heimlich* "becomes increasingly ambivalent, until it finally merges with its antonym *unheimlich*," and that the uncanny or unhomely "is in some way a species of the familiar" or homely (134).[13] As Petra Eckhard puts it, the uncanny has been "a dominant motif in Western art and culture" since the eighteenth-century Gothic revival, but it took Freud to make the connection to the human unconscious (10n), a pertinent observation for the present argument. For although Lawrence was generally hostile to psychoanalytic theory and his interest in "devouring" mothers would seem to be at odds with Freud's fixation on the bogeymen of "castrating" fathers in the oedipal complex, the concept of *unheimlich* as here defined has surprising application to Lawrence's novel, where the uncanny can be both the strange familiarized and, as Freud would have it in his essay, the familiar made strange.[14]

The Rainbow features the simultaneously strange and familiar, for example, in Tom Brangwen's immediate reaction to seeing Lydia Lensky for the first time in the celebrated scene where, without any apparent motivation, he seems paradoxically to recognize a complete stranger – "'That's her,' he said involuntarily" (*R* 29) – or in Ursula Brangwen's turning to Rouen Cathedral "as if to something she had forgotten, and wanted" (*R* 422), though in point of fact she has never seen it before. Such uncanny moments in the novel tend to occur during crises of attachment often triggered by the presence, prospect, even image of a child, an indication of a textual awareness that there is an emotional residue underlying the adult attachment problems that derives from childhood and the maternal bond. Because of that link, the novel's uncanny encounters and their related interpersonal crises illustrate and elucidate the recurring Lawrentian paradox of attachment whereby characters seem to fight against the very relatedness they ardently seek.

Encounters with the uncanny in *The Rainbow* provide a psychologically satisfying way of dealing with the contradiction inherent in a paradoxical situation, since the uncanny appears to grant standing to both sides of a dichotomy, to place any contradiction in suspense so that it need not be resolved. It provides Lawrence's principal characters in *The Rainbow* with a seemingly magical means of dealing with the paradox of relatedness, what Gāmini Salgādo has called the "pattern of attraction and repulsion" in each Brangwen generation (111). More specifically as regards attachment, what we might call the uncanny's negative capability regarding the strange and the familiar seems to offer a symbolic and therefore safe break with the engulfing mother without the risk of rejection, and to represent a reconciliation with the estranged mother even in the act of breaking away and even beyond death. In this nexus of emotions, marriage seems to offer a means of simultaneously working through residual childhood anxieties and forging ahead toward an independent existence. Of course, at some level Lawrence also realizes that the conflicts he is exploring have no such easy, magical solution in reality, and there is a parallel awareness in the novel that any attainment of a secure and liberating attachment is as ephemeral as a rainbow.

Tom Brangwen is the youngest in his family, and he is somewhat insecurely attached as a child because his mother's affection is conditional. We see enough of his early life to understand that he "was his mother's favorite" (*R* 16) but is unable to live up to her expectations of him simply because she fails to take into account his true nature. Tom gives way to his mother's desire to have him schooled, for example, even though he realizes that he is not suited to formal education and is bound to do poorly: "He believed his mother was right in decreeing school for him, but he knew she was only right because she would not acknowledge his constitution" (*R* 16). This lack of maternal attunement to his true self makes Tom feel "as if he were guilty of his own nature, as if his being were wrong, and his mother's conception right. If he could have been what he liked, he would have been that which his mother fondly but deludedly hoped he was" (*R* 17).[15]

When Tom is ready to break out from a "shut off" and "enclosed" Marsh (*R* 13) in order to promote a budding autonomy by exploring the larger world, he goes in search of the far-off and strange. It is "the hour of the stranger," as Lawrence once called the first urge of a young person to set out into the larger world (*PFU* 133). However, because Tom's primary attachment is insecure, he unconsciously feels that, as his exploratory desire becomes focused as an exogamous urge, he puts at risk his near relationships back home, where his mother still presides. When he encounters a prostitute for the first time, Tom's emotions are telling: he is shocked and "startled" (*R* 20), the latter word associating him with the early Brangwen men's reaction to the foreign in the form of invasive change. Even while he seeks the novel, it would seem that this encounter is far too strange for Tom; with no element of the familiar to it, such an experience cannot be domesticated. No narcotic to the brain here. The prostitute is *unheimlich* in the literal meaning of the word: not belonging to the home. Indeed, most of Lawrence's description of Tom's reaction to her is an apparently unrelated but psychologically apt encomium to the familial woman of the home, one that makes the emotional fallout of Tom's pursuit of the strange all the plainer: the presiding woman at the Marsh always "occupied the supreme position"; the men "depended on her for their stability"; and Tom is "rooted in his mother and his sister" (*R* 20). Dependence, stability, and rootedness all suggest close connection and familiarity, the opposite of what Tom is ostensibly pursuing here. Tom's hankering for the strange and far-off in this scene, in short, triggers fear of attachment loss because the unassimilable strange/foreign here evokes the prospect of emotional estrangement: "He had something to lose which he was afraid of losing, which he was not sure even of possessing" (*R* 21), a fitting characterization of his fear of abandonment, even of a predisposition to anticipate abandonment, because his attachment, which "he was not sure even of possessing," is not secure to begin with.

The solution for Tom that enables him to assert some independence and explore the new while retaining his precarious hold on the attachment at home is a trick of the mind involving the uncanny. He will, in effect, assimilate the unfamiliar to the familiar, the foreign woman Lydia Lensky to aspects of the internal working model of his mother, and assure himself that by making the strange familiar he is avoiding maternal estrangement. Thus the literally outlandish and yet somehow familiar Lydia functions for Tom both as his means to seek autonomy and as a proxy for the emotionally far-off parent, the estranged attachment object that must be secured as far as possible. Tom's sister Effie is being sarcastic when she says to him while indicating the strange Polish woman after church, "'There's your woman for you ... You'd better marry *her*'" (R 34), but she is unknowingly expressing Tom's own intuition: Lydia *is* the woman for him, and he *will* marry her *because* she is strange but in a way that paradoxically makes her familiar. Lawrence is writing out of his own deep emotions here: the fact that the very first time Tom sets eyes on the Polish woman Lawrence presents it as a kind of recognition and the fact that he gives Tom's future wife his own now-deceased mother's name suggest how invested Lawrence is in his portrayal of the complicated psychological process going on in Tom's unconscious.[16]

Thus, by means of a trick of Tom's mind, whereby the internalized image of the estranged mother finds an external if partial analogue in the strange woman,[17] Lydia seems both unfamiliar and familiar, thereby offering – if she can be won over – the magical formula whereby autonomy can be pursued without attachment loss because estrangement is symbolically overcome in the very act of pursuing the strange. The first time Tom sees Lydia, the uncanny feeling that he and the stranger "had exchanged recognition" (R 30) possesses him, and when his servant Tilly informs him that Lydia is Polish, he unaccountably feels a "curious certainty about her" and "a profound satisfaction that she was a foreigner" (R 32). The more foreign she is, the more he is certain that he wants her, as he instinctively realizes that Lydia's air of aloofness, her strangeness, and her foreignness will make the triumph of securing her all the greater. One day in church, his mother having just recently died, Tom views Lydia distinctly in terms of the far-off come near: "She was strange, from far off, yet so intimate. She was from far away, a presence, so close to his soul" (R 32). The situation is superficially odd in that Tom, by mentally bringing the far-off close, is apparently trying to overcome an estrangement from someone to whom he is not yet even connected, but that is because of what Lydia represents for him in terms of maternal attachment. Indeed, it is a "profound satisfaction" to Tom not only that Lydia is a foreigner, but also that she is a mother and thus can the more easily represent for Tom his unconscious emotional struggle with maternal estrangement, even the ultimate abandonment through death.[18]

According to Lawrence's unstable equilibrium model of attachment, the very need for the reassurance of closeness eventually and inevitably slides into a fear of merger, so, as much as Tom wishes to secure Lydia, he also senses, even early on, that he needs to escape her overwhelming influence, to be more autonomous, as the paradox of Lawrentian attachment takes hold: thus the very figure that initially represents for Tom an exploratory move away from the dependency of home attachment all too quickly takes on the additional mantle of a too-powerful bond, as Tom's unconscious pattern of anxiety reasserts itself. For example, at a time when they are barely acquainted, Lydia, acting as she would in her native Poland, knocks on the seldom-used front door and enters Tom's house uninvited to borrow some butter. This seemingly trivial transgression functions symbolically as a violation of Tom's self-boundaries, as I suggested earlier (see Introduction). Her entry "startled him. It was the custom for everybody to wait on the doorstep till asked inside" (R 34). As the colliery, canal, and railway were felt as a trespass and invasion by the Brangwens of 1840, Lydia's crossing the threshold of Tom's home is a symbolic encroachment on his precarious sense of self. Tom's feelings of inadequacy, projected outward as "unreal, barren, mere nullities" all around him (R 32), can be overcome only with the prospect of winning Lydia before him, and yet when she arrives unannounced he feels vaguely threatened.

Despite all the upheavals she has experienced, Lydia has a strong kernel of selfhood; whereas Tom's self-boundaries are rather fluid, hers are firmly demarcated: "These staked out and marked her horizon ... She scarcely noticed the outer things at all. What was outside was outside, non-existent" (R 96). This is in marked contrast to Tom's sense of self at Matlock, where, prior to meeting Lydia, his encounter with the foreign stranger prompted boundary questions: "Where was life, in that which he knew or all outside him?" (R 25). Strongly rooted in his locality as he is and living in a part of England where his family has been settled for generations, Tom is at a tremendous advantage, objectively speaking. Nevertheless, his own somewhat diffident sense of self is threatened by the relationship because, like Geoffrey Wookey in "Love Among the Haystacks," he is so dependent and feels that "he was only fragmentary, something incomplete and subject ... without her he was nothing" (R 40).[19] And it is apposite here to recall Schapiro's useful formulation: "[w]hat the self lacks internally it craves in the external world, and thus it risks being overpowered or enslaved precisely by what it urgently seeks." Tom realizes at a deep level, then, one of the paradoxical truths of Lawrentian attachment discussed in the Introduction: that relational closeness is both necessary and dangerous (the corollary being that relational distance is both attractive and frightening). For Tom, it is a complex, irrational, and recurring psychological process inculcated in childhood whereby the powerful need to approach relational merger prompts the countervailing urgency to protect the integrity of a vulnerable self through a distancing that in turn activates latent fears of abandonment: "Was she there for ever? Or might she go away?" (*R* 58).

The key crisis in the marriage of Tom and Lydia comes when she is carrying Tom's first child and she becomes emotionally removed: "there was ... silence and distance between them. She did not want him ... he was cast out" (*R* 61). As Lydia neglects Tom more and more during her pregnancy, "his existence was annulled" (*R* 62), "null" and variations of it and related words (as in "mere nullities" and "he was nothing," above) being key indicators of attachment and selfhood crises throughout the novel. In Schapiro's words, their relationship at such times "is emotionally charged with a child's acutely conflicting feelings toward a withdrawn, affectively nonattuned mother" (81). When Lydia goes into labour, various interrelated attachment crises become conflated: Tom's feeling of estrangement in his marriage, his link to his deceased mother, Lydia's maternal connection to the child about to be born, and little Anna's now-heightened emotional dependency on her mother. In the last-named relation, Anna feels bereft, cut off as she is temporarily from Lydia, but Tom's method of consoling her is inspired. In a much-admired scene, he takes her, wrapped in a shawl, into the dark, womb-like space of the cow barn. The action also indicates how Tom, even on the cusp of fatherhood, seeks signs of maternal attachment as he travels mentally back to his own childhood: "He looked down at the silky folds of the paisley shawl. It reminded him of his mother. She used to go out to church in it" (*R* 76). Feeling rejected as a son by his birthing wife, he resorts to memories, enhanced by nostalgia, of his time as son to his now-dead mother – in effect, the inverse process of his attraction to Lydia in the first place, in that he is returning mentally to his mother-attachment in reaction to what he feels is a wifely rejection.

At one point in the marriage, Tom seeks to articulate his anxieties and frustrations to Lydia, a turn of events that results in a real attempt to work out a *modus vivendi* between them. As Tom gradually yields to Lydia's caresses in this scene, he "opposed the mingling with her, even whilst he most desired it" (*R* 90), a characterization that sums up Tom's narcissistic and lifelong search for an impossible return to an infantile merger that yet leaves him autonomous. Tom's pursuit of the chimera of a secure yet liberating attachment ends only when the flood caused by a breach in the canal embankment takes his life in chapter 9. His death by drowning is significant in terms of the attachment issues that have coloured his emotional life all along. For Lawrence associates the flood with the biblical deluge in Genesis and Tom with Noah, who is cut off by God's wrathful flood from the same earth, as it were, that for the Brangwen men "clung to their feet with a weight that pulled like desire" (R 10). As Christine M. Connell has suggested, in this novel, "the materiality of the body is aligned with the materiality of the earth, and this association is the basis for emotional attachment and intimacy" (75). Schapiro claims that Tom's "psychologically resonant" death by drowning suggests a "narcissistic fantasy" of "annihilation through passive refusion with the mother" (85), and I would agree that Tom's unconscious and recurring need for merger plays a part. But what the flood imagery here and elsewhere in the novel specifically connotes is a male Brangwen neediness that drives the fantasy and is overwhelming – literally overwhelming in Tom's case – to both the men themselves and to the women they yearn for. Tom had sought in Anna an additional attachment object to "[relieve] the main flood to his wife" so that his neediness "did not foam and flood and make misery" (R 79). Now, with Anna married and no longer available to contain a portion of that emotional deluge for Tom, an actual flood overwhelms and kills him.

Where the young Tom Brangwen had been strongly if ambivalently attracted to the unfamiliar, his stepdaughter, Anna, is somewhat xenophobic, and understandably so given an early childhood that included the death of Lensky, her father, a transplanting to a new country, and the acquisition of a stepfather. The last development is ultimately stabilizing; nevertheless, Anna is generally wary of outside forces impinging upon her: "She hated people who came too near to her. Like a wild thing, she wanted her distance. She mistrusted intimacy" (R 92). So part of Will Brangwen's attraction for Anna is that he seems to her to embody simultaneously the unfamiliar and the familiar, distant and near, a cousin whom she vaguely remembers from very infrequent meetings in the past and yet not related to her by blood. He is *safely* "foreign": strange and yet family and very much "at home" at the Marsh (R 101). His status is inherently uncanny for her from the start, so no need for tricks of the mind to transform him. Given that Will seems to personify the formula for an attachment that promises both the security of the familiar and the independence of exploring the unknown, Anna unconsciously assumes that, in choosing him for her marriage partner, she will be able to have it both ways: to remain attached to her familiar environment even while asserting her autonomy. However, in this she is quite mistaken, for while "similarity can create a false sense of familiarity" (Hazan and Zeifman 342), equally, familiarity can create a mistaken assumption of security. Subsequent developments amply indicate Will's propensity to violate personal boundaries and thereby imperil Anna's independence and individuality. Will is driven to do so, of course, because of his own attachment deficits. As with Tom, flood imagery in Will's case denotes the overwhelming nature of a male neediness that seeks fusion yet ultimately estranges the loved one. Well into the marriage, for example, Anna "clung fiercely to her known self. But the rising flood carried her away" (R 155).

The attachment problems that blight the married life of Anna and Will are foreshadowed in the sheaves-stacking scene in chapter 4 of the novel, one of those Lawrentian *tour-de-force* dramatizations that so skillfully parlay a realistic depiction into something of deeper significance. It is a charming scene of rustic ritual wherein if the young man overtakes the young maiden in the field, it is "his privilege, to kiss her" (R 115). Beyond that, the entire episode readily symbolizes estrangement and attachment since it is centrally about setting up a space between the two characters and then reducing the distance incrementally until they finally come together. Anna repeatedly turns away from Will as they work: "And always she was gone before he came. As he came, she drew away, as he drew away, she came. Were they never to meet?" (R 114). Only by deliberately altering his tempo of work is Will able to engineer their meeting and embrace.

Viewing this engaging scene as a simple account of the awakening of a first love is entirely plausible, but it is also a foreshadowing of how Will's attachment issues will play out in the marriage and how Anna will resist him (as her "keen clash" when she brings two sheaves together betokens the conflict to come [R 114]). He is the pursuer in the sheaves ritual they are enacting, and the focalization is clearly his at this juncture. As Earl G. Ingersoll has suggested about this scene, Will wishes "not so much to meet [Anna] as to impose his will upon her" (75). In sum, the scene initially sets up a distance and then works to eliminate that distance, a far-off-come-near process that is recapitulated even in the embrace itself. As they kiss, Anna calls "in a low voice, from afar" and seems to "call to him from far off … And he drew near, and she drew near" (R 116). The attainment of the desired object is, of course, the more satisfying in the end for its very elusiveness, but there are also deep-seated psychological reasons to do with attachment anxieties that explain why the expunging of distance is so satisfying. For, like Tom's successful courtship of Lydia that familiarizes the strange, it seems that, for Will, bringing the far-off near symbolically represents the overcoming of estrangement and thereby a lessening of residual anxieties from an insufficiently secure childhood. Though Lawrence provides the reader with little of his past, the idea that Will's attachment problems stem from the maternal bond is strongly suggested in the language of a later passage: "In his soul, he was desolate as a child, he was so helpless. Like a child on its mother, he depended on her [Anna] for his living" (R 176).

What is, on the surface, a charming enactment of spatial diminution in the sheaves scene takes on a much darker aspect in Will's desire to close in like a predator on its prey even early on in the relationship: "They had looked at each other, and seen each other strange, yet near, very near, like a hawk stooping, swooping, dropping into a flame of darkness" (R 110). It is clearly Will who is the bird of prey here, as numerous descriptions before and after this one suggest. Anna's resistance to Will's need to absorb and her own countervailing drive to individuation come out in an uncanny encounter early in the marriage (described in a flashback) when she and Will pay a visit to Baron Skrebensky. For all three generations of Brangwens, the Skrebenskys, as established friends of the family, represent the uncanny, foreign/familial juxtaposition that is so attractive and so important for the working out of their attachment issues. For the now-married Anna "[t]hese strange Skrebenskys made her aware of another, freer element, in which each person was detached and isolated" (R 184–5), thus allowing her to realize that the close, reassuring feeling of kinship familiarity with Will was smothering her independence in her marriage: "the curious enveloping Brangwen intimacy, so warm, so close, so stifling, when one seemed always to be in contact with the other person, like a blood-relation, was annulled. She denied it, this close relationship with her young husband. He and she were not one" (R 185).

It is, however, Will's relationship with the uncanny that Lawrence explores in greater detail as the text's focalization shifts to his point of view after the wedding at the Marsh. Will's sense of self is weaker even than Tom's was, and he is much more assertive, even sadistic, in seeking to ensure his attachments. The less assured he feels the more he seeks the security of merger, but the more he insists on fusion, the greater is Anna's tendency to hold him separate from her. Needing Anna to bolster a frail sense of self and "driven by fear of her departure" (R 141), Will has a compulsion to dominate that is an expression of both the degree of his dependency and his profound reluctance to accept it: "Dread and desire for her to stay with him and shame at his own dependence on her drove him to anger" (R 141). Lee Kirkpatrick points out that when efforts to achieve adequate proximity to a primary attachment figure are rebuffed, some people "turn to God as a substitute attachment figure" (812). Although for Kirkpatrick it is most often the personal elements in a religion (such as Christianity's God the father or Mary the mother) that can best perform such a role, in Will's case, quite early on, he turns to church buildings for "a dark, nameless emotion" which is manifestly related to Anna – "somehow, she felt he was conveying to strange, secret places the love that sprang in him for her" (R 148) – and to his own infantile narcissistic need to merge with something greater than himself. As Lawrence writes in the Hardy essay in a manner that almost seems to be a pun on his own fictional character's name, when a man's need for stability is no longer fulfilled in a particular woman, "he must seek elsewhere ... for the centre to himself. Then either he must seek another woman, or he must seek to make conscious his desire to find a symbol ... so that he may have it at will, for his own complete satisfaction" (STH 57).

Functioning somewhat akin to a transitional object for a child, the Church becomes an unconscious attachment substitute for Will that will ease the unbearable feeling of estrangement from Anna. To do that it must have uncanny properties: both the distance of the strangely mysterious – and he insists on the mystery ("He did not want things to be intelligible" [R 147]) – and the familiar nearness of maternal acceptance. Indeed, in the chapter "The Cathedral" we see that, though also mystical, the Church does represent for Will the ideal, accepting, all-giving mother,[20] and Lawrence's imagery here strongly connotes merger, even the same kind of spatial reduction dramatized in the sheaves scene. The embrace in the sheaves scene is recalled in "the meeting and the consummation, the meeting, the clasp, the close embrace" that Will feels in Lincoln Cathedral (R 187). So instead of seeking a human stranger at this point for the uncanny experience he needs, Will goes to these "strange, secret places": to a cathedral or even, one further step removed, to a book on Bamberg Cathedral written in German, a language completely foreign to him (R 153). Anna partly intuits Will's need, resents it, and is able, by unwisely mocking it, to devalue it for him since he is partly ashamed already of his over-investment in the objects of his devotion, connected as they are with his deepest feelings of inadequacy. She "resented his transport and ecstasies" because they threaten her individual freedom and make the cathedral "the ultimate confine" (R 188). So she latches onto the impish gargoyles, which, she feels, undermine the monolithic, merging aspect of the cathedral.[21]

As in the first generation of Brangwens, the crisis comes in connection with a child, when Anna is pregnant with Ursula. Like a "narcissistically enraged child" himself (Schapiro 86), Will "raged in torment, wanting,

wanting" (*R* 166). At this point, the coming child is a like a sibling rival for the mother's attention, and Anna's sense of Will's compulsion to absorb her leads to the crucial conflict and Anna's naked dance of victory. Will needs more from Anna than she can give, but her dancing his "nullification" (*R* 171) – and we note the root word "null" again here – is hardly calculated to allay the attachment insecurities that drive his compulsion to begin with. And it is the pregnant Anna's strangeness that throws Will into crisis. To him, she is now "a strange exalted thing having no relation to himself" (*R* 171). His dependence on her, like Tom's on Lydia, is almost literally overwhelming, as suggested in telltale imagery harking back to Noah in Genesis: "She was the ark, and the rest of the world was flood" (*R* 173). Such language once more evokes the emotional kernel of a child ironically cut off by its own very neediness from its mother, who is represented by the unavailable earth, of which the ark is a frail synecdoche. Indeed, once embarked on her "fecund storm" of producing baby after baby, Anna "felt like the earth, the mother of everything" (*R* 193). The Lawrentian paradox expressing Will's ambivalent neediness sums up one variation of the attachment dilemma of the Brangwen men and many other male protagonists in Lawrence: "A woman, he must have a woman. And having a woman, he must be free of her" (*R* 173).

Soon enough, Will sees Ursula as a surrogate for Anna. Despite some charming aspects to it, the relationship is an unhealthy one in which Will's sadistic tendencies occasionally surface and Ursula quickly develops protective strategies to resist him. To shield herself, she tends to "[assert] herself only. There was now nothing in the world but her own self"; she learns to "harden herself upon her own being" (*R* 208), a defensive manoeuvre that will later have consequences for Ursula's relationship with Anton Skrebensky. Finding himself resisted on all sides and his beloved church devalued for him by his wife, Will eventually looks farther afield for his attachment substitute. As the Hardy essay remarks, "Every man seeks in woman, for that which is stable, eternal. And if, under his motion, this breaks down ... in the particular woman ... then he must seek elsewhere for his stability, for the centre to himself" (*STH* 57). This is the context in which Will meets the Nottingham girl, a stranger he wishes to keep unfamiliar: "[H]e did not want to know anything about her" (*R* 214). And yet, in keeping with the uncanniness so pervasive in the novel, there is something familiar about her as well. What appeals to Will in her takes us back to the role of the cathedral in Will's emotional life as a substitute for Anna. In fact, the girl's body curves have an effect on Will similar to the arches of Lincoln Cathedral: "And his hand that grasped her side felt one curve of her, and it seemed like a new creation to him, a reality, an absolute, an existing tangible beauty of the absolute" (*R* 213). Thus, for Will, the yearning for maternal attachment by proxy culminates ironically in the attempted seduction of a virtual child as his continuing if unavailing search takes the form of his efforts to control first his wife, then his daughter, and finally a strange girl.

Ursula Brangwen, the protagonist of the novel's third generation, does not marry in the course of *The Rainbow*. She does, however, form an on-again-off-again pair-bond with Anton Skrebensky over a number of years and seriously considers marriage with him. Both her choice of mate and her eventual repudiation of marriage with him are intimately bound up with her attachment struggles and his deep attachment deficits. Ursula has a strong longing for autonomy. Times have changed – especially for women – since her Brangwen grandfather set out to encounter life outside of the Marsh, but it is also, in Ursula's case, a matter of temperament and of a constraining home environment that has made autonomy seem attractive, even salvational. Where Tom and Will, as they draw back in defence of a vulnerable self, enact the Lawrentian paradox by resisting at times the very merger they fervently seek, in Ursula's case, the paradox becomes an inverted one according to which, by the end of the novel, she is on the verge of accepting the very attachment she has fought so hard against, an inversion that is very much a function of gender in a novel where men are needy and women determined.

A series of uncanny encounters dramatizes the attachment issues at stake for Ursula from the start. For example, it is striking that the first man Ursula feels passionate about, apart from her father, is her Uncle Tom, who, though he is family, also represents, like his mother, Lydia, "the superior, foreign element in the Marsh" (*R* 224). When Anton Skrebensky enters Ursula's life for the first time it is in the company of Uncle Tom, an apt connection since the two men have roughly the same function for Ursula's desire to explore the unfamiliar while retaining if possible the security of the familiar. A second early link to the uncanny for Ursula comes through Lydia's storytelling. After Tom Brangwen's death by drowning, the young Ursula forms a strong bond with her widowed grandmother, who recounts to the child stories of her girlhood and youth in Poland: "The child's heart beat fast as she listened … she seemed to feel far-off things" (*R* 241). For Ursula this is a fascinating experience of the "far-off" brought near that later contributes to her initial attraction to, and misjudgment of, the Polish-descended Skrebensky. In addition, her adolescent reading at this time nourishes family-romance fantasies that include a Poland that is simultaneously ancestral and exotic: "[S]he was truly a princess of Poland ... in England she was under a spell" (*R* 250). These early encounters with the uncanny function as precursors to Ursula's central relationship with Anton Skrebensky.

As a Skrebensky, Anton is part of a family with a longstanding connection to the Brangwens and to Lydia's stories of Poland. He is vaguely familiar, then, but, like Lydia to Tom, he is also the foreigner, wearing his hair "in the German fashion" and bringing to Ursula "a strong sense of the outer world" (*R* 269). When he kisses her for the first time, "[a] terrible and magnificent sense of his strangeness possessed her" (*R* 278). In short, he is to Ursula the embodiment of the uncanny she is more than ready for at this stage in her life, and "[s]he laid hold on him at once for her dreams" (*R* 271), an oneiric status that eventually turns nightmarish. For Ursula mistakes Anton's character. Her early view of him as "self-contained, self-supporting" (*R* 271) is a misjudgment (like Anna's initial misreading of Will's character) that is a product of a projection of her own needs.[22] In fact, as the novel makes plain, Skrebensky's sense of self is severely stunted, and what Ursula initially sees as his strength is actually a debilitating weakness. Feelings of isolation and abandonment have resulted from a too-early, and therefore spurious, autonomy that is forced upon him by circumstances rather than sought from a base of secure attachment. Skrebensky is an orphan who considers the army to be his only home, one that seems to supply him with a needed male identification and paternal authority, a crucial attachment that Ursula later undermines (just as Anna had belittled Will's attachment to the Church). In any case the army can offer only so much, and no maternal nurturing at all.

Lacking an authentic self and therefore unable to stand alone, Skrebensky looks to Ursula for surrogate maternal attachment, even merger. But there are several ways to effect interpersonal fusion: unlike Will, Skrebensky's default attachment style is self-effacement and a need to *be* absorbed. That need makes being part of the larger *corps* of the army crucially important to him, and it helps explain his masochism, which surfaces in sudden, bizarre descriptions such as this one, which implicitly figures Ursula as a carrion eater: "He wanted to kill himself, and throw his detested carcase at her feet" (*R* 283). Essentially, he is unconsciously compelled to adopt the submissive, masochist position because his fear of abandonment was strongly activated at a young age, when he was orphaned. Ursula eventually realizes that Anton has simply built up strong and misleading defences around a vacuous interior. Her cutting remark to him later on in the relationship that "'[i]t seems to me ... as if you weren't anybody ... You seem like nothing to me'" (R 289), cruel as it may be, hits the mark and does so with language that relates to the male Brangwens' feelings of nullity during attachment crises. As Schapiro notes, "[s]adomasochism flourishes in the absence of a real other" (89).

Once again the child figure plays a significant role. When Ursula and Skrebensky encounter the canal-barge couple and their infant, the parents are so charmed by Ursula that they decide to name their own baby after her. Thus, the barge infant also becomes a symbol of Ursula's palpable, living, even new-born self in contrast, implicitly, to Skrebensky's miscarried self, "the soul that ... lay dead, still-born, a dead weight in his womb" (R 304). The striking imagery suggests his incapacity to develop a viable selfhood and his need to be absorbed by a woman to be born a whole person. His affective investment in Ursula as a compensatory primary attachment is thus so great that he is shattered by her final repudiation, which must inevitably reactivate for him emotions related to the early loss of his parents. The failure of the relationship between Ursula and Anton is overdetermined by their respective earliest attachment experiences. Much as she was attracted to them, Ursula has had to fend off a father and an uncle bent on dominating her, and she prizes her independence. Skrebensky, in contrast, has lost both parents and needs to merge with a stronger individual. They are hopelessly incompatible. However, the intrusion of the Boer War, which sends Skrebensky off to fight in Africa, postpones the inevitable, final break between them. Ursula's last impression of him at the train station is ominous: "he was always so strange and null – so null ... Strangely nothing he was" (R 307).

When Skrebensky arrives back from exotic Africa he is eager to marry and take his wife to a privileged colonial life in far-off India.[23] Ursula, now in her last year at college, is able in some moods to see this older, world-travelled Skrebensky as attractively foreign, but it is inauspicious to say the least that, on their very first re-acquaintance, Ursula knows immediately that they are "enemies" (R 410). For it quickly becomes obvious to Ursula, at least at a pre-conscious level, that Skrebensky is far too dependent on her to allow her much autonomy. And if Ursula is sure of one thing it is that she must protect her authentic self in any relationship: "She had never been more herself. It could not occur to her that anybody, not even ... Skrebensky, should have anything at all to do with her permanent self" (R 418).

The question of marriage is the actual and symbolic catalyst to Skrebensky's collapse. He is so emotionally invested in Ursula that her reluctance to consider marriage and his sense that she is distancing herself from him magnify all his insecurities. His reaction is a deep and alarming sense of abandonment: "He began to tremble, he grew feverish with the fear of her departure ... Her absence was worse than pain to him. It destroyed his being" (R 423). Like Tom and Will vis-à-vis Lydia and Anna respectively, he sometimes "felt himself a mere attribute of her" (R 429). And yet everything proceeds normally on the social surface. They even become officially engaged, but when Skrebensky realizes that he and she will, in fact, never wed, he feels "as if he were being strangled" (R 432) and weeps uncontrollably in public. The reaction involves a residue from childhood attachment insecurities: "As if he were a child, she again wiped away his tears ... His face had always the same still, clarified, almost childlike look, impersonal" (R 434, 435). For Ursula, "[h]e seemed completed now. He roused no fruitful fecundity in her. He seemed added up, finished" (R 438). They both know it is over between them, and Skrebensky can only think that he must marry someone quickly and escape to India. His inspired solution combines the paternal support of the military with the prospect of a new maternal substitute: he will propose to his colonel's daughter "to screen himself from the darkness" (R 447) of his own nullity.

The final crisis of attachment for Ursula, like so many others in the book, is triggered by a child, or in this case the prospect of one. For after Skrebensky has departed for India, Ursula finds that she is pregnant with his child. So the "fruitful fecundity" he failed to rouse in her, metaphorically speaking, has become a physical reality. It is as if the "still-born" soul "in his womb" has somehow been revivified in hers, and as if by making her a mother-to-be he has transformed her more securely into the maternal attachment object he so obviously needed – but too late. Ursula begins to believe that she was wrong in rejecting Skrebensky even as Lawrence makes it clear that her attachment to him can be effected only through her own virtual self-annihilation. At this juncture, she has lost her integrity, and now it is her selfhood that seems null: "It seemed, this child, like the seal set on her own nullity. Yet she was glad in her flesh that she was with child ... What did the self, the form of life, matter?" (R 448). Thus the paradox of attachment for Ursula is the inverse of Tom's and Will's: she is about to accept the very attachment she has latterly fought so hard against, as one extreme of the double gyre of emotion kicks in with her contemplation of her isolation, bereft of her long-time partner, and subject to social ostracism as mother of a child born out of wedlock. She writes to Skrebensky telling him of the child, offering to marry him after all, and promising to "'serve [him] in all things'" (R 449). Fortunately for her own development toward individuation, he cables her back to say that he is already married.

Ursula's uncanny experience with the herd of horses in the rain, her subsequent severe illness, and her vision of the rainbow at the very end all reinforce her healthy separation from Skrebensky, a development brought about in part by circumstances and by the unconscious motivations symbolized by the horses that have elicited much diverse critical commentary over the years. As Cornelia Nixon has suggested, "since Ursula both runs for her life from the horses and is reborn into a new life arguably because she meets them" (123), a bifurcated critical approach to the scene has resulted.[24] I would suggest that the horses are yet another instance of the uncanny and are symbolically connected with Ursula's attachment complications. One of Freud's examples of the uncanny in his essay refers to animals that are normally *heimliche*, "tame and accustomed to humans" (126), but have become wild. In Ursula's world, horses are familiar, domesticated beasts: the Ur-Brangwen men, for example, "drew the heaving of the horses after their will" (R 10). But the fantasy horses of her encounter are anything but *heimliche*; they are wild, strange, and menacing. They thus combine the elements of the familiar (or domestic) and strange (or wild) that constitute the uncanny in this novel. For this is what Ursula's unconscious realizes she needs at this crucial point in her development: she must be strong enough to risk the estrangement of the familiar since it is the familiar, the near, and the domestic that represent a serious threat to her being. Skrebensky has been associated with horses and a herd mentality in the military, and for Ursula now to accept a domestic existence as she is tempted to do and "marry and love her husband and fill her place simply" (R 449) would be disastrous. It would also contradict her earlier determination *not* to emulate her mother's "limited life of herded domesticity" (R 329). An attachment with Skrebensky would have satisfied his needs but virtually destroyed her.

Having escaped the horses, Ursula feels "inviolable," her core "impregnable" (R 455), wording that suggests that she may already have lost the child at this point and, more symbolically, that Skrebensky's invasive presence has now been negated through Ursula's getting back in touch with her core self. She must still fight through a feverish illness and work on her relationships at a barely conscious level, but she realizes the necessity to refuse any role that is the projection of the needs of others: "her mother and father and Anton, and college and all her friends, all cast off" (*R* 456). Her miscarriage and Skrebensky's cable simplify matters. At the very end, the rainbow becomes the symbol of Ursula's potential for achieved autonomy while also suggesting secure attachment. She sees it "forming itself"; it is *sui generis*: "it took presence upon itself" (*R* 458); but it also allows the earth to fit into heaven. In *Kangaroo*, we read that for Somers (and, presumably, for Lawrence), the rainbow was always "[a] pledge of unbroken faith, between the universe and the innermost" (*K* 155). Keith Sagar has written that the rainbow "has no business in the novel except as a symbol" (72).[25] But precisely as a symbol, it is a powerful indication that, as the rainbow is self-forming and allows the earth to fit into heaven, Ursula has the capacity to achieve a balanced attachment in the future, having survived the flood of Skrebensky's neediness and accepted the creative potential of separation on the way to establishing her autonomous selfhood.

"My heart leaps up when I behold / A rainbow in the sky," wrote William Wordsworth (160), a poet whose work Lawrence knew quite well.[26] Apart from a romantic and expressionist sensibility, what the two writers have in common is the realization that our earliest emotions and patterns of attachment stay with us throughout life even if our childhood perceptual wonderment fades: "The Child is father of the Man," says Wordsworth, a paradoxical statement from the same poem, "My Heart Leaps Up," that he reuses (along with the concluding two lines of the poem) as the epigraph to his great Immortality Ode. Whether or not Lawrence was thinking of the Wordsworthian rainbow when he came to pen his own *Rainbow*, the novel clearly depicts the pervasive influence of childhood attachment patterns of relating on marriage.

4

CLASS

Deep, deep is class hatred and it begins to swallow all human feeling in its abyss.
  D.H. Lawrence, *The Captain's Doll* (*Fox* 128)

They're not any better than we are / the upper classes – they're worse. / Such bloomin' fat-arsed dool-owls / they aren't even fit to curse!
  D.H. Lawrence, "Up he goes! –" (*Poems* 480, ll. 17–20)

"Upper? Why all their uppishness amounts to is extra special greedy guts, ten-thousand-a-year minimum. Upper classes! Upper classes! Upper arses."
  Willie Struthers's speech in D.H. Lawrence, *Kangaroo* (*K* 311)

Class is a multifaceted area in Lawrence studies, encompassing not only an important theme in his writing but also a crucial component of his personal history and aspects of the reception of his work during his lifetime. When Lawrence died on 2 March 1930, the obituaries said much more about sex and censorship than about class, according to Dennis Jackson's review of over two hundred English-language death notices and obituaries from the time (33–72). In the essay "We Need One Another," one of the last pieces he wrote, Lawrence expresses a degree of exasperation regarding his unshakable reputation as sex-obsessed: "I am so tired of being told that I want mankind to go back to the condition of savages" (*LEA* 302).[1] Even now, suggests David Ellis, "[a]sk any reasonably literate members of the general public about Lawrence and they will tell you that his chief interest was in sex" (*Love and Sex* xi). This was not always the case, but the sensation surrounding the publication of *Lady Chatterley's Lover*, its suppression, and the later trial to determine whether its publication violated obscenity laws has forever linked Lawrence and sexuality in public consciousness.

Nevertheless, Lawrence has also been associated with issues of social class from the start of his career even by people unfamiliar with his writing.[2] Lawrence's prospects certainly got a boost early on because of his perceived working-class background. Influential enablers and mentors such as Ford Madox Ford (or Hueffer as he was then) were thrilled to have "discovered" a natural literary genius among the rustics and coal-shovellers of the East Midlands. In the words of Neil Roberts, Ford "adopted and promoted Lawrence as the working-class genius the literary world had been waiting for" ("Writing" 21). In fact, when Ford visited Lawrence, he was astonished to find a small but thriving intellectual coterie that Lawrence was part of in Eastwood (Nehls, vol. 1, 151–2). A genuinely working-class author was rare, and Lawrence's emergence was certainly an exceptional and, to some, an exciting phenomenon. Among a number of contemporary arbiters of taste, however, Lawrence's unusual class origins were far from celebrated, as we see in T.S. Eliot's "scathing, High Church contempt" or Virginia Woolf's "faint uppercrust sneer," as Sandra M. Gilbert puts it ("Apocalypse" 238). In any case, the early class-tinged interest, whether positive or negative, was soon enough overshadowed by establishment outrage over Lawrence's sexual frankness as his writing moved beyond *Sons and Lovers*, and Lawrence's reputation became something quite different until the 1960s sexual revolution brought Western culture closer to his liberal views on human sexuality and rendered him a cultural champion of sorts for a brief period. At that point, general social developments and the Kate Millett smackdown in her book *Sexual Politics* (1970) conspired to create the caricature of Lawrence the misogynist, which still persists to some extent today alongside more nuanced views of his work.

F.R. Leavis took on the task of rehabilitating Lawrence's reputation when it was at a low ebb, critically speaking. In his book *D.H. Lawrence: Novelist* (first published in 1955), Leavis has a long chapter entitled "Lawrence and Class," which deals mostly with the early story "Daughters of the Vicar." Leavis's discussion offers some insightful comments about a few of the details of the tale but is otherwise fairly pedestrian in its analysis. His central point about Lawrence and class, however – "no writer is more wholly without class-feeling in the ordinary sense of the term" (100) – seems badly off the mark. Leavis's magisterial style can at times be persuasive, but it too often becomes defensive or indulges in special pleading. From our perspective today, the argument seems to be as much about Leavis himself and his various feuds (especially with T.S. Eliot) as it is about Lawrence. The "class-feeling" remark, for example, seems to be a direct rejoinder to Eliot's comment on Lawrence, quoted by Leavis, that "'no man was ever more conscious of class-distinctions'" (85). Leavis reactively claims that the precise opposite is true. His mid-twentieth-century intervention remains a crucial one in the history of Lawrence's reception, but, in terms of the role of class in particular, there is some truth to Graham Martin's contention that, in emphasizing what he viewed as Lawrence's key concern with a vitality that transcended class, Leavis effectively "removed 'class' from the agenda of relevant discussions of Lawrence's work" (36). And yet Leavis was partially right to decentre class as a Lawrentian concern, if not necessarily for the reasons he posits. For his discussion points to an interesting wrinkle in Lawrence's portrayal of class in a number of works: that it can function as an issue that partially screens a much different one.

Lawrence was indeed acutely conscious of class, but the consciousness was inextricably linked to his feelings about his class-crossed parents. He could not divorce his ruminations about middle-class aspiration from his tangled emotional attitude to his class-ambitious mother, and he inevitably associated working-class traits with his collier father. As a result, in much of his fiction, class concerns have a tendency to become a means of exploring complex emotions in relationships rather than the nominal focus of interest itself.[3] His true area of expertise was much more the world of human affect than that of social analysis. For Lawrence, the material struggle of one class against another missed the real point, which for him, he writes in the essay "The State of Funk," is "the change inside the individual ... The great social change interests me and troubles me, but it is not my field" (*LEA* 221). The change "inside the individual" that Lawrence would explore during his career includes the evolving emotional vicissitudes related to attachment. In short, attachment and class are mutually complicating concerns in Lawrence's writing.

Class, then, had a personal significance for Lawrence: it was involved in the violent conflicts of his childhood home and in the formation of his very sense of self. Often considered "the only writer of working-class origin accorded canonical status," he was, in reality, not simply of the working class (Milne 203). In "Which Class I Belong To," Lawrence wrote: "My mother belonged potentially to the middle-classes ... Nevertheless, ours was an absolutely working class home. My mother, in a shabby little black bonnet, was a working-man's wife, in spite of her shrewd, 'different' face. And we were brought up as working-class children, pure and simple" (*LEA* 36). There was actually nothing "pure and simple" about Lawrence's class affiliation. His nuclear family consisted of two distinct English classes: his father was decidedly working-class in speech, culture, and viewpoint, while his mother spoke standard, educated English and was emphatically middle-class, at least in aspiration and outlook. "My father hated books," he writes in *Studies in Classic American Literature*, "hated the sight of anyone reading or writing. My mother hated the thought that any of her sons should be condemned to manual labour" (*SCAL* 83). That Lawrence became a writer of books, let alone a reader of them, speaks to his early identification with this mother's rather than his father's class values. From an early age, Lawrence admits, he wholly identified with his mother's outlook: "I was foreordained to accept all her values" (*LEA* 28). Even the literal values of the two classes differed markedly within the family. When, in *Sons and Lovers*, Walter Morel learns that his son Paul is to earn twenty guineas for a painting he has done, he is incredulous: "'But twenty guineas for a bit of a paintin' as he knocked off in an hour or two – !'" (*SL* 296).

It is a rare thing for a major writer to emerge as Lawrence did from the pressure cooker of a family that consisted internally of two classes. The uncommon admixture is memorably portrayed in *Sons and Lovers* and in the cognate play *A Collier's Friday Night* (probably written in November 1909 and posthumously published [*Plays* xxvii]) and is repeatedly recalled in late, non-fictional writing. In "[Return to Bestwood]," "Getting On," "Which Class I Belong To," "[Autobiographical Fragment]," and other essays written between September 1926 and September 1929, Lawrence vividly describes his class-conflicted childhood home. In the late essay "Myself Revealed," Lawrence writes that "I was born among the working classes and brought up among them. My father was a collier, nothing praiseworthy about him. He wasn't even respectable, in so far as he got drunk rather frequently, never went near a chapel, and was usually rather rude to his little immediate bosses at the pit" (*LEA* 177). His mother, he suggests, was "superior. She came from town, and belonged really to the lower bourgeoisie. She spoke King's English, without an accent" (*LEA* 177). Initially, the attraction between Lydia and Arthur no doubt included the frisson of an inter-class union by means of which Lydia unconsciously aspired to mitigate an inescapable puritan upbringing and Arthur could imagine the prestige in having a "superior" wife. But the gulf in values and temperament proved to be too gaping in the long run. In a chapter of his Lawrence biography entitled "A Disastrous Marriage," Jeffrey Meyers claims that "Lydia had no tact or patience with her husband, taunted and provoked him, treated him with icy disdain, mocked his coarse habits, condemned his drinking, refused to sleep with him, and taught the children to look down on their father" (16). While some of Meyers's details may be fanciful or exaggerated, it was, indeed, a disastrous marriage and one that produced class-conflicted offspring.

In the poem "Red-herring," Lawrence describes how, as children, he and his siblings were "in-betweens": "indoors we called each other *you*, / outside, it was *tha* and *thee*" (*Poems* 425, ll. 9, 11–12). John Worthen has suggested that Lawrence saw writing as a "glamorous, middle-class profession" and as his ticket out of the working class (*Outsider* 39).[4] Worthen has also speculated that it was Hueffer/Ford who persuaded

Lawrence to write about the working class in the first place (*EY* 217). Given his own familiarity with both classes, Lawrence probably had no idea how fascinating middle-class readers would find an insider's description of working-class life. While he may have yearned for a bourgeois existence early on, later in his life, Lawrence saw his former class aspirations as futile and the middle class as duplicitous. In the poem "The saddest day," the speaker describes the day

> when I had to tell myself plain:
> the upper classes are just a fraud,
> you'd better get down again.
> (*Poems* 482, ll. 38–40)

And in "Prestige," he describes his realization that he will never fit in with the middle class: "at last I saw the reason: they were just a bloody sham" (*Poems* 483, ll. 23–4). Similarly, in poems such as "Finding your level," "Climbing up," and "Up he goes!–" Lawrence describes (here in a distinctly working-class voice) his disillusionment with his class ascent:

> it damn well wasn't worth it,
> goin' up an' bein' refined;
> it was nowt but a dirty sell, that's all,
> a damn fraud, underlined.
> (*Poems* 480, ll. 13–16)

Lawrence's feelings about class shifted over time, but it is fair to say that they were also conflicted at all times. Referring to the play *Touch and Go*, Peter Scheckner suggests that "Lawrence never seems to be able to locate his sympathies in this play. The workers no doubt have been wronged by the mine owners, but nothing looks worse ... than the unruly mob" (80). All in all, it is no wonder that critical opinion about Lawrence's status has been so varied in studies of working-class fiction. Pamela Fox, for example, in her book *Class Fictions: Shame and Resistance in the British Working-Class Novel, 1890–1945*, virtually ignores Lawrence, while Nicola Wilson's *Home in British Working-Class Fiction* considers him foundational.[5]

Lawrence makes it clear in the late essays and other writing that, while "[o]ne can belong absolutely to no class" (*LEA* 180), if he does identify with any class it is with his father's: "They are the only people who move me strongly, and with whom I feel myself connected in deeper destiny" (*LEA* 22). However, as Paul Eggert suggests, the late bias of sympathy for the working class "forgets the far more guarded, self-conscious and spiritualising young man [Lawrence] had once been" (160). In the highly autobiographical novel *Kangaroo*, the Lawrence stand-in, Somers, tells his neighbour Jack Callcott that "'[m]y father was a working-man. I come from the working people. My sympathy is with them, when it's with anybody,'" but then adds significantly, "'Mostly it's with nobody, I assure you'" (*K* 46). This mature Lawrence figure is still a red herring, an in-between: Jack is not quite sure what to make of Somers, who seems to be "a gentleman and not a gentleman ... [n]either one thing nor the other" (*K* 37). Keith Cushman traces the end of Lawrence's bourgeois aspirations to the time when, in his early twenties, Lawrence lodged for a few years with the middle-class Joneses of Croydon, at the beginning of which period he was still "actively attempting to sever his ties with his working-class origins" ("Domestic Life" 222). A few months after leaving the Croydon family, "he was forced to conclude that, though he had lived among the suburban bourgeoise [*sic*], he was not one of them" ("Domestic Life" 227). Without his mother's ambitions and values, in fact, it is doubtful that he would ever have become a writer. He knew that it was not the working-class half of his dual class inheritance that made him an artist, although it certainly contributed to the material that he fashioned into his art. Scott Sanders points out the irony in Lawrence's literary breakthrough with the publication of *Sons and Lovers*: at the very time he was fictionally describing the working-class life in his home district, he had found "a place amidst the middle-class intelligentsia and aristocratic dilettanti of London" (22).

Lawrence's partial shift in sympathy over time from the middle to the working class parallels his evolving feelings towards both of his parents as he more and more closely examined his childhood emotions under the microscopic lens of his adult analysis. From a certain perspective, it seems that, paradoxically, as Richard Wasson puts it, "Lawrence comes to lose all sympathy with the class to which he aspired" (292). But the aspiration itself was never unmixed and the loss of sympathy never complete. In his first novel, *The White Peacock*, the conscious loyalty to Lawrence's mother and her class is obvious. The father is essentially eliminated from the portrayal of the central family; he makes only one brief appearance before conveniently expiring. Lawrence uses his mother's maiden name, Beardsall, for that family as if to create the ideal, immaculately conceived, fatherless, middle-class family of his young fantasy. (Where the family income comes from is a bit of a mystery.) Yet, even here, one might suggest that the fictional mother's concealment of the father's existence is an expression of a subliminal realization on Lawrence's part that his father's true worth has been kept from him and his siblings. In one scene in *Sons and Lovers*, the young adult Paul Morel, who in many ways represents how Lawrence saw his younger self, declares to his mother that "'I don't want to belong to the well-to-do middle class. I like my common people best. I belong to the common people'" (*SL* 298). But his mother's rejoinder, also a product of Lawrence's memory and imagination, is unanswerable. She points out to Paul that he does not mix with the common people and that it is he who is "snobbish about class" (*SL* 298). At this point we can discern evidence of an unconscious resentment of Paul's mother's narcissistic domination and an unacknowledged attraction to his father, which comes out here as a declaration of class loyalty that strikes his mother as fanciful but is a much safer avowal of preference than would be a partisan alliance with Walter within the family. The attraction is also observable in the way Walter is portrayed more sympathetically than Lawrence intended.[6]

In the final analysis, Lawrence was torn in terms of his class identification between a desire for the kind of self-realization prized by his mother's culture and a yearning for the kind of warm community that he saw in his father's. But there is a further complication. The quest for individuation almost by definition involves a weakening of the communal bond, but while Lawrence, in countless works, proclaims or portrays the value of individual self-development, he also sought for many years to establish a utopian community, his Rananim. Since we know, as Benjamin puts it, that "[t]he route to individuality ... leads through identificatory love of the father" (133), the relationship between Lawrence's conflicted class affiliation and the attachment dichotomy of merger-autonomy is a complex one that involves Lawrence in a double bind. If we use the situation of *Sons and Lovers* as paradigmatic of his own family, we see that Lawrence grew up in a situation where the parents' roles in attachment were unusual or, as John Turner puts it, the "gender roles in the Morel family are reversed" (*Psychoanalysis* 86). The very figure who, in the normal course of development, represents for the child the move toward independence, i.e. the father, in Lawrence's life also embodied warm communal life; the potentially engulfing mother stood for self-realization, conceptually the opposite of merger. In addition, the young Lawrence (like the young Paul Morel) would have seen his mother rather than his father as a protector. So the necessary struggle for separation in the name of individuation also seems paradoxically to involve the repudiation of his mother's values, which included self-development.[7]

It may be because of this inherent contradiction in the intersection of class with attachment that the Lawrence character faced with a crucial life choice involving an inter-class attachment is much more often female than male, as if Lawrence needed the extra buffer of an opposite-gender character to distance himself from the excruciating dilemma. The split is his own, but by using a female protagonist he could explore the issue at one remove. In any case, it is remarkable to note that there are some two dozen female characters in Lawrence who are faced with a choice between two classes (although in some cases the choice is more theoretical than actual and at times the dilemma is peripheral to the main plot). The most obvious examples are Lettie Beardsall in *The White Peacock* choosing between Leslie Tempest and George Saxton, Alvina Houghton in *The Lost Girl* torn between various respectable suitors and the Italian peasant Ciccio Marasca, and Connie Chatterley choosing the gamekeeper Mellors over her aristocratic husband, Clifford. In a less clear-cut way, there is the situation in "Second-Best" (1914), for example, where Frances perforce chooses the working-class Tom over the "gentleman" Jimmy. Juliet, in the story "Sun" (1925–26), estranged from her middle-class husband, Maurice, and attracted to the married Italian peasant who watches her sunbathe in the nude, must finally admit to herself that "she would never come to him – she daren't, she daren't, so much was against her" (*WWRA* 38). There is also the implicit choice of Carlotta Fell in "Glad Ghosts," hinted at by the materially poor narrator, between himself and Luke, a prosperous man from her own upper class: "She hated her own class: yet it was also sacrosanct to her" (*WWRA* 175). There are many other occurrences.[8] When the point of view shifts to the male, as it does on occasion in these narratives, as detailed below, it is a signal that the class conflict is opening up to reveal the relational crisis it has been screening, and the complications of maternal attachment then make themselves felt.

Over time, Lawrence's class identification became increasingly convoluted and somewhat paradoxical, but what is constant is the laminating of the emotions stemming from attachment with Lawrence's complicated feelings about class. As John Goode argues, "The [new] national education system gave [Lawrence] an opportunity unavailable to previous generations to achieve middle-class status," but it also involved him in "the painful process of deracination" inevitable to a working-class intellectual. It alienated him from both of his classes, for his reading made him skeptical of his mother's Chapel values as well as distancing him from his father's (110). In the essay "Which Class I Belong To," Lawrence admits that "I myself could never go back into the working class, to the blindness, the obtuseness, the prejudice, the mass-emotions. But neither can I adapt myself to the middle-class, to sacrifice the old, deep blood-affinity between myself and my fellows" (*LEA* 39). Referring to the very dissimilar families of Arthur and Lydia Lawrence, Worthen asserts that "[t]he differences came to a complex kind of flowering and expression in the life and work of D.H. Lawrence. He contained the differences within himself, as the product of his upbringing; and he was continually articulate about them, in his ceaseless attempts to come to terms with them" (*EY* 27). While realizing the limitations of both classes, Lawrence could also see decided attractions in both. In Paul Morel's words, "'from the middle classes, one gets ideas, and from the common people – life itself, warmth'" (*SL* 298). He needed both and continually attempted to imagine their alliance through fictional embodiments despite the evidence of misalliance in his parents' marriage.

Since the emergence of the middle class as a large and important segment of British society, and certainly since the Industrial Revolution, there has been movement between social classes as well as opposition to that fluidity. The negative connotations of words such as "upstart" and "degraded" suggest some of the social resistance to new members when birth and fortune collide as metrics to determine class worthiness. Lawrence would later reject both standards in favour of intrinsic character as the basis of a "natural" aristocracy, a neat if perhaps disingenuous squaring of the circle of his internal class strife. Undoubtedly also derived in part from the Great Chain of Being, the hierarchical and spatialized concepts of "upper" and "lower" classes are so entrenched in the English language and culture that they have become dead metaphors. One of the things that his dual-class experience gives Lawrence is a means to explore significant issues of attachment and self-realization through a questioning and revitalization of these moribund figures of speech.

The personal associations that class had for Lawrence became a repeated source of his fictional structure and of his characteristic imagery. The flame is Lawrence's frequently occurring symbol for lower-class, usually male, vitality and warmth,[9] for example, and it is interesting that several critics have fastened onto that one indicator to the exclusion of others. So we have Daleski's *The Forked Flame* and Anthony Burgess's biography *Flame into Being*, *Kindled in the Flame* by Sarah Urang, *Pillar of Flame* by Barbara S. Miliaris, and Tennessee Williams's 1951 play about D.H. Lawrence called *I Rise in Flame, Cried the Phoenix*. But the flame is only one element in a multifaceted association. Lawrence came to connect the middle class not only with ideas but also with cold, light, and ascent and the working class not only with "life itself" but also with warmth, darkness, and descent. Although he generally favoured the latter cluster of images and concepts, he tended to explore the complexities of his own dual inheritance and personality components by projecting aspects of himself onto his fictional characters of various classes. In the novella *The Captain's Doll* (1923), for example, the Lawrentian protagonist, Captain Hepburn, climbs up the ice of a glacier and proclaims his intention to write a book, thus symbolically establishing, through the motifs of ascent, cold, and intellect, his upwardly aspiring class bona fides in pursuit of the aristocratic Countess Hannele. This fictional display of mating fitness might be seen in some sense as a belated and displaced answer to Frieda's mother, the Baroness von Richtofen, who, upon first meeting Lawrence in 1912, according to a letter Lawrence wrote to Edward Garnett, asked, "'Who was I, did I think, that a Baronesse [Frieda] should clean my boots and empty my slops: she, the daughter of a high-born and highly-cultured gentleman[?]'" (*1L* 429), an event that Lawrence dramatized in his play *The Fight for Barbara*, where there is very little change from his epistolary description in the words of Lady Charlcote (*Plays* 259–60).

Lawrence's mature writing, however, mostly values working-class characteristics (as he saw them) as if in atonement for his early rejection of his father, to lessen the too-powerful hold on him of his mother, and to critique a middle-class English culture that was, in his view, destructively puritanical in its attitude to the body. He does so by using images of darkness, warmth, and descent that he associated with his father and with Arthur Lawrence's work. In the essay "Nottingham and the Mining Countryside," Lawrence talks about the "dark intimacy of the mine," the "naked sort of contact" there, and "a lustrous sort of inner darkness, like the gloss of coal, in which we moved and had our real being" (*LEA* 290). Lawrence knew that his father and the other miners literally descended every working day of their lives into the depths and darkness of the coal pit down to the warm "intimate community" they had created there (*LEA* 289), so that the otherwise dead metaphor of "lower" class was very much alive to him. The somewhat counterintuitive concept of a life-enhancing lowering/burial was undoubtedly reinforced by Christian, mythical (the Persephone myth in particular), and even botanical associations, links that Sandra Gilbert has shown are evident in Lawrence's poetry ("Apocalypse" 246–7). What we typically see in the fiction is a middle-class woman (or two women) who must choose between two men who represent the upper and lower worlds and are often of two distinct classes. With this pattern, Lawrence is, in a sense, reversing several hundred years of convention in the English novel. Whereas in works such as *Pamela* or *Tom Jones* or *Oliver Twist* (and many others) the movement is for a character from the serving classes or presumed to be from the working or farming class to be raised into the middle or upper classes (it often turns out that the secret origin of the character was the upper class all along), with Lawrence the movement is mostly a lowering for salvation.

In particular, we see variations of the dynamic throughout Lawrence's writings where darkness, warmth, and descent are opposed to light, frigidity, and ascent. In the story "The Blind Man," written in late 1918 (*EME* xxxv), for example, it is the darkness of the sightless Maurice, the husband of Isabel Pervin, that principally represents for her the choice of the lower, vital life over the upper, intellectual existence represented by her friend and cousin Bertie Reid. (See below for further discussion.) In *Sons and Lovers*, the association of Walter Morel and his working-class mates with warmth is pervasive, as in the description of Morel's escape from the frigid and isolating atmosphere of his home life to the enticements of the pub, where "[t]he men made a seat for him, and took him in warmly" (*SL* 57). In the late novella *The Virgin and the Gipsy*, it is the life-saving bodily warmth provided by the lower-class gipsy figure that symbolizes the vitality Yvette yearns for. It is also metaphorical warmth that Yvette seeks. When her father nastily criticizes her life-affirming curiosity and attraction to the gipsies and the Eastwoods, "a numb, frozen loneliness came over her," and "[i]t was hard to break the frozen, sterile silence that ensued" (*VG* 61). The gipsy woman who tells her fortune predicts that she will meet a dark man who "'will blow the one spark up into fire again, good fire'" (*VG* 30). Indeed, Yvette finds that even the gipsy's eyes are "full of the fire of life" (*VG* 74).[10]

There are also anomalous patterns in some fiction that ultimately conform to the positive Lawrentian associations of dark, descent, and warmth. In *The Ladybird*, the dark man is not a lower-class figure but a foreign aristocrat, Dionys Psanek, who, however, has been brought low as a wounded prisoner of war. Lady Daphne's choice is between the upper world of her likewise wounded husband, Basil, who wishes to worship her in a sexless marriage, and Dionys, who represents the dark underworld as a kind of Pluto figure and will have Daphne as a "night-wife" only (*Fox* 217). We looked briefly at the short story "The Princess" in the Introduction in terms of the security-exploration dynamic. The plot of the story turns on Dollie's need for warmth, which she gets in too large measure from Romero, so the association here is more complicated than in other fiction. There are elements of "The Princess" that resemble *The Lost Girl*, but, as we will see below, in that novel, Alvina is willing to put up with the peasant Ciccio's initially forced sexuality in order to warm herself with his physicality and to thumb her nose at social propriety by marrying him. Not so with the Princess, Dollie. She seeks Romero's warmth in the frigid mountain cabin, but, having had a vacant, narcissistic father, she cannot in the end accept the far-too-present Romero. In many of these works, because Lawrence's class associations were inevitably also connected to his parental attachments, the class plot will often give way to a relational consideration from childhood. What we see is that the binary choice between traits associated with Lawrence's two classes leads to a complication as the implicit betrayal of his early loyalty to his mother (and of his own earlier self) results in the return of the repressed: the emergence of a mother issue in a plot that does not necessarily call for it.

In the early story "Daughters of the Vicar," first written (as "Two Marriages") in 1911 and published in 1924 (*PO* xl), the two middle-class daughters of the title, as briefly discussed in chapter 3, are involved in a decision to opt for security in marriage or to hold out for love in a way similar to the kind of choice often faced by Jane Austen's upper-middle-class female characters, except that in Lawrence we have the added dimension of cross-class interaction complicating the situation. Mr Lindley, the titular vicar, "considered himself as belonging indisputably to the upper or ordering classes" (*PO* 40) even as, or especially because, he ministers to a mostly working-class population. His children are isolated from their inferiors and grow up "unwarmed" (*PO* 41). The eldest sister, Mary, opts for comfort in marrying a "measley little shrimp," the curate Mr Massy (*PO* 50), whose "body was almost unthinkable" (*PO* 48). Mr Massey offers Mary middle-class respectability and financial security if not much else. In Mrs Lindley's mind, "[w]hat did the man matter, if there were pecuniary ease!" (*PO* 49). Significantly, in choosing comfort and security, Mary has chosen the upper over the lower, for she "had sold a lower thing, her body, for a higher thing, her freedom from material things" (*PO* 56).

Her sister, Louisa, is made of more vital stuff. In her own mind, had Mr Massy proposed to her, "she would have flipped him from the room" (*PO* 56). Instead, she yearns for the working-class Alfred Durant, "a laughing, warm lad … [who] had made her feel warm" (*PO* 47). Unlike her sister, Louisa will decidedly descend to have the "lower thing," and even the very situation of the Durant cottage underscores the choice, for the dwelling is "below the road" in a kind of hollow as the garden "sheered down steeply" to the cottage, and the chimney is only just level with the road (*PO* 63). The cottage is also near a crossroads and a quarry, locations that suggest the necessity for making a crucial choice and digging deep within oneself to make it. Louisa believes, however, that Alfred seeks to avoid an attachment to her by "calmly placing her in a superior class, and placing himself inaccessibly apart, in an inferior" (*PO* 54). The potential for an inter-class romance that, for Leavis, transcends class in favour of vitality (87 *et passim*) is thus clearly set up, but a funny thing happens on the way to the resolution. For after Alfred's domineering mother, Mrs Durant, dies, it appears that the class barrier has largely been a screen for a different kind of obstacle. Lawrence describes how Alfred now realizes for the first time that (like Lawrence himself) "he had been centralized, polarized in his mother" (*PO* 78) and is bereft without her.[11] While she was alive, Mrs Durant was a barrier to Louisa's romantic intentions regarding Alfred, and, once deceased, she remains a hindrance, since Alfred is now in no emotional state to contemplate a new attachment. Using the tell-tale imagery of flooding and drowning that is often (most prominently in *The Rainbow*) a symbol of male neediness, Lawrence describes how Alfred becomes "lost in a great, bewildering flood" without his mother and feels "like a swimmer who forgets to swim" (*PO* 78).[12] Louisa wins him over in the end only because in his eyes she becomes a maternal substitute, making up the fire, preparing his dinner, and washing his back. Alfred even wants Louisa to occupy his mother's place in a literal sense and wonders why Louisa "wouldn't use his mother's round arm-chair" (*PO* 80). Louisa's own attraction to Alfred earlier in the story also seems bound up in his maternal connection: "Her heart, her veins were possessed by the thought of Alfred Durant as he held his mother in his arms" (*PO* 53).

Apprised of her daughter's plans, Mrs Lindley scolds Louisa: "'You don't want to marry a collier, you little fool'" (*PO* 85); but Louisa is quite prepared to be foolhardy by defying her parents and ignoring the class differences between her and Alfred. He, however, is not initially inclined to buck convention, and only the life crisis of losing his mother and the prospect of replacing her brings about Louisa's desired conclusion. Mark Kinkead-Weekes has argued that the maternal element seen in the Louisa-Alfred relationship in the early version of the story is downplayed by Lawrence in the finalized text (*TE* 141–2). To be sure, the motif of substitution is more subtle in "Daughters of the Vicar" than in "Two Marriages," but it is there, and the idea of Louisa as stand-in mother substituting for Mrs Durant is the culmination of a series of substitutions announced in the very title, for a "vicar" is by definition a substitute (from the Latin *vicarius*). When Mr Lindley falls ill, Mr Massy arrives to fulfill his duties temporarily, Louisa replaces Mr Massy with Alfred as a potential suitor, and at the end of the story, England will be replaced by Canada as the mixed-class couple looks abroad to escape social disapprobation.

This last plot development has led Graham Martin to argue that Lawrence is ultimately evading the very class issues he has raised by opting for "the colonial solution" (the departure for Canada) in this story and elsewhere (42), but I would contend that the deeper issue for Lawrence was always psychological rather than social, as he explores areas of human reality that Jane Austen was not particularly interested in. Lawrence is following Louisa's life and choices in the context of the class-conscious Lindley family, but as soon as he switches focalization in order to explore Alfred's feelings, he is propelled into the territory of his own intensely fraught relationship with his mother, and the story diverts into this highly emotional region. Alfred's mother wanted to make a gentleman of him (*PO* 66) as Lawrence's mother wished to propel her boys into the middle class. He is attuned to her emotionally as Lawrence was to Lydia Lawrence: Alfred "noticed when she was tired, or when she had a new cap. And he bought little things for her occasionally. She was not wise enough to see how much he lived by her" (*PO* 66). Alfred's sensitive, somewhat unmanly nature (what Lawrence's local culture would have called "mardy"), so different from the other colliers, sounds quite a bit like Lawrence's own: "In his innermost soul he felt he was not a man" (*PO* 67). So he joins the navy and then enters the pit to prove his masculinity to himself if to no one else. This is all in the final version of the story. Lawrence strongly implies that Alfred's general difficulties with women and with Louisa specifically are directly related to his emotional dependence on his mother. His deep grief at her death surely derives from Lawrence's experience of his own mother's passing.

Essentially, then, in "Daughters of the Vicar" we have two narratives: a class conflict that seems to be an obstacle to a romantic relationship and a mother-son attachment that seems to inhibit the full individuation of the son and is the real barrier. Lawrence makes it more difficult to see through the screen of class in that he emphasizes the class differences with the changes he made to "Two Marriages," where Mrs Durant is "a burgess' daughter" (*PO* 211). This detail is left out in the final version, and Alfred has now become a collier. The class and attachment narratives dovetail rather nicely except that the resolution of the class issue – ostensibly the central one in the tale – turns on the attachment issue. Sanders has criticized Lawrence for his tendency to convert social categories into psychological ones (24). In fact, for Lawrence the two cannot be separated.

A similar screening is at work in the play *The Daughter-in-Law* from early 1913 (*Plays* xxxv), a kind of kitchen-sink drama *avant la lettre*. The domineering mother figure, Mrs Gascoyne, is a version of Mrs Morel in *Sons and Lovers*, except that she is decidedly working-class. She complains that her daughter-in-law, the genteel Minnie, twice turned down her collier son Luther's offer before agreeing to marry him because "he wor in collier's britches, i'stead o' a stool-arsed Jack's" (*Plays* 348), but Minnie, like Miriam in the novel, argues that the mother will never let her sons go and that the problems in her marriage with Luther, on the face of it due to class differences, are actually rooted in the mother-son relationship, specifically the mother's dominion over her boys and their emotional dependence on her: "*You* held him, and persuaded him that what he wanted was *you*. You kept him, like a child" (*Plays* 348). Luther's brother, Joe, declares before everyone that Minnie has spoken the truth. The essential problem, it turns out, is a smothering mother and an emotionally dependent son. Contrary to Sanders, here class is a displacement of an emotional difficulty onto a social one as Lawrence somewhat compulsively visits and revisits the turmoil of his coming to maturity and works through his dawning realization that the narcissistic needs of his beloved mother seriously impaired his own development.

In the novella *The Fox*, we see a similar dynamic at work. The middle-class Jill Banford and Nellie March are trying their hand at farming during and just after the war when their *ménage à deux* is invaded by the recently demobilized Henry Grenfel, who used to live on the farm with his grandfather. Jill's objections to Henry's impulsive plan to marry Nellie are mostly class-based – he is "a beastly laborer" who would lower their standing in the community (*Fox* 37) – but March's reason for initially resisting his importunities is that, as she says to Henry, she is "'old enough to be your mother'" (*Fox* 25). In this, one of his richest shorter works, Lawrence is interested in many issues including the dislocation of gender roles during the war, but it is striking that the class issue once more seems to give way to a mother-son scenario and that, once again, the "colonial solution" is invoked at the end with Henry and March intending to travel to Canada, which for Lawrence seems to be the frequent refuge of a mixed-class couple, as it is again in *Lady Chatterley's Lover*.

In the story "The Blind Man," we see most of the events unfold through the consciousness of Isabel Pervin, who is married to Maurice, blinded during the war. Maurice is not working-class in origin; he is more or less a gentleman farmer, but he enjoys doing menial jobs around the farm such as milking the cows and mashing the turnips, and he is associated with the Lawrentian lower-class attributes of feeling, darkness, and warmth. He is close to the "hot animal life" on the farm (*EME* 52), and his physicality is emphasized: "a big fellow with heavy limbs" (*EME* 48). He lives in darkness and in "unspeakable intimacy" with Isabel (*EME* 46), and they are expecting a child in a few weeks. But Isabel also yearns for the world of light and intellect to balance her life with Maurice. That alternate world is represented by Bertie Reid, her distant cousin and old friend. He is a bachelor, a barrister, and an intellectual man of letters who has a marked aversion to physical contact, an "incurable weakness" that, in spite of his worldly success, makes him view himself as "neuter, nothing" (*EME* 58). Maurice "was just the opposite to Bertie whose mind was much quicker than his emotions" (*EME* 48). So the usual class-related opposition is clearly set up and comes to a head when Bertie arrives for a visit to the Pervins. Isabel need not make an actual choice between the two men (she has long ago chosen Maurice as her life partner), but she is torn between the two worlds that Lawrence tended to associate with the working and middle classes respectively: darkness, warmth, and close physicality versus ideas, light, coolness, and physical standoffishness.

In a sense, the two men represent Lawrence's own divided nature and his attachment conflict between the attractions of merger and the promise of individuation. Bertie represents the aspiring middle-class man of letters, "our Bert," as Lawrence was known to his family, and Maurice embodies his identification with the robust physicality of a father who worked in the dark.[13] But as was the case with "Daughters of the Vicar," as soon as we leave Isabel's point of view and enter into Maurice's own thoughts, there is a drastic change in the narrative focus away from this class-inflected opposition and toward childhood attachment issues. Just as Bertie is arriving, Maurice has gone upstairs to change and shave. He hears the initial conversation between his wife and Bertie and unaccountably feels "a childish sense of desolation ... He seemed shut out – like a child that is left out ... He was fretful and beside himself like a child, he had almost a childish nostalgia to be included in the life circle ... By some fatal flaw, he could not be by himself, he had to depend on the support of another. And this very dependence enraged him" (*EME* 55). Apart from the obvious oedipal constellation that this scene sets up, with Maurice as the child shut out of the intimate life of mother and father, there is the Lawrentian attachment paradigm propelling events here. It takes only a hint of abandonment, Isabel greeting his rival in his absence, to trigger a crisis of rage and a sense of being bereft on Maurice's part. We are in the childhood territory here of a dependency that ineluctably encourages merger for security but at the same time triggers a resentment that creates a countervailing anxiety of abandonment.

The apparent theme of the story "Hadrian" (initially published in *Land and Water* as "You Touched Me" in 1920) is the importance of touch (also emphasized in "The Blind Man") and the related subplot of an awakening Sleeping Beauty that we see in numerous other Lawrence narratives. The Sleeping Beauty role here is split between a man and a woman, both of whom are awakened in different ways. But there is a very strong undercurrent of abandonment from the very start, and it is with the insecurely attached individual's fear of abandonment that the class theme interacts in this story. The setting is the Pottery House within a disused pottery. There is a "desolate yard," the "great doors of the yard permanently shut," and the two daughters, Matilda and Emmie, of the well-to-do resident Rockley family, "already old maids" (*EME* 92). (Two other daughters live elsewhere and do not figure in the plot.) In the local industrial town, there seem to be no acceptable suitors of the right class for the two girls, who are expecting sizable legacies when their father dies. Matilda and Emmie are marginalized within the family and, because of their class, within the local community, but the pervasive feeling of abandonment is particularly focused on the father, Ted Rockley, a widower, now dying of kidney disease.

Years earlier, Rockley identified himself with an abandoned, abject thing when he adopted a working-class charity boy, then six years old, with the grandiose name of Hadrian. He is a rather ordinary lad with a cockney accent who always got on poorly with his adoptive sisters in part because of their class snobbery. When Hadrian was thirteen, Matilda made an effort by means of what she considered to be the proper education "to make a little gentleman of him, but he refused to be made" (*EME* 94). He leaves altogether at the age of fifteen for Canada, enlists when the war breaks out, and, after the armistice, returns for a brief visit while on leave. He intends to travel back to Canada, where, he believes, class differences matter much less than in England. As he tells Rockley, "'there's too much difference between the men and the employers over here – too much of that for me'" (*EME* 97). To Matilda and Emmie, he now seems "charged with plebeian energy" (*EME* 98). The identification between the old and young men is clinched when Hadrian occupies Rockley's usual room upstairs so that the invalid may remain downstairs at night. This is also the crucial plot device that leads to the turning point when a sleepwalking Matilda enters her father's old room and strokes Hadrian's forehead, a touch that results eventually in the denouement of the two getting married. One of the significant aspects of the plot turn is how the substitution reinforces the sense of identification between Rockley and Hadrian, and when Rockley insists on the marital union, threatening otherwise to financially cut off both daughters, the identification is complete.

Matilda is at least a decade older than Hadrian, so there is a similar kind of symbolic mother-son dynamic at play to what we see in Henry Grenfel's courting of March in *The Fox*, written around the same time as "Hadrian." In fact, like March to Henry in *The Fox*, Matilda says to Hadrian that "'I'm old enough to be your mother,'" and she adds, "'In a way I've been your mother'" (*EME* 106). Lawrence does not provide any details about Rockley's childhood or his marriage, but the implications of the plot dynamics might suggest a deep if perhaps irrational resentment at being abandoned, a feeling that is projected onto a plausible younger double who happens to be from the working class and was abandoned as a child. The mother factor certainly points to attachment issues, most obviously for Hadrian. In the case of Rockley, we are told that he "seemed to have a strange desire, quite unreasonable, for revenge upon the women who had surrounded him for so long, and served him so carefully" (*EME* 104). Unreasonable, yes, but revenge for what? Rockley's threat to cut off his daughters financially, a form of abandonment, and transfer the entire legacy to Hadrian is, in effect, also a transference of abandonment from the abject son who is his symbolic double to the daughters. He will become Rockley's heir and occupy the place of the son Rockley never had while the daughters will be cut off. The virtually enforced marriage is, in one sense, Rockley's dying manipulation of events so that, emotionally speaking, by means of a union with a proxy, the mother-wife-daughter undoes the sense of abandonment he has felt and that has been symbolically projected onto the abandoned pottery works. Rockley's insistence, in a "strange and unrecognizable voice," after Hadrian and Matilda are wed that she kiss him and Hadrian in turn suggests a symbolic incest wish. Matilda "had never kissed him before, not since she was a tiny child" (*EME* 107). Hadrian's own motive for wishing to marry Matilda is partly class-based. He is attracted to the "high-bred sensitiveness" that, in his mind, she shares with her father, and "he wanted to possess himself of it, he wanted to make himself master of it" (*EME* 100). In the end we have a working-class "son" uniting with a high-bred mother figure as the class conflict and attachment feelings interact.

In the novel *The Lost Girl* (1920) we see the symbolic use of upper and lower fully exploited. The novel announces a descent-ascent trajectory in the very first two chapter titles: "The Decline of Manchester House" and "The Rise of Alvina Houghton." At one point, the titular lost girl, the respectably middle-class Alvina, finds herself in the same dilemma faced by Mary and Louisa in "Daughters of the Vicar." She considers a proposal of marriage from the eminently eligible if somewhat elderly Dr Mitchell, whom she does not love, and she is tempted to choose as Mary Lindley did in the earlier story: "She would be so comfortable, she would be so well-off for the rest of her life" (*LG* 265), and she would have respectability. But she ultimately follows Louisa's example and seeks passion in an inter-class relationship with a foreigner. Alvina is a member of the local bourgeoisie; her father was once the "crème de la crème of Woodhouse society" (*LG* 2). She must discover the paradoxical Lawrentian truth that to find herself she must lose herself and that to be degraded in social standing is to be upgraded in vitality. The fact that Lawrence in this novel calls his home town of Eastwood "Woodhouse" may easily be attributed to various place names in the East Midlands area, as John Worthen suggests in his explanatory notes (*LG* 361), but one might also suspect a sly dig at Austen's Emma Woodhouse and her very different conception of the importance of maintaining one's class position in society, especially when it comes to one's choice of marriage partner.[14]

Alvina learns through her life experiences that class respectability is highly overrated and can stifle any chance a woman might have at a satisfying life, but it takes courage to oppose the ingrained notions of the importance of social standing and the proper behaviour of middle-class women. She initially finds warmth with a dusky suitor from Australia, Alexander Graham, a connection opposed by her aptly named governess, Miss Frost, whose cold and light upper world ultimately wins the day. In "periods of lucidity, when she saw as clear as daylight," Alvina is immune to Alexander's attractions and sees him as an "inferior," but the attraction returns at night and "[s]he felt the dark, passionate receptivity of Alexander overwhelmed her" (*LG* 24). Alvina's search for a spark of life continues in her training as a maternity nurse and then in a visit to one of her father's many dubious business ventures, a coal mine, where she is "wound down in the iron bucket to the little workings underneath" (*LG* 46) and becomes strongly fascinated by the dark, underworld life of the colliers, in whom "the force of darkness" bubbles up (*LG* 48). Her quest, then, has taken her down under, so to speak, in terms of geography (the Australian beau), anatomy (obstetric nursing), and geology (underground in the coal pit).

The life-enhancing movement from high to low (and north to south), from cold to warm, and from light to dark culminates for Alvina in her relationship with the Italian peasant Francesco "Ciccio" Marasca, who is part of a theatrical troupe working at her father's cinema to fill out the program with live entertainment as was the custom at the time. Alvina's association with the troupe degrades her in the eyes of her home town: "Alvina did not care. She rather liked it. She liked being déclassée" (*LG* 117). Ciccio is "a dark-skinned foreigner" in England (*LG* 215) and knows the importance of warmth: "'You can live without food, but you can't live without fire,'" he says to Alvina (*LG* 220). It is at this point that maternal concerns make themselves felt. Madame Rochard is "a wonderful mother" for the men of the troupe and, in a manner reminiscent of Louisa Lindley's substitutive role in "Daughters of the Vicar," Alvina takes instruction from the older woman in the domestic arts as if in preparation for proxy motherhood.

Although concern for her class standing periodically returns to trouble Alvina, her overall trajectory is downward and toward fulfilment. Madame Rochard tries to warn her about Ciccio that "'you will go down, with him'" (*LG* 180), but Alvina asks, "'Why should life always go up?'" (*LG* 183). Thus it seems ironic that their journey ends with a steep hike upward in the Italian Colli Albani, at the end of which Alvina finds herself in a freezing cold cave-like dwelling. After her long journey downward to fulfilment and warmth, it seems odd that Alvina's question "Why should life always go up?" seems to be mocked by the long ascent toward frigid conditions. We learn little of Ciccio's own motivations, but possibly he is attracted to Alvina as the means for "goin' up an' bein' refined" as Lawrence's poem "Up he goes! –" has it (*Poems* 480, l. 14), so that the ascent represents his class aspirations rather than Alvina's vitalistic imperative. But more likely the fact that seven years elapsed between Lawrence starting the novel and finishing it, with the war's intrusion stranding the manuscript in Germany (*LG* xxiv), may explain the curious inconsistency. For by 1920 Lawrence was about to enter his leadership period in which female quests give way to male priorities and female passivity is highly valued, a period that also features, as we have seen, the climbing of a glacier by Captain Hepburn in *The Captain's Doll* to prove his fitness and upward aspirations. Toward the end of *The Lost Girl*, Alvina feels "[t]hat there was nothing for her but to yield, yield, yield" (*LG* 321). As in other work, the "colonial solution" for inter-class couples is at play here, too, as Alvina and Ciccio have now left England, and Ciccio must go off to war while a pregnant Alvina awaits his return so that they may travel to America. She is about to become a mother, and Ciccio's departure, realistic enough as a result of conscription, may represent the movement away from interpersonal merger and toward individuation.

In the autograph manuscript of the first-person narrative "Elsa Culverwell," the initial iteration of what eventually became *The Lost Girl*, we can see that Lawrence had already developed many of the elements that would later appear in the novel: the middle-class family of the protagonist, the mother's ineffectuality, the father's delving into one failed scheme after another, the governess Miss Niell (who becomes Miss Frost), and the sewing-room overseer Miss Venner (who becomes Miss Pinnegar). Lawrence just gets to the point where Elsa may have found a lower-class catalyst to a more vital life when the manuscript breaks off after a mere twenty pages (*LG* 398). What is interesting here is the detailing of the class backgrounds and expectations of Elsa's parents, something that is much less emphasized in the final version. Elsa's mother is the daughter of a squire who is a scion of an old but no longer wealthy family, while her father is the descendant of well-to-do tradespeople. The problems in the marriage are partly temperamental ones, but class also plays a part. One of Lawrence's tentative titles for the story at one point, "Mixed Marriage" (*LG* xixn), may refer to Alvina's eventual union with Ciccio, but might equally be meant for Elsa/Alvina's parents. The mother "really was a lady, and really was superior to most folk," while the father "was not a real gentleman" (*LG* 349). The father builds a house-cum-shop in Bestwood (changed to Woodhouse in the finished novel), but for his wife, "[t]he idea of a shop was disgusting ... When she heard the ping of the bell, and realised that a collier was in her house, under her roof, she felt a kind of insecurity and horror ... She loathed the shop" (*LG* 345).

It is striking that in the published version of the novel, Alvina chooses to "degrade" herself to an extent that would have horrified her mother in this earlier version. In "Elsa Culverwell" there is little to indicate the determination and willing debasement of Alvina Houghton but much to suggest that some of the conflicts of Lawrence's own family have been displaced or taken up a notch, so to speak, and presented as a clash between representatives of a cash-poor squirearchy and an upstart but monied merchant class. The working class makes an appearance only at the end of the manuscript when we meet the Holderness family. The father, a stone-mason, complains about the attitude of his son, who has just broken a chisel: "'He's only just back from the High School, you see,' sneered the father. 'He's such a gentleman, just now'" (*LG* 358).

The oddness of *The Lost Girl* continues in *Aaron's Rod* in that we have the by-now-familiar set-up of two men, the working-class Aaron Sisson, a miners' check-weighman, and the middle-class intellectual Rawdon Lilly, potentially representing two ways of life, but the structure floats aimlessly insofar as there is no woman to choose between them, contrary to what Lawrence has conditioned us to expect in these structures. However, in *Lady Chatterley's Lover* (1928), Lawrence reprises the pattern we have been considering. The novel was written just after he returned to Italy from his last visit to his home region, which was in the midst of industrial strife and class warfare (Ellis, *DG* 316). Once again, we have the familiar Lawrentian situation of a woman, Connie Chatterley, who must decide between two ways of life embodied in two men, both of them projections of aspects of Lawrence himself. Her husband, Clifford, is upper-class, intellectual, wheelchair-bound, and devoid of a "lower" self because of war wounds. Significantly, his animus toward the body preceded his disablement, as we can most clearly see in *Version 2* of the novel: "he had always believed in the immortality of the soul ... and the comparative worthlessness of the body" (*FLC* 408). Connie's lover and Clifford's gamekeeper, Oliver Mellors, is lower-class, sexually potent, and close to the earth. One striking aspect of the novel is how Lawrence, because of his parents' marriage and his own marriage to the daughter of a German baron, can imagine an upper-class woman involving herself with a lower-class man initially for the purpose of producing a child. This turns on its head the common tendency in the British novel, where, in works such as George Eliot's *Adam Bede* (1859) and Thomas Hardy's *Tess of the d'Urbervilles* (1891), an upper-class man exploits a lower-class woman and the birth of a child leads to tragedy. But what is noteworthy about the final version of the novel is how Lawrence sets up class as the central differentiating element among the characters but then removes it as a serious factor by creating a confluence of class positions among the major actors and emphasizing attachment inclinations instead.

As Sanders and many others have noted, if we look at the three versions of the novel chronologically, we see that Lawrence gradually lessened the class barriers between Connie and the gamekeeper to the point where Mellors (Parkin in the earlier versions) becomes, in effect, "a gentleman in disguise" (181). As David Ellis puts it, "No longer a homogeneous working-class figure, Mellors has risen from the ranks during the war and gained a commission. He not only looks like a gentleman to several of the other characters but is perfectly capable of speaking like one when it suits him." He is now an educated man, well read and someone "who easily switches registers from dialect to standard English" (*DG* 390–1). He is, in short, an "in-between," to use the term of the poem "Red-herring." He is a fantasy Lawrence avatar who, like Lawrence, was once considered somewhat effeminate (*LCL* 276), has had pneumonia (*LCL* 196), is troubled with a persistent cough (*LCL* 112), was a scholarship boy (*LCL* 145), and describes relationships with two women that parallel Lawrence's experiences with Jessie Chambers and Helen Corke (*LCL* 358). Mellors rose in the army to officer rank and became "quite the gentleman," in the view of Mrs Bolton, Clifford's nurse, until he returned to Tevershall to work as a gamekeeper (*LCL* 145), an occupation that is not a clearly demarcated working-class one. A gamekeeper is in a precarious, conflicted, inter-class position: paid by the landed gentry to protect its property against the predations of the same lower class of which he is nominally a member. A further shift in the final version is the elimination of the Tewson family and, with that excision, the long debate on class that occurs when Connie visits their home in the first two versions. Also, Parkin's objections to the thought of living off Connie's money as an affront to his manhood dissipate a fair bit in Mellors. What these developments do is allow Lawrence to create two hybrid characters in Mellors and Mrs Bolton so that the relationship between Mellors and Connie more closely parallels that of Clifford and his nurse. The result is a decentring of class as the prime focus of the novel, for Lawrence's principal interest lies elsewhere even as he writes his novel in the midst of a major industrial strike that pitted one class against another and at the centre of which were the coal miners of northern England, the very people Lawrence knew best.

Mrs Bolton, then, is another class migrant. After her collier husband dies young in a mining accident she goes on to upgrade her education and qualify as a nurse. Working among the colliers, "she felt very superior to them ... At the same time, a resentment against the owning class smouldered in her" (*LCL* 81). Nevertheless, she is now thrilled to be working with a "titled gentleman" (*LCL* 100). Her partial assimilation into the negative values of the upper class is suggested by her gambling at cards with Clifford. The activity is competitive, aggressive, and profane, and may be contrasted to the division of the week's takings (the "reckoning") done with great courtesy and delicacy on a Friday night among Walter Morel and his colliery stall-mates in *Sons and Lovers* (a scene that also appears in the play *A Collier's Friday Night*). The reckoning is a communal, decorous, and almost sacred activity that, together with their common and dangerous work, binds the men together in trust. The gambling at cards may suggest only negative values, but it also indicates Mrs Bolton's shifting class affiliation. Not quite so thrilled as Mrs Bolton with that same "titled gentleman," Connie, too, moves toward an in-between status. Her class is "the well-to-do intelligentsia," and Clifford, as minor aristocrat, is her class superior (*LCL* 10). Her sympathies are often with working-class people and against her own husband, and, in one love scene with Mellors, she tries to speak in his Derby dialect, albeit with mixed success (*LCL* 177). That Mellors's daughter is also named Connie suggests Connie Chatterley's potential for inter-class sympathy. Clearly, with Mellors's background of class ascent and Connie's willingness, like Alvina Houghton's, to "lower" herself, the prospects of meeting somewhere in the middle look better than in the first two versions of the novel, where Lawrence painted himself into a corner by keeping Parkin decidedly lower-class, as Ellis has argued (*DG* 392).

The strange thing is that Clifford, the obvious incarnation of everything negative about English society, in Lawrence's view, including an affinity for mechanical solutions and a hankering after money, also has something in him of Lawrence, the ultimate in-betweener. David Ellis references Frieda Lawrence for the suggestion that her husband identified with both Mellors and Clifford (*DG* 327).[15] One possible, proleptic indication of the identification is evident in the early short story "The Shades of Spring," a fictionally transmuted recounting of Lawrence's return visit to the beloved Haggs Farm and the Chambers family (Worthen, *EY* 246–7), a story we will examine as a homecoming tale in the next chapter. The Lawrence figure, John Adderley Syson, on his way to visit Willeywater Farm after a long absence, is accosted by a "manly and good-looking" gamekeeper "taut with animal life" named Arthur Pilbeam (*PO* 99). Pilbeam is now courting Hilda Millership, the Jessie Chambers figure with whom Syson had been intimate. The tension between the two men is palpable, but the point is that Lawrence is imagining himself in a love triangle involving a gamekeeper, and in terms of the later, comparable *Lady Chatterley* triangle, he is in Clifford's position. Moreover, in the final version of the novel, Clifford has become a writer of some note, and his debility, though it works symbolically well enough for Lawrence's purposes, also easily suggests Lawrence's own chronically debilitating illness.

The Clifford-Lawrence identification may have emotional roots, but it is also tactical. By splitting the plot late in the novel between Connie-Mellors and Clifford-Mrs Bolton in a kind of chiastic criss-cross involving class and gender, Lawrence finally avoids the problem of mother trouble intruding where it does not belong. It is hived off onto one half of the composite Lawrence figure, but it is unavoidably there. Clifford's development serves Lawrence's argument that the industrial system is created by and in turn produces stunted human beings, but the stunting seems intimately linked to mother issues. All along, Mrs Bolton has been "half mistress, half foster-mother" to Clifford (*LCL* 112), and, after Connie leaves her husband, he clearly appears in the role of the "child-man" he has never really outgrown, literally at Mrs Bolton's breast (*LCL* 291). Sungho Kim calls this a "cross-class pseudo-sexual relationship" that depends on Mrs Bolton accepting the role of "a potent mother" (146).

Lawrence is tempted to imagine a class truce or meeting of minds by means of mixed-class characters and inter-class relationships. As Wasson writes, "he struggled to show that the politics of *eros* could resolve class war" (301). But he was too honest a writer to endorse the kind of sentimental rapprochement-cum-romance seen in Elizabeth Gaskell's *North and South* (1855), for example. There can be no class-based solution: "It only remains for some men and women, individuals, to try to get back their bodies and preserve the other flow of warmth, affection, and physical unison. There is nothing else to do" (*LEA* 284). In the end, Lawrence once more goes for the "colonial solution" and has Connie and Mellors contemplate a life in Canada. In his final novel, then, Lawrence has come no further than in his early work in terms of envisioning a new dispensation in industrial Britain, but then that was never his goal. In a preface to his play *Touch and Go*, he argues that the class war is the fight of two dogs over a bone that is hardly worth the having. The material struggle misses the real issue (*Plays* 366–7), and it is not, in any case, his struggle. To repeat, in the essay "The State of Funk" he wrote: "The great social change interests me and troubles me, but it is not my field" (*LEA* 221). Lawrence never really did escape his complex class origins or heal his divided nature, but they gave him some of the crucial tools necessary to become the writer he had it in him to become. As Neil Roberts remarks, "[w]orking-class realism was not, despite the achievement of *Sons and Lovers*, to be Lawrence's métier" ("Writing" 23). Instead, as interested as Lawrence is in class issues, in the end they become part of his never-ending exploration of attachment.

5

STORIES OF HOMECOMING

> "I think my coming back home was just *reculer pour mieux sauter* [retreating the better to jump]"
> Gudrun to her sister Ursula in D.H. Lawrence, *Women in Love* (WL 10)

> When you have run a long way from Home and Mother, then you realise that the earth is round, and if you keep on running you'll be back on the same old doorstep. Like a fatality.
> D.H. Lawrence, *Studies in Classic American Literature* (SCAL 131)

> "Myself, my desire to go onwards takes me back a little."
> D.H. Lawrence, "Glad Ghosts" (WWRA 188)

Homecoming is a notable, if under-analyzed, theme in a number of Lawrence's fictions. With this subject, Lawrence seems often to be expressing an adult version of Mahler's "rapprochement" stage of psychic development in childhood maturation (see Introduction), the in-between stage that arises from the dilemma that, on the one hand, the child needs to recognize its separateness as the ego develops, but, on the other, it is not yet able to stand alone (Mahler, *Psychological Birth* 229). The start of life involves a necessary total dependency that gradually gives way to a crucial and healthy desire for exploration, with periodic returns to the safety of the caregiver, temporary retreats to security that are needed until the achievement of full (or a degree of) independence anchored in a secure attachment. Returning to the caregiver for the child, then, is a kind of recharging of the emotional/attachment batteries by plugging into the power source of safety before further exploration on the way to individuation can take place. If the attachment is relatively secure, a child can proceed in a fairly linear and progressive fashion from a necessary fusion to a healthy autonomy. However, what Lawrence's writing mostly explores, as we have seen, is the genesis and consequences of insecure attachment, and the development is not linear but rather to and fro, both within individual works and across his fictional oeuvre.

As the epigraphs above serve to suggest, Lawrentian homecoming involves a tension between a nostalgia to return to the known world of the past and maternal security and a desire to forge ahead and explore the new, or, as Lawrence expressed it at the age of forty, having returned for a visit to Eastwood, "I feel at once a devouring nostalgia and an infinite repulsion" (*LEA* 15). The narratives of homecoming are, then, portrayals of the conflict between the urge to explore the unknown and the pull of nostalgia for the known, or, as Weldon Thornton expresses it, the tension "between the need for openness and venturesomeness and the fear that manifests itself in self-protection and defensiveness" (26). In chapter 2 we looked at a good example of just such a struggle in Tom Brangwen's process of maturation in *The Rainbow*. With the help of the model of the double gyre of emotion related to attachment and of Mahler's concept of rapprochement, we can suggest that the two feelings in the conflict are interconnected: the nostalgia is an expression of a desire to reconnect after a period of separation has weakened the always-precarious feeling of attachment, and the repulsion is a function of that very reconnection, as the return home either provides the requisite emotional ballast to resume the journey forward or serves to reawaken the old fear of fusion. "Nothing depresses me more," Lawrence writes in late 1927, "than to come home to the place where I was born, and where I lived my first twenty years" (*LEA* 50).[1] The attachment perspective also helps us to see that the intricacies of character portrayal in Lawrence's stories of homecoming are projections of his own attachment complications as his insights deepened into his upbringing and debilities.

Certain manifestations of the homecoming urge in Lawrence seem natural enough. It is no surprise, for example, to see Paul Morel in *Sons and Lovers* long to return to the succour and security of his mother after being badly beaten in his fight with Baxter Dawes. He wrenches himself off the ground, where Baxter has left him prostrate, and heads for home, to his mother: "He wanted to get to his mother, he must get to his mother" (*SL* 411). It is more surprising to see the same basic homecoming urge in Lawrence's much later fragment "The Flying-Fish," which starkly registers the yearning for the security of home in the face of threatening circumstances – in this case, grave illness. Lawrence reportedly characterized the work as "written so near the borderline of death" (*SM* xxxv).[2] Composed in March of 1925, when Lawrence was suffering from both malaria and a resurgent tuberculosis, the incomplete story that Ross Parmenter calls "almost straight autobiography" (332) depicts a deep longing for home but breaks off part way through the homeward voyage. Parmenter suggests that "the home that Lawrence was envisioning was part of the country near Eastwood that had seemed particularly lovely to him in late adolescence" (333).[3] There is a character in "The Flying-Fish" named Lydia, Lawrence's mother's given name (and a name Lawrence used in both "Love Among the Haystacks" and *The Rainbow*). Rather than the mother in this case, she is the sister of the protagonist, Gethin Day, but a sister old enough to be his mother. Lawrence's own illness, in effect, is combined with the memory of his mother's terminal cancer and displaced onto Day's sister, and she dies while he is in transit to get home, a journey he undertakes when he is informed that Lydia is gravely ill. Having spent most of his life abroad, Day now "felt that home was the place ... [h]e wanted to go home" (*SM* 210). Relatively insignificant in Lawrence's body of work, "The Flying-Fish" nevertheless portrays the strong pull that coming home to the security of a mother figure could have in Lawrence's life and imagination even as he neared the age of forty. For him, as he writes in *Fantasia of the Unconscious*, "a man never leaves his first love, once the love is established" (*PFU* 148). We also see nostalgia for home strongly expressed in *Kangaroo* at a time when Lawrence is very far from home himself: the protagonist, Somers, "longed for Europe with hungry longing ... He felt he would have given anything on earth to be in England ... he wanted to go back, to go home" (*K* 19). Somers also thinks back to his (and Lawrence's) time in Cornwall after the authorities ordered him to leave the coast as a "[t]orture of nostalgia" (*K* 248).

For Mahler, the rapprochement stage is the origin of "many uniquely human problems and dilemmas – problems that sometimes are never completely resolved during the entire life cycle" (*Psychological Birth* 99). Prominent among them is the difficulty of achieving an equilibrium of attachment: "There is an oscillation between the longing to merge blissfully with the ... 'all good' symbiotic mother, and the defense against reengulfment by her" (*Psychological Birth* 230). As I have been suggesting throughout this study, that balance is always tricky in Lawrence and at the centre of his fictional embodiments of relationships, but the theme of homecoming brings the dilemma clearly into focus. The fictions of homecoming in Lawrence, indeed, reflect the never-ending struggle to attain secure attachment while avoiding fusion and protecting a vulnerable sense of selfhood without triggering abandonment anxiety. Unsurprisingly, paradoxical situations arise in this effort. For one thing, adaptation to the very strangeness of the new, from which a momentary respite into the known world of the past is often sought through homecoming, guarantees that, upon return, the home one left behind will itself seem different, even strange, though it may in actuality be unaltered. Joyce Wexler suggests that "[t]he claim that the strange is commonplace is a logical contradiction, yet as a paradox it figuratively conveys the perspective of an expatriate returning home. Seeing his native land with more sophisticated eyes, he finds it both strange and familiar" (28).[4] Wexler's reference to the perspective of an expatriate is quite apt given, for example, this description of the feeling of the

Lawrence stand-in, John Adderley Syson, on his return to the country of his youth: "Like an emigrant, he had returned on a visit to the country of his past to make the comparison" (*VicG* 141).[5] Similarly, in *Kangaroo*, Somers thinks back to the time during the war when his sister took a cottage for him in his old home district: "And so he returned, after six years, to his own country. A bitter stranger too, he felt" (*K* 251). Lawrence exploits this paradox inherent in homecoming in many of these stories in order to work through his emotional attachment complications that seemingly have no solution.

As "The Flying-Fish" suggests, returning home for Lawrence generally means an overt or sometimes more implicit return to the mother or what the maternal represents of a desired security and an unwanted dependence. Thus, his portrayal of homecoming tends to shift as his attitude to the maternal changes with Lawrence's continuing exploration of the emotional import of, and the toll taken by, his earliest attachment. Lawrence's fictional mothers come in many guises that range from the formidable Mrs Witt in the novella *St Mawr* or the authoritative matriarch Gran Ellis in *The Boy in the Bush* to the weak-willed Clarissa Houghton of *The Lost Girl*, whose death early in the novel is barely mourned by her family and hardly noticed by the reader. Some Lawrentian mothers are engulfing, while others are withholding; few if any are adequately attuned to their offspring. In *Mr Noon*, as we saw in the Introduction in connection with the briefly appearing character Stanley (a portrait of Harold Hobson [*MN* 329n]), the narrator baldly observes, "But there you are – men shouldn't have mothers" (*MN* 256). If there is any overall arc to the portrayals it can be said to be a development from reverence to revenge. Within that trajectory, we can identify three stages in Lawrence's attitude to mothers or the maternal and corresponding homecoming stories that belong more or less to each stage, but it is important to keep in mind, even as we look at them sequentially, that the stages are overlapping since Lawrence's attitude tends to shift back and forth over time even within an identifiable general pattern.

As we saw in chapter 2 with gender identification, there is a gradual lessening of the maternal attachment when it comes to homecoming and a strengthening of the ties to the paternal. In other words, Lawrence eventually imagines in his fiction, sometimes in merely symbolic terms, a successful masculine attachment he was never able to create satisfactorily in life. The return to the mother is, in the end, at least in theory, in the service of being able to leave her, just as it is in the rapprochement stage of attachment that Mahler theorizes. However, as noted above, the evolution is not always strictly unidirectional. In fact, as late as 1924, a full thirteen years after Lawrence's mother's death, we may discern Lawrence fantasizing a better life for his mother than the one she actually had in the story "Jimmy and the Desperate Woman," a tale that has always been taken to be about something else entirely (as it is, primarily). The fiction is one of Lawrence's so-called Murry stories from the mid-1920s in which he skewers the character and actions of his erstwhile good friend, John Middleton Murry.[6]

A highbrow magazine editor essentially rescues a literary-minded woman unhappily married to a miner in northern England and invites her and her child to live with him in London, apparently as Murry more or less actually did at one point (Ellis, *DG* 166). While the miner, Pinnegar, speaks standard English and finds solace outside of his marriage with another woman rather than at the pub, there is a similarity between him and Walter Morel and a parallel between the editor's visit to Mrs Pinnegar and Mr Heaton's call on Mrs Morel in *Sons and Lovers*.[7] A comparison of the two scenes at the miners' respective homes suggests a rescue fantasy on Lawrence's part in "Jimmy and the Desperate Woman" that involves a woman in a situation analogous to that of Lydia Lawrence as well as Gertrude Morel. So even relatively late in his career Lawrence occasionally reverts to his early-life loyalty to his mother and a sympathetic view of her life as "desperate."

Certain early and some later works show the catastrophic results of losing a mother. One thinks, first and foremost, of the death of Mrs Morel in *Sons and Lovers* and its effect on her son Paul, but we also have the life crisis of Alfred Durant in "Daughters of the Vicar" when his mother dies, and the attempted suicide of Mabel in "The Horse-Dealer's Daughter." Where Alfred Durant feels "like a swimmer who forgets to swim" (*PO* 78) after his mother's death, Mabel sets out deliberately to drown herself in the wake of hers, though the crisis is triggered years after the death. Mabel is twenty-seven when the story opens; her mother had died when she was fourteen, and ever since then, Mabel "lived in the memory of her mother" (*EME* 142). When the household is about to break up after the death of the father, who has left nothing but debts, Mabel feels that her only legacy is "the world of death she inherited from her mother" (*EME* 143), and she walks into a pond to drown herself, only to be rescued by Dr Fergusson and returned to the world of the living. Lawrence is expressing *inter alia* his genuine grief at the death of his mother in these works of fiction, but, with the help of the more objective observations of both Frieda and Jessie Chambers, a process was set in motion whereby he began to question his own cherished view of her. Moreover, the indications of unease with the strong maternal relationship are noticeable even in those narratives that mourn the mother: Paul, Alfred, and Mabel are all nearly destroyed by the lingering power of the relationship after the mother departs or when some other life crisis confronts them.

The stories of homecoming that belong to this first phase generally feature a strong desire to return to the maternal or to a proxy mother with only hints of any reservation. There are both male- and female-centred homecoming stories, but the emotions portrayed are invariably ones Lawrence experienced himself. In chapter 1, we saw a clear link between coming home and returning emotionally to maternal care in *The White Peacock*, where the landscape of Cyril's home region takes on the characteristics of a nurturing mother. From his exile away from the valley of Nethermere, he retrospectively remembers "a day when the breast of the hills was heaving in a last quick waking sigh" (*WP* 126). In "Hadrian" and *The Fox*, the coming home to a mother figure is not literal but quite clear nonetheless. As discussed in part in chapter 4, in both stories we see a young man who has gone to Canada and, when the war broke out, joined the military. When the stories open, the war is winding down, and each youth is on leave. He returns home, and eventually marries a woman who is considerably older than he is. In "Hadrian," Matilda tells Hadrian, who was adopted into the family as a boy, "'I'm old enough to be your mother. In a way I've been your mother'" (*EME* 106). In "The Fox," Henry Grenfel returns to the farm where he had lived with his grandfather before he ran away to Canada only to find that the grandfather is dead and two women are running the farm. When he proposes marriage to one of them, Nellie March, she responds, "'What nonsense! I'm old enough to be your mother'" (*Fox* 25). Far from dissuading Hadrian and Henry, the age discrepancy is an attraction, and the homecoming becomes the means to unite with a mother of sorts.

Sometimes the homecoming to a mother figure within this grouping of stories is slightly less direct. "A Prelude," one of Lawrence's earliest tales (written in 1907), opens with a description of a character based on Sarah Ann Chambers, Jessie's mother (*LAH* 223n), in whose presence the husband and sons are emotionally anchored. The story is about the relationship of one of those sons, Fred, with a neighbour, Nellie Wycherley, whose family has become much more prosperous than Fred's and whose parents are both dead. Nellie has been away in town for some time, and when she returns, she finds the neighbouring family "cool and estranged" (*LAH* 11), for they believe that she has become proud and arrogant with her wealth and town ways. It is a classic romantic-comic plot of two lovers separated by an obstacle, in this case the relative inequality between the two families and the misunderstandings that result. Nellie says to a friend, "'I wish this miserable farm and bit of money had never come between us'" (*LAH* 12). The central device that ends the estrangement is the Christmas play of St George, which Fred and his brothers, disguised as "guysers," come to Nellie's farm to perform on Christmas Eve. There is a further misunderstanding based on the symbolic significance of the money thrown to the guysers, after which Nellie returns the visit and makes her true feelings known. She embraces Fred's family, and "kissed the little mother" (*LAH* 15). The last words of the story are: "Already she was at home" (*LAH* 15). The orphaned Nellie has crossed the divide between the two families and found a proxy mother.

"The Last Straw," formerly known as "Fanny and Annie," (1921) ends somewhat similarly, but, like some other female-centred homecoming stories, the return home here is in the context of settling for second best, a compromise that highlights the importance of finding, or returning to, a mother figure even at some cost. Fanny "had loved her brilliant and ambitious cousin, who had jilted her, and who had died" (*EME* 154), and she has now come back to marry the foundry worker Harry, who had been her first love attachment. The title is somewhat puzzling as there does not seem to be any "last straw" that determines Fanny's decision to return home and marry Harry after keeping him dangling for a dozen years. It is a decided "come-down" for Fanny and not a happy return: "she had come back for good. And her spirit groaned dismally. She doubted if she could bear it" (*EME* 154, 153). Lawrence gives us no insight into her motivation except that she has simply made up her mind to return and marry Harry. Thornton intriguingly suggests that Fanny is pregnant and that this is the reason for her return and her determination to marry (25). That would explain a number of anomalies in the story, including Fanny's aunt's suggestion that her niece may be taking advantage of Harry, Fanny's remark that he may be getting more than he bargained for, and her willingness to overlook Harry's possible paternity and admitted sexual liaison with a local woman, Annie Nixon (Thornton 26). What remains unexplained is why Lawrence would be so cagey about the pregnancy (consideration for the magazine audience for which the tale was intended is a possibility) or why Fanny would have informed her aunt about the pregnancy if she is so determined to conceal it by a hasty and less than ideal marriage. For, if we accept Thornton's argument, Fanny's aunt's remark about taking advantage of Harry must mean that she has learned that he will unknowingly be raising another man's child.

Fanny's somewhat humiliating return may simply be another instance of Lawrence, disillusioned and rather bitter as he was after the war, gleefully dramatizing an ambitious woman being cut down to size and agreeing to marriage on a man's terms, such as we see, for example, at the end of *The Captain's Doll*, where, as Peter Balbert puts it, Captain Hepburn "makes it clear that he will not back down from the non-negotiable terms for marriage that he proposes to Hannele" (*Marriage* 85).[8] However, in "The Last Straw" there may be another, psychological explanation for Fanny's homecoming related to attachment: that, in keeping with Lawrence's rapprochement tendencies, it is, in effect, to find a mother. There are two mother figures in "The Last Straw." There is Fanny's Aunt Lizzie, who seems to be *in loco parentis* in relation to Fanny, admires and pities her, and does not think that Harry is good enough for her. She makes only a brief appearance in the story, however. Harry himself is "something of a mother's lad" (*EME* 157), and the second figure is his mother, the working-class Mrs Goodall, a strong and vocal woman, between whom and Fanny "there was naturally no love lost" (*EME* 157). The question is, rather, whether there is love to be gained. Mrs Goodall is flattered by Fanny's return to her son but angry as well: "'I towd him mysen … 'Er's held back all this long, let 'er stop as 'er is. 'E'd non ha' had thee for *my* tellin', tha hears'" (*EME* 158).

It is evident to Mrs Goodall and her family, as well as to the entire village, that Fanny is settling for second best in accepting Harry. At Sunday tea, there is an unexpected development. After Mrs Nixon has publically accused Harry of impregnating her daughter, everyone expects Fanny either to call off the wedding or, if she is still determined to marry despite the allegation, to accompany Harry back to chapel for his choir singing, but she does neither. Instead, Fanny declares that she will stay home with Mrs Goodall: "'I'll stop with *you* to-night, Mother,' … 'Best you had, my gel,' said Mrs Goodall, flattered and assured" (*EME* 166). Fanny thus declares her loyalty to her new family and to their class. In effect, she has chosen the erstwhile hostile Mrs Goodall over her aunt as a substitute mother. As Thornton puts it, there is an "interplay between venturesomeness and self-protection that works itself out in Fanny's psyche" (21), and we should not be surprised that self-protection or security wins out in the end for a woman who appears to have no parents alive and who has seen her great love abandon her and then die. With her security and confidence in the world attenuated, Fanny needs a rapprochement with a caregiving figure, and the very force that formerly characterized Mrs Goodall's hostility to Fanny, when converted to a welcome, is extremely enticing. In coming home and wedding Harry, Fanny is gaining a protective mother.

In the middle stage of Lawrence's working through his relationship to his mother and the maternal in general, the force of nostalgia battles with a growing sense of estrangement, and he portrays maternal figures as less than dependable, even destructive. One senses the need for masculine identification and a growing determination to move on in life.[9] So we have the unreliable Mrs Crich of *Women in Love* (see chapter 1), for example, and Hester, the mother of Paul, in "The Rocking-Horse Winner," who pretends to love her children but knows in her heart that her devotion is a sham: "She had bonny children, yet she felt they had been thrust upon her, and she could not love them" (*WWRA* 230). Squires would have it that in this story Lawrence "returns to his painful Eastwood past to portray a boy obsessed with pleasing his mother" (III). If that is so, then the obsession certainly proves detrimental. Cowan calls Hester an "inaccessible mother" to Paul, whose "ineffectual father" is an unavailable model for masculine identification (*Self and Sexuality* 126). Notwithstanding how deeply that other Lawrentian Paul, namely Morel, mourns his mother's death in *Sons and Lovers*, Cowan suggests that Gertrude Morel shares with Hester a crucial characteristic derived from Lydia Lawrence: "Each of these mothers appropriates her young son's instinctual being and exploits it for her own needs, without regard for his developmental needs and possibly without full awareness of the consequences for him" (*Self and Sexuality* 128). In this short story, Lawrence expresses a conscious realization that he had not fully taken on board in writing the earlier work but that existed "as an undercurrent of meaning in the novel" (*Self and Sexuality* 129). He now begins to acknowledge the damage done to him by what had been his most valued relationship.

Intellectually, Lawrence knew there was no turning back once he was embarked on the life that took him both physically and emotionally very far from the Eastwood of his childhood and his mother's engulfing embrace, and, equally, from Haggs Farm and Jessie Chambers, his first relational proxy for and rival to his mother. In a letter dated 23 February 1922 written to his mother-in-law in Germany, he muses that he "mustn't look back" (*8L* 53). Even more strikingly, in *Aaron's Rod* he uses an evocative metaphor to suggest the dangers of turning back even for a brief glimpse at what one has left behind. When the eponymous protagonist of that novel returns for a fleeting look at his home and family after having deserted them, Lawrence calls the chapter "The Pillar of Salt," invoking the biblical story of Lot's wife, who, in violation of the divine sanction not to look back at the destruction of Sodom as the family group flees for their lives, was turned into a pillar of salt when she could not resist the urge to turn around and look (thus the high saline content of the Dead Sea, according to legend). Obviously, then, Lawrence is suggesting that Aaron has made a mistake by coming back, even if just for a peek. He repeats the backsliding yet again later, in a chapter entitled "More Pillar of Salt." Tempting as it is, looking homeward can be dangerous.[10]

Nevertheless, Lawrence himself cannot help looking back from time to time in his fiction as he compulsively revisits the complications of his early attachments and their consequences for his personality and emotional make-up. As late as November 1928, he could write nostalgically to David Chambers, Jessie's brother, that "whatever else I am, I am somewhere still the same Bert who rushed with such joy to the Haggs" (6L 618). The nostalgic yet reluctant review of the past often manifests in the fiction as a sour, not to say salty, taste in the mouth. "A Modern Lover" (originally called "The Virtuous") was first published in 1933 but most likely written by the end of 1909, well before the death of Lydia Lawrence. It is based on Lawrence's relationship with Jessie Chambers (LAH xxvi–xxvii) but also contains elements of fantasy and wishful thinking. The background to the story, Andrew Harrison tells us, was Lawrence's protracted, on-again-off-again relationship with Jessie and a new connection with Agnes Holt, a woman he met through his new Croydon associations. Agnes was "an independent-minded woman with whom he could talk and flirt" (Harrison, Life 33). Lawrence introduced the two women to each other, Harrison surmises, "to show Jessie that he was moving on and resolving the impasse in his emotional life," but being rebuffed by Agnes about a sexual relationship "pushed him back into the arms of Jessie" (Life 43). And it is that return and the ambivalence infusing both nostalgia and moving on that are reflected and fictionalized in "A Modern Lover."

As with other stories of homecoming ("The Witch à la Mode" perhaps most obviously), there are strong elements of nostalgia in "A Modern Lover" but, inevitably, those of estrangement as well, given the pressure of the underlying, if temporarily repressed, realization that there is no going back. Cyril Mearsham, a namesake of *The White Peacock*'s Cyril Beardsall, has been away in the great city in the south for two years and now returns to Muriel and her family with whom he had been so intimate, as Lawrence had been with Jessie and the entire Chambers clan. On the way to the farm, Cyril notes that the "old, wide way, forsaken and grown over with grass, used not to be so bad," and he stops "to look around and to bring back old winters to the scene." He wistfully senses a glamour "in the old places that had seemed so ordinary" (LAH 28). Once ensconced in the parlour of Muriel's home, Cyril remembers that the family is soon leaving the farm, and he begins to "call up the old days, when they had romped and played so boisteriously [sic]" (*LAH* 33). In fact, Cyril will rather cynically use the past he shared with Muriel in an attempt to reclaim her for himself.

The elements of estrangement here, even from one's former self, are as strong as the nostalgia, and the clash of the two feelings creates the emotional tension of the story. Looking at a photograph of himself in the parlour, Cyril feels that "nothing is so hateful as the self one has left" (*LAH* 33), perhaps an oblique self-reproach for returning. For Cyril, it seems, even nostalgia is not what it used to be. The brothers arrive home from the pit, and their coal-dust-covered faces make them strangers in effect (*LAH* 30), while at dinner the family members feel ill at ease in Cyril's presence: "His nicety contrasted the more with their rough, country habit. They became shy and awkward, fumbling for something to say," and their mode of dress at table accentuates his strangeness (*LAH* 32). In spite of the estrangement and the distinct feeling that the family belongs to his past, Cyril makes a play for Muriel even though – or perhaps because – she now has a new boyfriend, Tom Vickers. Lawrence is remarkably self-critical in having the narrator liken Cyril to a scavenging bird on this point. His soul is "like a sea-gull over the waters, stooping now and again, and taking a fragment of life – a look, a contour, a movement – to feed upon" (*LAH* 29).

When Tom arrives, the three young people converse for a while and also engage in singing old songs, but all the while Cyril is insinuating himself back into Muriel's heart, possibly without entirely knowing what he is about: "Perhaps Mersham did not know what he was doing. Yet his whole talk lifted Muriel as in a net, like a sea-maiden out of the waters, and placed her in his arms, to breathe his thin, rarified atmosphere" (*LAH* 43). As the narrator suggests, the development is not going to be healthy for the sea-maiden taken out of her natural element. If there is a surprising development in the story, it is the strong attraction Cyril feels for Tom as they go out to the barn to get Tom's bicycle, as he must be off. "'After all,'" thinks Cyril, "'he's very beautiful, she's a fool to give him up'" (*LAH* 44), as Lawrence begins to reach out for masculine identification (see the earlier discussion in chapter 2). Cyril is honest about his admiration for Tom when he and Muriel walk together in the dark, telling her, "'He is very desirable – I should choose *him* in preference to me – for myself'" (*LAH* 46). Still, Cyril suggests to Muriel that they become intimate without marrying since he cannot afford to marry, and Muriel's hesitation on this point provokes him. The tale ends inconclusively since Lawrence himself does not yet know where his relationship with Jessie is going. The two characters have stumbled in the dark crossing a muddy meadow "where there was no path" (*LAH* 45).

The early story "The Witch à la Mode" (first published posthumously in 1934) is a homecoming tale that is also one of Lawrence's so-called Croydon stories. It was originally called "Intimacy" and written "as early as March or April 1911" (*VicG* xxvii). The time of composition is significant, for it is shortly after Lawrence's mother's death in December 1910 and in the midst of Lawrence juggling a frustrating relationship with Helen Corke and his then-engagement to Louie Burrows (Worthen, *EY* 301–2). "The Witch à la Mode" is ostensibly the story of a love triangle involving Bernard Coutts (the Lawrence figure), Winifred Varley (Helen), and Coutts's fiancée Connie (Louie); however, Connie appears only as a shadowy figure in Coutts's mind, waiting for him at the vicarage in Yorkshire, so the triangle is an internal rather than an eternal one. Nevertheless, Connie represents a potential onward movement for Coutts, countering his homecoming urge.

The fact that Lawrence had problems placing this tale and never saw it published in his lifetime suggests some serious weaknesses. Indeed, though there are some fine touches here and there, there seems little point to the story beyond the feeling of homecoming and what happens to that feeling in the course of the narrative. It is notable that in a letter to his sister Ada of 1 March 1911, Lawrence expresses ambivalence about his own anticipated homecoming at Easter. Ada and Arthur Lawrence were moving out of the family home, Lynn Croft, and moving in with Lawrence's married sister, Emily, in the wake of Lydia's death and Arthur's reduced working hours (Harrison, *Life* 54). In the letter, Lawrence asks his sister to "tell me plainly … all that concerns the home," and then, in apparent reply to her question as to whether there is anything he wanted from their old home, he says, "No, there is nothing I want – saving the woman, and, if you like, the black vases, which will always remind me of home: not, God knows, that one wants too much to be reminded thereof" (*1L* 233).

In the story, Coutts has just arrived from France after an absence of ten months, and he evidently left an unresolved relationship with Winifred behind him when he departed. Instead of going on to London, which was his original plan, he chooses to make "concessions to his desires … against his conscience" (*LAH* 54), stay overnight in Croydon, and visit old friends in nearby Purley, the widowed Mrs Braithwaite and her elderly father, Mr Cleveland. Coutts had been a frequent visitor there on Friday evenings, as had Winifred, who has also been invited this night in anticipation that Coutts would show up. Most of the significant plot, such as it is, takes place later at Winifred's home after Coutts has accompanied her there. There is much banter and debate between them and a mutual recognition that their relationship would never have worked out. The climax of the story occurs at the point where Coutts is about to leave and he and Winifred begin to get physically intimate. In the midst of an embrace and with "[a] sudden involuntary blow of his foot" (*LAH* 69), Coutts overturns a gas lamp, starting a small fire that prompts him to escape into the night "with burning-red hands" (*LAH* 70). The burning-red hands may be a literalization of the idea of being caught red-handed, as he is in his own mind's eye, in an act of infidelity, given his engagement to Connie, or possibly the burning hands suggest a pent-up frustration and rage, since, apparently, as in the past, he "knew that she wanted no more of him than that kiss" (*LAH* 69).[11] In any case, the homecoming can hardly be called successful in this case.

From the moment the story opens, we get a sense of Bernard Coutts's pleasurable feeling of coming home, embracing the familiar after being in foreign parts. He may as well stay the night in East Croydon "'where I am used to the place ... I know it so well,' he thought. 'And love it'" (*LAH* 54). The evening star seems to greet him (*LAH* 54). Even the tram-car he boards "ran on familiarly" and, at the terminus, seems to be "like an eager dog, [running] in home, sniffing with pleasure the fume of lights" (*LAH* 54, 55). The Braithwaite residence reinforces this homey feeling: "'You know where to put your things,'" Mrs Braithwaite remarks to the returning friend (*LAH* 55); his visits have been missed. Once Winifred arrives, we see that she and Coutts have had a fraught relationship involving emotions more or less corresponding to the mixed feelings Lawrence expressed at his own impending homecoming. It is a rapprochement, but a tense one, a return to an ambivalence corresponding to the conflicting desire for merger and the fear of engulfment: "after months of separation, they dove-tailed into the same love and hate" (*LAH* 61). Winifred believes that Coutts's engagement with Connie is an uncharacteristic search for a security that he has previously eschewed in favour of exploration, whereas for Lawrence the contrary appears to be the case, given the structure of the story: the engagement to Connie, like Lawrence's to Louie, is an exploration away from home but one that is doomed to fail. Coutts and Winifred have been holding hands along the way, but it seems that both are deliberately stoking their old hostility, perhaps to lessen the pain of the definitive break sure to come.

The story enacts a return geographically for Coutts, but also a return to a familiar relationship before he embarks on consolidating his new one. At Winifred's, Coutts feels at home and a sense of freedom. He goes upstairs to wash his hands, and, while doing that, thinks of the contrast between the two women. He senses that his betrothed will bore him in the long run and admits to himself his dangerous fascination with Winifred. Adumbrating the blaze at the end of the story, Coutts thinks that he and she "really played with fire" (*LAH* 64). He is at a fulcrum point between an emotional rapprochement and an advance to the new. Back downstairs, he sinks into his usual chair. The homey feeling for Lawrence here seems to be expressed by an indirect reference to Lydia Lawrence. Twice we read that Winifred's eyes are dark blue and heavy (*LAH* 65), often a cryptic reference in Lawrence to his own mother, as R.E. Pritchard, to my knowledge, was the first to suggest in a parenthetical aside (25).[12] Both characters admit that any relationship between them would not be a success, and then at the point of Coutts leaving, they have the intimate embrace. It is Winifred who ends the rapprochement; at least Coutts feels it is: "Already she had had enough ... as she lay in his arms, she was gradually dismissing him" (*LAH* 69). The fire that precipitates the final break is, like Winifred's eyes, "a bluish hedge of flame" and "blue, with a yellow tongue" (*LAH* 69), and, as she clutches Coutts in fear, Winifred "almost strangled him" (*LAH* 69), an ominous sign for the relationship.

If anything, "Intimacy," the earliest version of the story, published for the first time in 2009 in the Cambridge edition of Lawrence's work, emphasizes the feeling of homecoming even more than does "The Witch à la Mode," and this earlier version of Coutts seems even more in need of rapprochement to the security of home. Sounding a bit like Paul Morel at the end of *Sons and Lovers* (whose final chapter is entitled "Derelict"), he expresses the need for stability (as he does in "Witch") but adds here, "'I am anchored to nothing ... I merely drift like a derelict with this current and that'" (*VicG* 131). In addition, the sense of the fear of re-engulfment is more pronounced in "Intimacy" than in the later version; the Winifred character, here called Margaret, does not send dismissive signals during the embrace, and Coutts deliberately rather than "involuntarily" sends the lamp crashing down. In both versions, Bernard Coutts returns to a home of sorts, to a would-be lover who has been left behind, and makes a break. The rapprochement story features a very strong desire to go back to the familiar and an equally powerful resolve to get beyond, to make a break and embrace the unfamiliar. Home has its attractions, like the black vases of Lynn Croft Lawrence wrote about, but it is dangerous in its regressive appeal for the sojourning individual.

The final stage of Lawrence's attempts to come to terms with the maternal, seen most clearly in later works such as "Mother and Daughter," "The Lovely Lady," and "The Blue Moccasins," reflects a desire for a kind of literary revenge on the mother figure on behalf of a Lawrence who is now beyond mere conscious realization and, justified or not, has become more and more resentful of the psychological wounding his close attachment to Lydia Lawrence inflicted on him. In "Education of the People" (written in 1920 in the form we now have), he would go so far as to say: "There is the devil in mothers ... babies should invariably be taken away from their modern mothers and given ... to rather stupid fat women who can't be bothered with them. There should be a league for the prevention of maternal love, as there is a society for the prevention of cruelty to animals" (*RDP* 121). And a good deal of *Fantasia of the Unconscious* can be read as a sometimes savage critique of the way his mother brought him up.[13]

The corresponding homecoming stories naturally bear the impress of this development. The figure of the defeated mother suggests Lawrence's need to express a stage in life where he has attained freedom from the iniquitous aspects of the maternal bond, although the very thoroughness of the defeat depicted may be a protesting-too-much that throws into question any suggestion that his psychic liberation could be anything but tenuous. Like a former atheist turned proselytizing convert, Lawrence seems to put great energy into these stories, but the result is not always convincing. In *St Mawr*, for instance, the otherwise fine portrayal of Mrs Witt is distorted by the author's determination to do mothers down. She is a mother who stubbornly fights to get her way and yet unaccountably wishes to embrace defeat. We read at one point that "she would have been glad at last to be defeated by it [something indestructible in men]. That was the point. She really wanted to be defeated, in her own eyes. And nobody had ever defeated her" (*SM* 100). Readers will be forgiven for their skepticism on this point.

In "Mother and Daughter," written in mid-1928 (*VG* xix), Mrs Bodoin, after many years of companionship and a close if sometimes testy relationship with her daughter, Virginia, finds herself jettisoned in an almost gleeful manner by that daughter. Virginia's determined efforts to free herself of her mother's influence in this story owe a great deal to Lawrence's evolving views on his own mother and his continuing attempts to liberate himself of her posthumous influence even as he ironically continues to return compulsively to the attachment in his imagination. Tired of her mother's interference in her relationships with young men, Virginia finally opts for the grandfatherly Arnault, who is more than a match for Mrs Bodoin and who sees, "first and foremost, the child" in Virginia (*VG* 117). It is apparent that Lawrence's earlier experience of his mother's emotional influence on his own love life plays into Virginia's actions, and the fact that Virginia, in effect, switches her allegiance from her mother to a father figure reflects Lawrence's changed perspective on both of his parents. Where Mrs Witt supposedly wished in vain to be defeated, in "Mother and Daughter" the definitive statement of defeat is much more persuasive: "Her mother was beaten" (*VG* 120). Moynahan has characterized the mother in stories like this one as "the strong-minded, aging woman who has fastened herself parasitically onto someone younger and less clever than herself" (179), an exaggeration perhaps but one that indicates how far Lawrence has come in the portrayal of mothers.

The eponymous lady in "The Lovely Lady" (written in 1927), Pauline Attenborough, is just as thoroughly overcome as Mrs Bodoin. She is a wealthy, cultivated widow in her seventies who has maintained a youthful appearance and considers her life to be her "work of art" (*WWRA* 256). But appearances belie the almost parasitic nature of her youthfulness (to use Moynahan's word): her vivacity is bought, so to speak, at the expense of the vitality of her family. She is described on the last page as "a woman hardened to her own will: she never lives, she only knows what it is to force life" (*WWRA* 274). Residing with her are a son, Robert, and a niece on her husband's side, Cecilia (Ciss), who is dependent on her charity. Pauline is an unreliable mother to Robert, sometimes generous with money, sometimes mean, so that "[h]e never knew exactly where he was" (*WWRA* 246). Instead of the mother being attuned to her son, he is constantly alert to her needs, much as Paul Morel is to his mother's in the earlier *Sons and Lovers*: "And Robert was always on the *qui vive* to attend to her. It was as if his mother absorbed all his faculties" (*WWRA* 248). As for Cecilia, Pauline treats her with courteous contempt. Altogether, Pauline tyrannizes the other two, who, it turns out, are attracted to one another.

Ciss sees Pauline as an obstacle to what she hopes could be a fulfilling life with Robert, while Robert himself will make no move, for "[h]is will was prostrate ... almost prostituted to his mother's will" so that "he could never shake off his mother. He could never even think of it" (*WWRA* 250). When, purely by chance, Ciss discovers that Pauline harbours guilty secrets to do with her two sons (one has died young), she uses that knowledge to torment her without Pauline realizing what is actually going on.[14] Her famous loveliness crumples almost overnight, and she soon dies. The word "murder" is bandied about in the story, and Ellis is justified in comparing Ciss's subtle and intuitive attacks on Pauline to Henry Grenfel's tree-felling killing of Banford in *The Fox*

(*DG* 344), except that where Henry's goal is to rid himself of a rival for the mother figure, Ciss's is to eliminate the mother herself, thereby removing the obstacle to her own happiness. As Ellis also suggests, the "leisured" class setting of this story, so far removed from Lawrence's actual background, tends to obscure an intense authorial investment in the characters and any analogy with Lawrence's evolving attitude to his mother. Pauline feels she may have driven her son Henry to an early grave by interfering in his marriage plans, and, for Ellis, Henry's death is a reimagining of the death of William Morel and of Lawrence's brother Ernest (*DG* 344). Altogether, "The Lovely Lady" "confirms the hardening of Lawrence's heart against his mother" and "suggests that he was now blaming Lydia Lawrence more bitterly for the man he had become ... and doubting that she had cared for him with anything like the fervor with which he had been devoted to her" (*DG* 345).

In "The Blue Moccasins," Lawrence's last completed short story (*VG* xliii), we see how Lawrence's resentment of his mother's overwhelming influence on his young life and her interference in his romantic attachments lingers almost two decades after her death. The centrality of the colour blue here is the key indicator of his emotional involvement in what he is writing, and the fantasy of the thoroughly defeated mother figure points to a continuing struggle with his insuperable childhood attachment to Lydia Lawrence. While there are countless Lawrence characters with blue eyes, in this case, the link between the blue-eyed Lina McLeod and Lawrence's mother seems definite. As we have seen (see note 12 of this chapter), Lawrence tended to associate blue with his mother, and that was especially so when she was on her deathbed and the blue of her eyes seemed to intensify: "They seemed to grow darker as she came to the edge of death / And I could not bear her look upon me," he writes in the early poem "Bereavement" (*Poems* 1439, ll. 6–7). In *Sons and Lovers*, after Paul has struggled home from his violent encounter with Baxter Dawes, he wakes up next morning and "found his mother looking at him. Her blue eyes! – they were all he wanted to see" (*SL* 411).

"The Blue Moccasins" depicts a marriage between the forty-seven-year-old Lina McLeod and the twenty-four-year-old Percy Barlow. Lina is quite obviously a mother figure to her husband; unlike both March in *The Fox* and Matilda in "Hadrian," she is literally old enough to be her husband's mother. Lawrence emphasizes her "long, thick white hair, done perfectly" (*VG* 167), and, in keeping with a symbolic incest taboo, the sexual side of their relationship quickly dies out (*VG* 170). A crisis in the marriage arises over the pair of "lovely turquoise-blue" moccasins that Lina had purchased years earlier in New Mexico and has hung up in Percy's room. The blue of the moccasins is repeatedly associated by the narrator and by Percy with Lina, with her "very blue" or "vivid blue" or "forget-me-not blue eyes" (*VG* 170, 177). When Lina wants the moccasins for a still-life she wishes to paint and finds them missing, Percy denies all knowledge of their whereabouts, but in fact he has taken them as costume props for a local play he is acting in with the flirtatious, young Alice Howells. They are to adorn her feet in the play in which she is the romantic heroine to Percy's hero. When Lina arrives unexpectedly to watch the theatrical production, she discovers not only Percy's lie about the moccasins but also the obviously intimate feelings between her husband and Alice. Lina suffers "shame and torment" in viewing the performance (*VG* 174), and she seems vanquished at the end of the story even as she leaves with the confiscated moccasins. In fact, Lawrence revised the ending to emphasize precisely that defeat, as we can see in a comparison with the deleted early manuscript-version ending (*VG* 248–50).[15]

The stories of homecoming that I would group in this third stage of Lawrence's developing attitude to the complicated emotional mix related to the maternal display a range from disappointment and rationalization to gleeful revenge. Two homecoming stories involving Jessie Chambers, "The Shades of Spring" and "The Shadow in the Rose Garden," belong to the former end of the range in the process of maternal reckoning. In them, unsurprisingly, the roles of mother/wife/lover become conflated. "The Shades of Spring" describes a dynamic similar to some of the other Jessie stories, but this time the Lawrence figure, John Adderley Syson, is recently married to someone else while the Jessie character, Hilda Millership, has also moved on and, unbeknownst to Syson, is more or less engaged to a gamekeeper, Arthur Pilbeam. There is a strong sense of nostalgia here, as in so many of the homecoming stories, but whereas, in Mahler's terms, rapprochement functions as a reassurance that the caregiving attachment is still there if needed, Lawrence seems by the end of this story to want to reassure himself that the break with the past was inevitable and necessary and that the attachment never was what it seemed to be. This conclusion comes across mostly as a rationalization, but it is also an early indication of Lawrence moving toward a realization that his mother was not what he had believed her to be.

The note of estrangement in "The Shades of Spring" is sounded early on even as the feeling of homecoming initially enlivens Syson. As he approaches his old path to Willeywater Farm (based on the Chambers' Haggs Farm), Syson is seen by a watching blacksmith and his mate as a "trespasser" (*PO* 98). There has been an absence of six or eight years since Syson has been this way, but he feels that "[h]e was back in the eternal" (*PO* 98). He is "extraordinarily glad" as "he had returned to the country of his past, and he found it waiting for him, unaltered" (*PO* 98). The seeming lack of change, so emphasized in Syson's reaction to the landscape he is once again traversing after a long absence, represents a rapprochement to a source of security. As with Gerald Crich's worship of the mechanical principle in *Women in Love*, redolent for him of security and permanence, changelessness in the landscape, which is so satisfying for Syson here, symbolizes the reliability in caregiving that alone can give a child a secure attachment. But Syson is soon disabused of the illusion: things have indeed changed, and nothing represents that change so obviously as the keeper who now "was standing a few yards in front, barring the way" (*PO* 98) like some archangel blocking the return to paradise and as if Syson were indeed a trespasser. The encounter startles him out of his complacency of nostalgia. To the keeper, Syson is an "intruder," perhaps even more so when Pilbeam finds out that he is the man who used to be involved with the woman he himself is now courting (*PO* 99).

Given Syson's marital status, the homecoming is under false pretenses, so to speak, but he seems to need to return in order to move on. It is of course easier, if still painful, to be the one who leaves than the one left behind: "this was his past, the country he had abandoned, and it hurt him to see it so beautiful" (*PO* 101). Once Syson learns of the relationship between Hilda and the keeper, his self-satisfied bubble of touring the scenes of his past connections is burst: "What a fool he was! What god-forsaken folly it all was!" (*PO* 101), but it is not any god who is the forsaking agent. In spite of the bravado of his having abandoned this place and in particular Hilda, Syson seems to have needed the return to a state of attachment as it had been. He may be free to explore new attachments, but he seems to want the base of security from the past to remain unchanged, there for his reassurance whenever needed.

The feeling at the heart of estrangement, that one does not belong, undercuts the hoped-for rapprochement that nostalgia promises in the very urge to come home in the first place. The feeling of alienation continues and increases when, in a scene very similar to one in "A Modern Lover," Syson enters the well-known farmhouse and finds the family, with whom he had once been so familiar and friendly, at their dinner. They welcome him rather coldly and assume that he has become far too refined for the old intimacy to be appropriate. This rebuff hurts Syson, who "loved the place extraordinarily" (*PO* 102). As for Hilda, "[h]er brief, sure speech, her distant bearing, were unfamiliar to him"

(*PO* 103). This barrier to a successful return to a sense of surety is similar to the dark side of the uncanny: the familiar made strange.

Although Hilda is friendly enough, even to the point of being willing to revive an element of their old closeness, the feeling of estrangement has now overcome nostalgia, and, in Syson's mind at least, she is a different person from the Hilda he had known or thought he had known: "He knew quite well what she had been for him. And gradually he was realising that she was something quite other, and always had been" (*PO* 104). In the onward movement toward individuation, it is comforting to know that any regrets about a past attachment left behind are unjustified. And so Lawrence has the Jessie/Hilda figure take part in the rationalization that she had never been what Lawrence/Syson had taken her to be: "She saw the scales were fallen from him, and at last he was going to see her as she was ... He would not love her, and he would know he never could have loved her" (*PO* 104). She is generous and honest enough to admit that Pilbeam has his limitations while Syson could create a sense of wonder about the natural world (*PO* 107), but, at the same time, she complains that "'[y]ou took me away from myself ... You bullied me'" (*PO* 108). So the story turns into more of a leave-taking than a homecoming as Syson must admit that he did not appreciate Hilda for the real person she was. As we saw in connection with the internal working model in the Introduction, Syson concludes that the Hilda he believed was the Beatrice to his Dante had existed only in his own mind.

The keeper re-enters the scene, and the three of them walk toward a gate that would seem to represent the boundary now definitively created between Syson and Hilda, and, as in many of these stories, there is a gesture toward masculine identification. The two men feel a kinship "almost like friends" (*PO* 110). This could have been the end of the story, but Lawrence adds an odd coda. There is little doubt that Syson has been hurt if not shocked by his return to the scene of his youth. Using an incongruous image for the natural beauty that Syson finds himself surrounded by, Lawrence underscores the pain: "He felt as if it were underground, like the fields of monotone hell ... Inside his breast was a pain like a wound" (*PO* 110). He seems to use the gate and the edge of the woods to demarcate his current self in contrast to the one he has come back to look at. And he rationalizes his pain away: "He knew now it never had been true, that which was between him and her, not for a moment" (*PO* 110). Though this is a story of a rapprochement that fails in reviving the old feeling of attachment, the failure itself may be a salutary one in terms of separation-individuation.

In "The Shadow in the Rose Garden," the homecomer is a woman, and the homecoming is something of a disaster. The overt presence of a mother figure is very slight, although, as the title may be taken to intimate, there is a shadowy one. The genesis of the short story goes back to August 1907, when the Lawrence family was vacationing at Robin Hood's Bay in Yorkshire with Jessie Chambers in tow (*VicG* xix, 219). The earliest version of the tale, "The Vicar's Garden," features a first-person narrator and recounts a young man and young woman (standing in for Lawrence and Jessie) visiting a beautiful garden at a vicarage, which, they later learn, is inhabited only by the vicar's mad son and the son's minder. Lawrence drastically re-imagined and revised the story, probably in August 1911 (*PO* xlv), now using a third-person narrator, retaining a few key elements from the original tale, but turning it into a story of homecoming. It was first published in March 1914 in the American magazine *Smart Set* (*VicG* xx), and then revised again for publication in November 1914 by Duckworth in the volume *The Prussian Officer and Other Stories*. The fact that the story began as a first-person narrative and was based on Lawrence's own experiences suggests that, indirect as the connection may be in the final version, Lawrence is emotionally invested in the tale.

It is the unnamed woman in the story who has insisted that the couple holiday at the seaside town where she had lived years earlier because, she says, "'I am at home here – it's not like a strange seaside place to me'" (*PO* 122). In the *Smart Set* version of the story, the husband, Frank, objects, in words similar to Cyril Mersham's thought in "A Modern Lover," that "'there's nothing as miserable as going back to places where you used to live'" (*VicG* 13). The difference in sentiment signals the tension between the two of them but also the dichotomy between moving on and looking back typical of these stories and characteristic of the rapprochement stage of attachment.[16] Lawrence's own ambivalence between the urge to return and the desire to move on, then, is split between the two main characters in this story, and the division reflects their positions in their marriage: she dissatisfied and longing for a past love and he hoping for a stronger commitment from her than she has shown him to this point.

Near the beginning of the tale, in both versions, Frank views himself in the mirror in a self-satisfied if perhaps narcissistic way. In the earlier version of the story, his smart jacket sits on "a healthy body" (*VicG* 11), whereas in the final version it sits "upon a confident body" (*PO* 121), the latter emphasizing his positive self-image.[17] In terms of the primary attachment relationship, however, the mirror may suggest his need to provide his own positive mirroring in the absence of any meaningful acknowledgment from his wife: "She looked apart from him and his world, gazing away to the sea" (*PO* 121). This lack of attunement suggests a maternal narcissism whereby the caregiver uses the child as a mirror to reinforce her own deficient sense of self. The establishment of an integral sense of self in a child, on the contrary, requires a supportive caregiver who is the mirror for that child.[18] Although Frank is anxious for her approval and recognition, unlike many Lawrence male protagonists, he is not desperate. Schapiro astutely interprets the story as one of a mutual failure at positive mirroring and points out how important the motif of vision and eyes is here, as elsewhere in Lawrence's writing. The emphasis "draws its emotional and psychological force from the eye contact, the subtle but profound attunement play of early mother-child interactions" that lays the foundation for "a sense of subjective self" (58). So it is significant that when the woman enters the vicarage garden she touches some roses "as a mother sometimes fondles the hand of her child" (*PO* 125). Her affectionate motherliness, though, is not meant for her husband. For him, she is the embodiment of the unreliable mother who fails to offer unconditional love.

The wife believes that her great love of years ago, the gentlemanly vicar's son, Archie, has died, but she wishes, nevertheless, to return to the location she associates with their passion of the past, the garden of the vicarage. She discovers that he is actually alive when he suddenly appears and approaches her, without, however, any recognition in his eyes. As in "The Vicar's Garden," he is quite mad. And the chance meeting throws the woman into a psychological crisis: "She had to bear his eyes. They gleamed on her, but with no intelligence" (*PO* 127). The virtually abandoned vicarage – it seems "sterile ... as if it were still used but not inhabited" (*PO* 125) – becomes the emblem of both the vicar's son's vacant mind and the woman's feelings of being abandoned, in effect, for the second time, by the lack of recognition. Schapiro points out that she is wearing a white muslin dress that makes her blend into the background of the white roses she sits among: "the frozen center, the lack of authentic self-experience, the feeling of one's existence lapsing into a white nothingness recall, for instance, Mrs Morel's thwarted emotional life and her swooning into the white lilies, as well as the frigid lives and snowy deaths of Gerald in *Women in Love* and Cathcart in 'The Man Who Loved Islands'" (58). Seeing Archie as a "lunatic" (*PO* 127) affects the woman deeply: "The whole world was deranged" (*PO* 126). She leaves the garden "blindly" and returns to the cottage "as if some membrane had been torn in two in her, so that she was not an entity that could think and feel" (*PO* 128).

The wife's metaphorical blindness makes impossible any recognition of Frank or his needs when she returns, so that he is thwarted and exasperated. He feels that "she was no more sensible to him than if he did not exist ... He did not exist for her, except as an irritant" (*PO* 128). He realizes that she has never really loved him and had "taken him on sufferance" (*PO* 129). The woman in the tale finally if reluctantly tells her husband what has happened in the garden, and he resents the fact that she kept her affair with Archie a secret from him all this time. He may be named Frank, but she has not been frank with him. So although the husband is attuned enough to his wife to recognize that something is seriously amiss, the story ends with both characters feeling stymied, unsatisfied, and unrecognized in a marriage that is bound to founder. The breach between them at the end is far greater than in the *Smart Set* version. Perhaps the woman's wish to return was in the interests of moving on, but the past has had such a hold on her that, even before her discovering the vicar's son alive and mad, there were troubling signs. The only positive indication for the two of them at the end is the mutual recognition of each other's boundaries: "He could not go near her. It would be a violation to each of them to be brought in to contact with the other" (*PO* 132).

In this tale, Lawrence may be imagining aspects of his parents' relationship, particularly the feeling in retrospect that, in marrying Arthur Lawrence, his mother was settling for "Second-Best," as the title of a companion story in the *Prussian Officer* volume would have it.[19] The woman in "The Shadow in the Rose Garden" is not wholly satisfied in her marriage to a working-class man, "a laboring electrician in the mine," who comments, "'You might as well be in pit as in bed on a morning like this'" (*PO* 129, 122). Given the physical description of the husband, "rather small, but alert and vigorous" (*PO* 121), and his interest in examining a painting hanging in the cottage, I would suggest that he is an amalgam of elements of both D.H. Lawrence himself and Arthur Lawrence. The landlady at the cottage, Mrs Coates, with her "china-blue eyes" (*PO* 122), is the only obvious mother figure in the story. She notes the class discrepancy in the couple: the man and woman are about the same height, but "he's not her equal otherwise" (*PO* 122). However, if we regard the couple as representative of Lawrence's parents, then the wife's lack of recognition of the husband contains elements of Lawrence's shadowy realization of his mother's narcissistic regard and conditional love. The husband's belated realization that his wife took him on sufferance reflects Lawrence's re-evaluation of the kind of conditional approval he had from his mother.

Since the novella *The Virgin and the Gipsy* features a symbolic homecoming, a defeated mother figure, and a turn to the masculine, it belongs to this third stage of Lawrence's attitude to the maternal, though the rich material of this work encompasses so much more. The novella was written about Frieda's Weekley family rather than Lawrence's childhood family; nevertheless, it reveals aspects of his own ongoing struggle with early attachments. There are several mother figures in the novella, but it is the absent mother who deserted her husband and children, as Frieda had done, that is a kind of black hole in the centre of the narrative distorting the orbits of all the relationships and attachments. The two Saywell daughters, Lucille and Yvette, to a certain extent idealize their runaway mother with her vitality and glamorousness, as they recall "their real home, the Vicarage in the south," but they also remember her "fearful selfishness" and the sense that she was "not very dependable" as a mother (*VG* 7). Cynthia, then, though she never appears in the story, joins the legion of Lawrence's unreliable mothers in his fiction, despite the fact that she is modelled on the very woman that Lawrence himself enticed away from her family. As Nancy Paxton argues, unlike the real-life scenario involving the visit of Frieda's daughter Barby, "Yvette is not given a similar opportunity to reunite with her mother in the novella," as it "register[s] shifts in [Lawrence's] view of his father as well as his mother" (59).

At one point, the protagonist, the now nineteen-year-old Yvette, meets a Mrs Fawcett (who styles herself Mrs Eastwood). She becomes for a time a stand-in of sorts for Yvette's mother until Yvette's father, the rector, nastily discourages the connection, even vaguely threatening his daughter with a "criminal-lunacy asylum" for her supposed moral depravity in what is obviously a displaced fit of anger at his wife's desertion (*VG* 60).[20] The rector's rectitude is all on the surface, for he seems to harbour a secret, repressed incestuous desire for his daughter Yvette. After he has scolded her over a rather trivial matter to do with money, the virginal Yvette feels "crushed, and deflowered and humiliated" (*VG* 28), in contrast to her feeling of safety with the gipsy even when he and she are nakedly embracing for warmth in the aftermath of the flood.[21] So Yvette seems to be bereft of any adequate parental model until she meets the gipsy man. Mrs Eastwood, like Frieda in real life and like Mrs Saywell of this story, has left her husband and children for a younger man, a Major Eastwood, and is waiting for her divorce to be finalized so that she can marry him (thus the rector's particular aversion to her).[22] Both the absent Cynthia and the forbidden Mrs Eastwood offer ambiguous modelling for Yvette but come across as strong and unbowed older females. We do have a defeated mother figure, however, in the Mater, a character based on Frieda's erstwhile mother-in-law, Agnes Weekley. The protagonist's grandmother rather than mother, the Mater is nevertheless a mother figure in the story as indicated by the family moniker for her, and the revenge Lawrence takes on this mother figure is terrible, so much so that he decided not to publish the story in his lifetime (Ellis, *DG* 288).[23]

The Mater is one of Lawrence's great comic-satiric creations. Balbert aptly uses the term "Dickensian caricature" to describe Lawrence's technique in portraying her (*Marriage* 215). She is grotesque in body and habits and determined to maintain her power in the family, which "was her own extended ego" (*VG* 9). Most significantly, she is a virtual parody of an attuned mother, using her intuitive understanding, especially of her son, the rector, for manipulation and to get her own way: "the Mater knew his weaknesses to a hair's-breadth. She knew them, and she traded on them by turning them into decorations for him, for his character" (*VG* 8). With this description of the Mater's "trad[ing]" and "decorations," Lawrence ironically calls to mind the Mater's oppositional counterpart, the gipsy man, who is a tradesman selling his decorated household goods. Yvette sees through her grandmother's power games: she "saw the stony, implacable will-to-power in the old and motherly-seeming Granny" (*VG* 16) and eventually comes to despise her: "It was Granny whom she came to detest with all her soul" (*VG* 63). The flood that kills the Mater and destroys the rectory is symbolic of Yvette's baptism into a new life by near-drowning and representative of her anger at the soul-destroying propriety of the Saywell family. (The surname references a hypocritical minor figure in John Bunyan's *The Pilgrim's Progress*.)[24] The defeat of the mother figure here is complete.[25] The flood is also the fulfilment of Yvette's wishes. Though she maintains a hard kernel of selfhood when the gipsy first stares at her, "the surface of her body seemed to turn to water," and later, just before the Eastwoods arrive at the gipsy camp to break the spell, Yvette "was only aware of the dark, strange effluence of him bathing her limbs, washing her at last purely will-less" (*VG* 24, 47).

The Virgin and the Gipsy is a homecoming story in the sense that Yvette has been searching for a real home since her mother absconded. She has variously fantasized family-romance scenarios including her childhood home in the south and then life with the Eastwoods. Now, while actually at home in the rectory, she indulges in another family-romance fantasy and imagines herself back in the gipsy encampment that she had visited some weeks earlier, as if it were her spiritual home: "And the man in the green jersey made it home to her. Just to be where he was, that was to be at home. The caravans, the brats, the other women:

everything was natural to her, her home, as if she had been born there" (*VG* 68). Here, obviously, the imagined homecoming is not to a mother but to a lover/father figure whose apparently chaste and life-saving naked embrace contrasts with Saywell's unconscious incestuous desire.[26]

In the uncompleted "The Woman Who Wanted to Disappear," Lawrence's last fictional work (*VG* xliii), the homecomer is likewise a woman, but one whose coming home begins with leaving home. It is quite remarkable that as late as January 1929,[27] Lawrence was still imagining in fictional form the temptations and satisfactions of homecoming, although, as with "The Flying Fish," illness may have been a prompting motive. The homecomer here is a wealthy woman with a husband and children who simply announces one day to her seemingly indifferent spouse, Peter, that she would like to disappear for a year and then promptly leaves home. The narrator tells us that what she is trying to do is "to get right away – from herself, really" (*VG* 252). She goes back to "her mother's country," the place "she had known by heart as a child" (*VG* 252). After a false start at an expensive mountain hotel, she finds that what she is searching for is a place "where she should become her own rare and magical self – her *true* self, that nobody knew, least of all she herself" (*VG* 252). In other words, like the wife in "The Shadow in the Rose Garden," she is looking for the authentic self that she has either not achieved through her marriage or that she has had stifled by it.

The woman ends up in a dark forest that gives her the sense of homecoming even as the fragment of a story takes on the characteristics of a fairy tale. It is a coming home that is both spatial, to a home country, and temporal, to childhood. Even so, or perhaps therefore, she feels alone and frightened "just as she did when she was a child" (*VG* 253). She now feels "the thrill and delight of her childhood, the glamour of the forest!" (*VG* 253). Her car breaks down and, in something of a panic, she continues on foot. Like Alvina Houghton in *The Lost Girl*, the unnamed woman realizes the Lawrentian paradox that she must lose herself to find herself, disappear in order to appear or be apparent – to herself and others. As Birkin puts it in the "Class-room" chapter of *Women in Love*, "'You've got to learn not-to-be, before you can come into being'" (*WL* 44), something the woman has intuited vaguely in her otherwise unaccountable desire to disappear, for she is decidedly not suicidal.[28] She finally finds a little wooden house in a clearing, a forest-keeper's hut. She is cold and frightened, and then, accosted by the forester himself, she is invited into the hut just as it is about to rain. The man lights the fuel in the stove, and the woman slowly warms up. There the manuscript ends.

The protagonist here carries within her Lawrence's strong feelings about his childhood and his home. The male or father figure is split into Peter, the husband, and the forester: the first is indifferent to her needs; the second, whose association with darkness and warmth harkens back to Lawrence's working-class father, caters to them and intuits them. It is the difference between an unreliable and narcissistic caregiver and an attuned, mirroring one. The fairy-tale atmosphere merely underscores the wish-fulfilment aspect of the tale: instead of the evil, devouring, forest-dwelling witch-mother of "Hansel and Gretel," we have the provident, good, forester father, and instead of food, what he provides is shelter and warmth. Lawrence is returning in his mind to his childhood to repossess the needed emotional nurturance he once thought he had, but he now imagines that the nurturing is provided by a father figure. He is finally able toward the end of his life, albeit in somewhat disguised form, to accept the sustenance that had been offered him by Arthur Lawrence, a proffering dramatized as early as the warm milk offered to Paul by Walter Morel toward the end of *Sons and Lovers*.

The Escaped Cock features an even more definitive turn to the paternal. It is a fictional depiction of a Jesus figure after his return to life that taps into what is perhaps the ultimate story of homecoming in Western culture, a return from the dead.[29] The unnamed man of Lawrence's story, indeed, exits the tomb and returns to some of the people from his messianic past and repeatedly goes back to the garden where he has been entombed. Resurrection is a theme seen elsewhere in Lawrence – in "The Horse-Dealer's Daughter," for example. But what is interesting in *The Escaped Cock* for our purposes here is that the man who died chooses his father over his mother, and Lawrence departs from the biblical source to make explicit his intention, at least in Part 1 (the second part was written later), to renounce the earthly mother in favour of the heavenly father. Meeting Madeleine (Mary Magdalene) in the garden for the second time, he sees that she has brought his mother and a woman called Joan with her. As the editors of the Cambridge University Press edition remark: "There is no suggestion in the Gospels that Christ's mother was ever at the tomb" (*VG* 276n). Madeleine urges the man to go to his mother, but he refuses: "'I must go to my Father,' he said. 'And you will leave us! – There is your mother!' she cried, turning round with the old anguish, which yet was sweet to her. 'But now I must ascend to my Father,' he said" (*VG* 136), in a final turn from maternal to paternal care.

Conclusion

THE OTHER SIDE OF OTHERNESS

> As we give greater value to the preoedipal world, to a more flexible acceptance of difference, we can see that difference is only truly established when it exists in tension with likeness, when we are able to recognize the other in ourselves.
> Jessica Benjamin, *The Bonds of Love* (169)

> The man who, as he grew older, increasingly and at times stridently insisted in his writing on the vital importance of experience of "the other," did so out of a very fearful knowledge of what the opposite experience was like.
> John Worthen, *D.H. Lawrence: The Early Years 1885–1912* (*EY* 266)

> To be sincere is to remember that I am I; and that the other man is not me.
> D.H. Lawrence, *Studies in Classic American Literature* (*SCAL* 27)

D.H. Lawrence's sensitivity to the natural world is extraordinary, and his ability to describe it in striking and memorable words of prose is arguably as great as any other writer in the history of the British novel. Whether he is applying his botanist-eyed interest to describing a flowering plant or his astonishing poetic power to the crashing of waves on a beach "like a rush of white serpents, then slipping back with a hiss that fell into silence for a second, leaving the sand of granulated silver" (*K* 340), Lawrence can take one's breath away. His keen emotional insights, earned from ruthless self-examination and penetrating observation of others, make him a psychological writer with few peers. As a philosopher, however, he can be hectoring, tiresome, and frequently unconvincing, so that when a philosophical reflection enters his fiction – often at tedious length and to digressive effect – it is usually to the work's detriment. One possible exception to this general rule is the concept of otherness, a kind of touchstone for Lawrence (perhaps most obviously in his poetry) that by general consensus represents one of the finest products of his thinking. Neil Roberts calls Lawrence "a significant theorist of otherness" (*Travel* 21) while M. Elizabeth Sargent and Garry Watson have written a thoughtful appreciation that places Lawrence's ideas about otherness in the context of thinkers who have "celebrated difference and heterogeneity" such as Mikhail Bakhtin, Martin Buber, and Emmanuel Levinas (410, 415). However, the enduring power of Lawrentian otherness may be explained not so much by its theoretical basis as by the fact that, in addition to its philosophical aspect, it is closely aligned with the nature description and the psychological insights that are his real strengths.

In concluding this study, I want to sketch out how the Lawrentian concept of otherness might be related to the central feature of the psychological aspects of his writing: the complex depictions of attachment. The two are interconnected in the very basic sense that there must be an other for an interpersonal attachment with the self to take place at all, and, as this study has detailed, a viable sense of self is possible only with the recognition of the other. Otherness, then, enters into the very core of Lawrence's paradoxical expression of the teeter-totter emotional swings attendant upon the desire to merge with an other and the countervailing need to be separate from that other in order to protect a vulnerable sense of self. In short, if we place Lawrentian otherness within the purview of the attachment paradigm we can better understand its full import, and we can see that there is a personal and defensive component to it. As Sargent and Watson themselves write, "those who are most sensitive to otherness may be precisely the ones who – possibly because of a greater vulnerability on their part – occasionally succumb to irritation with and fear of it" (410). It is not only, as Sargent and Watson suggest, a matter of Lawrence's practice at times failing to live up to his own principle (428); the discrepancy is baked into the very nature of Lawrence's habitual way of coping with his conflicted attachment tendencies.

The Lawrentian concept of otherness is a seemingly simple one. In theory, it is the opposite of bullying. As Lawrence writes in *Fantasia of the Unconscious*, "Most fatal, most hateful of all things is bullying. But what is bullying? It is a desire to superimpose my own will upon another person" (*PFU* 92). Otherness, in contrast, is the refusal to impose one's own ego, needs, knowledge, or perspective on another person, non-human living being, or even object, a respectful determination to eschew domination, a self-effacement deriving from the simple recognition that, as Lawrence puts it in the Hardy essay, "I see a flower, because it is not me. I know a melody, because it is not me. I feel cold, because it is not me" (*STH* 42). But beyond a simple matter of perception, otherness becomes a moral issue for Lawrence: "The essence of morality is the basic desire to preserve the perfect correspondence between the self and the object, to have no trespass and no breach of integrity, nor yet any defaulture in the vitalistic interchange" (*PFU* 27).[1]

In "Introduction to These Paintings" (written in early 1929), Lawrence famously praises Cézanne for his still-life depiction of apples as an honest attempt "to let the apple exist in its own separate entity, without transfusing it with personal emotion. Cézanne's great effort was, as it were, to shove the apple away from him, and let it live of itself" (*LEA* 201). It is very admirable for Cézanne to do so and wonderful for Lawrence to have the perspicacity to perceive what Cézanne did and approve of it. However, while the otherness of the apples may work perfectly well as an aspirational metaphor, the question is, does Cézanne actually do what Lawrence ascribes to him? Is it even possible to do such a thing, or has Cézanne's artistic method become grist to the mill of Lawrence's own outlook? Is Lawrence failing to let Cézanne "exist in [his] own separate entity, without transfusing" his own personal emotion into what he sees in the painter's work? After all, Cézanne is depicting a scene of *nature morte*, which sounds a lot more lifeless than the English equivalent, "still life."[2] The apple cannot "live of itself"; humans have already imposed themselves on it by picking it from its tree. Furthermore, the very idea of appleyness is a human construct. There is no "other" there, merely paint on canvas.

Of course, Lawrence is talking about an attitude that he feels comes through on the canvas, but Cézanne's apples are the product of human imagination. They were painted by someone who was interested in how they look to the human eye and how they might be portrayed. They are witnessed by viewers who might appreciate that certain way of depicting them, and they are written about by a human being, D.H. Lawrence. They are, then, to a greater or lesser extent, humanized, which is to say anthropomorphized, whether we want to think so or not. If they were not, they could hardly be depicted or appreciated through the medium of oil on canvas. This is not in the least to suggest that Lawrence's otherness is a fraudulent concept, merely that it is more complicated than it is sometimes assumed to be. Lawrence may have come closer to his own optimal understanding of otherness several years earlier when, in "Morality and the Novel" (written in mid-1925), he emphasizes that art is about relations between things or between beings rather than about the things themselves and writes of Van Gogh's sunflowers that "[h]is painting does not represent the sunflower itself. We shall never know what the sunflower itself is" (*STH* 171).

In studies of the Lawrentian concept of otherness, there are nuanced differences that seem to depend on where the critic looks, since the term tends to mutate somewhat in parallel with Lawrence's emotional life. Some critics examine the concept primarily in the poetry, where it manifests itself at times in perhaps its purest and least complicated form, while others focus on cultural and racial issues, where otherness may have a somewhat different connotation and genesis, and a third group looks at specific works of fiction in which otherness involves the much messier realm of relationships that develop over time. Going back some fifty years, in her study of Lawrence's poetry, *Acts of Attention* (1971), Sandra M. Gilbert points to the "purity of non-human life" as that which "constituted its chief 'otherness' for [Lawrence]. A peach was fully itself – *en soi* – as a man could never be fully himself" (162), a formulation which hints at a possible source of attraction for Lawrence in the struggle to maintain a selfhood that is "fully itself." David Cavitch's brief article from 1974 defines Lawrentian otherness as "a perfected relatedness with the object world" that has a tendency "to deteriorate into Lawrence's perception of his irremediable solitude" ("Merging" 177), an observation that parallels the double gyre of Lawrentian attachment we have examined in which autonomy can slide over into isolation. Cavitch also recognizes in the poem "Fish" the opposite attachment tendency, a longing "to return to bodily and psychological oneness with a maternal presence" ("Merging" 174). In a much more recent study, Elise Brault-Dreux also looks at non-human otherness in the poems of Lawrence (and Katherine Mansfield). She recognizes that language makes it virtually impossible for "the human poet not to humanize non-human otherness at least a little" (32) but that Lawrence attempts "to avoid the poetic expression of too much knowledge of the other" so that (as she quotes Christopher Pollnitz as arguing) we get "'a deepened sense of separateness for an ultimately unknowable object'" (28, 29).[3] Perhaps Brault-Dreux's most apposite comment (also derived from Pollnitz) is that "it is in facing the otherness of the other that the subject, too, becomes aware of his independent integrity" (29). This last observation comes close to Jessica Benjamin's formulation in the above epigraph, and to Barbara Schapiro's paradox that "the self's sense of its own subjective reality is contingent on recognition of the other's subjectivity, on the other's 'not-me' existence" (80), a key realization in Lawrence's struggle with the paradox of attachment. As Lawrence writes in "Aristocracy" (1925), "When the white cock crows, I do not hear myself, or some anthropomorphic conceit, crowing. I hear the not-me, the voice of the Holy Ghost" (*RDP* 373).

Both Howard J. Booth and Neil Roberts examine Lawrence's otherness from a cultural and racial perspective. According to Booth, Lawrence is open to "an encounter with the 'other' that transforms and changes the self" ("Race" 171), but, at the same time, "there is a fine line between an openness to transformation of the self and a failure to respect the other's difference" ("Race" 173). Booth could have added to the other side of that fine line the fear of the other's difference. Consciously, Lawrence is all for adventure and encounters that change him, but underneath that openness is a terrible anxiety about the prospect of opening up to an other. As we have seen, the Lawrentian self is vulnerable to a feeling of inauthenticity or hollowness whenever there is a major imbalance in attachment terms. Without external confirmation there is no basis for the establishment of a stable internal reality, but, by the same token, as Lawrence came to realize about his upbringing, there is no guarantee that the other will reliably support the needs of the self rather than seeking his or her own validation. Roberts focuses on the travel writing and on the fiction that reflects Lawrence's interactions with the other cultures he encounters, and he traces Lawrence's anxiety about otherness to fears of miscegenation. As many others have done, Roberts recognizes that Lawrence's otherness is most successfully imagined in connection with the non-human world (*Travel* 17). He warns against the "tendency to dismiss Lawrence's engagement with cultural difference as merely a psychological projection," but he also recognizes that "we have good reason to believe that [Lawrence's] complex feelings about cultural otherness were entangled with the family drama that shaped so much else in his life and writings" (*Travel* 30).

When we turn to otherness in the fiction, the depiction of relationships naturally becomes central. In a 1974 study of *The Rainbow* and otherness, T.H. Adamowski argues that, in the fiction at least, "the quality of the otherness of the Other makes itself felt as an attention to the distance between the selves" (60), a description which recalls the incremental reduction of distance between Will and Anna in the sheaves scene of *The Rainbow*. That scene was an early indication of Anna's determination to retain her autonomy and Will's desire to impose his longing for merger without due regard for Anna's otherness. Adamowski recognizes aspects of Lawrentian otherness that are related to the autonomy side of the attachment dilemma: "A concern with the uniqueness of the self always runs the risk of making the Other appear to be either inessential or an eternal adversary" (65). Nevertheless, Lawrence recognized the paradox that "[t]here is no way of being 'true to oneself' that does not involve the Other" (76). John Turner analyzes "The Man Who Loved Islands" as, among other things, a psychological fable, a story "about a man who needed solitude but who lacked the capacity to be alone" ("Capacity" 259), a man stuck, as it were, between the exclusively negative aspects of merger and autonomy and unable to deal with others. Turner helpfully defines loneliness (an alien concept for Lawrence) in terms related to what attachment theorists call the internal working model (see Introduction) and connects it to maternal attachment. According to this understanding, loneliness is a loss of an inner presence (or model) of people and objects, "a breach in the lifelong process of symbolization whereby the particular attachment to the mother's presence is decathected and spread widely throughout the human and natural world" ("Capacity" 261). Lawrence is highly ambivalent about encounters with others: "He was drawn toward other people, and he was impelled to reject them," a conflict Turner traces to "an over-cossetted childhood in which passion was disallowed" ("Capacity" 284–5). Finally, T.H. McCabe, in a study of "Odour of Chrysanthemums," which McCabe sees as Lawrence's earliest explicit exploration of otherness, understands the concept in an almost tautological manner as the simple recognition that all other life is "beyond the self and inside all other living things" (149), a recognition that is necessary perhaps only as a bulwark against a tendency to solipsism.

In the various pieces written about Lawrentian otherness, the same passages from his poetry, essays, and fiction tend to come up repeatedly. Certain poems, especially from the volumes *Look! We Have Come Through!* and *Birds, Beasts and Flowers*, are often cited and with good reason: in particular, there are references to "Wedlock," "New Heaven and Earth," "Manifesto," "Fish," and to some of what I would call the abject animal poems such as "Man and Bat," "Mosquito," and "Snake." As often as not, otherness in these poems is reactive. Toward the end of "Wedlock," for example, the joy of merger gives way to an insistence on separation or otherness:

> I am so glad there is always you beyond my scope,
> Something that stands over,
> Something I shall never be
> (*Poems* 202, ll. 77–9)

In the often-quoted "New Heaven and Earth," otherness is an escape from "the maniacal horror" of solipsism – "everything was tainted with myself" – (*Poems* 211, l. 27; 210, l. 15), and the discovery of otherness is connected to a resurrection to a new heaven and earth:

> I put out my hand in the night, one night, and my hand
> touched that which was verily not me
> verily it was not me.
> ... it was the unknown.
> (*Poems* 212, ll. 78–80, 86)

"Manifesto" similarly portrays a speaker relieved to discover the separate other: "she is all beyond me, / she is all not-me, ultimately" (*Poems* 219, ll. 106–7). The poem also contains one of the most hopeful iterations of an ideal attachment that combines security with individuality: "two of us, unutterably distinguished, and in unutterable conjunction" (*Poems* 220, l. 139), but that description is only an aspiration, for the woman "has not realized yet, that fearful thing, that I am the other" (*Poems* 219, l. 116). These poetic movements suggest otherness as a defensive manoeuvre as much as a doctrine. Almost invariably, the discovery or touting of otherness is in reaction to a solipsistic tendency (fusion by absorbing external reality) or attraction to merger (fusion by being absorbed); it rarely stands on its own or in an emotional vacuum.

Even in the abject animal poems, where otherness seems self-evident, the speaker gains a proper understanding or appreciation of the animal in question only once he can identify with it. In other words, at least a minimal degree of anthropomorphism or even merger is necessary in order, paradoxically, to maintain the ideal of difference. The profound dissimilarities between the human speaker of "Man and Bat," "Snake," and "Mosquito" and the non-human creatures depicted, in fact, lead to human aggression. Yes, there is a recognition that "[b]ats must be bats" in the first-named poem (*Poems* 299, l. 136), but the overwhelming feelings are fear and disgust until at the very end the bat and speaker in a sense become one; there is no suggestion of letting the bat "live of itself." In "Mosquito," Brault-Dreux claims, there is, to a certain extent, a dynamic "which balances an intense attraction to the other with a determination not to absorb it" (32). But there is anger and hatred toward the insect in this poem, not even a pretense of accepting it on its own terms. In the famous poem "Snake" there is respect, even reverence for a time, and we see regret at the end. But the speaker needs to domesticate or familiarize the reptile with similes such as comparing the sight of it at the water trough to drinking cattle or, later, to "a king in exile" (*Poems* 303, l. 16; 305, l. 69), and there is a horror at its snakey retreat into the wall face.[4] These are wonderful poems, but, again, if we look to them for expressions of a pure Lawrentian otherness we will not find it.

When Lawrence's non-fictional prose is brought into the discussion of otherness, it is often the psychology works, *Studies in Classic American Literature*, and shorter pieces such as "Love" and "Democracy" that are referenced. From the 1918–19 version of *Studies* we get praise for "the deep, tender recognition" in Crèvecœur "of the *other*, the other creature which exists not in union with the immediate self, but in dark juxtaposition. It is the tenderness of blood-knowledge, knowledge in separation" (he is referring to quails) (*SCAL* 199). In the chapter on Edgar Allan Poe, where Lawrence discusses the ultimate mingling of incest in some Poe stories, he proclaims that the "triumph of love …

does not lie in merging, mingling, in absolute identification of the lover with the beloved. It lies in the communion of beings, who, in the very perfection of communion, recognise and allow the mutual otherness. There is no desire to transgress the bounds of being" (*SCAL* 240). In fact and paradoxically, the self becomes "most burningly and transcendently itself" in the embrace of the other (*SCAL* 240). This is the bright side of otherness, an ideal state of union that maintains singleness: merger with autonomy. But the other side of otherness often creeps into the prose: a reaction to the fear of engulfment. In the final version of the Poe essay, we read, "The central law of all organic life is that each organism is intrinsically isolate and single in itself." No ideal union here, rather the isolation of the individual: the dark side of autonomy rationalized as necessary: "The moment its isolation breaks down, and there comes an actual mixing and confusion, death sets in" (*SCAL* 67). How then is equilibrium in attachment to be achieved? Somewhat less strident is the following from "Democracy": "One man is neither equal nor unequal to another man. When I stand with another man, who is himself, and when I am truly myself, then I am only aware of a Presence, and of the strange reality of Otherness" (*RDP* 78, 80). There is no hierarchy in this formulation. In "Love," we have, again, the rare recognition of the paradoxical and interdependent nature of the equilibrium between the need for coming together and that of remaining integrally individual: "In pure communion I become whole in love. And in pure, fierce passion of sensuality I am burned into essentiality ... into sheer separate distinction" (*RDP* 10).

Possibly the most referenced passage in the fiction that deals with otherness is the description of Birkin's and Ursula's love in Sherwood Forest in the "Excurse" chapter of *Women in Love*, where the balanced phrasing and the alliteration mirror the achieved interpersonal equilibrium: "She had her desire fulfilled, he had his desire fulfilled. For she was to him what he was to her, the immemorial magnificence of mystic, palpable, real otherness" (*WL* 320). More subtly, in *The Rainbow* there is a scene, where Tom and Lydia are discussing marriage, in which Tom feels Lydia's weight upon his body, and her palpable otherness helps to define and authenticate his own selfhood just as Lawrence sometimes theorized that it should: "It was rather splendid, to be so ignored by her, whilst she lay against him, and he lifted her with his breathing ... The strange, inviolable completeness of the two of them made him feel as sure and as stable as God" (*R* 46). We know, however, that, as the relationship develops, Tom by no means continues to feel divine, nor that "it was splendid" to be ignored by Lydia. In fact, her estrangement enrages him on numerous occasions because it is a threat to his very sense of self. Problems ensue, then, when the other's otherness becomes too strange or too overwhelming, for then it is threatening to the insecure self. The equilibrium that Lawrence sought his whole life is essential: "[D]ifferentiation requires, ideally, the reciprocity of self and other, the balance of assertion and recognition" (Benjamin 25).

As we have seen in the foregoing chapters, no Lawrence character can sustain a balance of attachment for very long. Insofar as the recognition of otherness partakes of the same psychological dynamic that we have seen in the equilibrium of attachment, it is an ephemeral one. Otherness can be proclaimed in the essays with no opposition except perhaps Lawrence's own reservations, enunciated in the poetry until other thoughts challenge it if they ever do, and enacted in the fiction until events of the plot and other characters push back or complicate the issue. To say that Lawrentian otherness contains a component of defensiveness does not make it any less admirable since, in fact, Lawrence had to fight against some of his own inclinations to develop the principle. To say that Lawrence insists at times on otherness in part because he himself was not always respected as an intrinsic other growing up makes it more understandable. Toward the end of his life, Lawrence could transform the vexing paradox of attachment into something positive, at least for a moment in time. In the essay "We Need One Another," which arrived at the offices of *Scribner's Magazine* one month before Lawrence died (*LEA* 371n), Lawrence insists on the interdependence rather than the struggle between what I have been calling merger and autonomy: "So that everything, even individuality itself, depends on relationship." And again: "We have our very individuality in relationship" (*LEA* 298).

NOTES

Introduction

1 In the course of this study, the dating of Lawrence's works will generally appear at and only at the first mention of the work in question. The date of publication will normally be provided, but it will sometimes be more appropriate to indicate the date(s) of composition, in which case the distinction will be made obvious.
2 In his essay "Morality and the Novel," Lawrence uses "trembling" to describe the kind of dynamic equilibrium between opposing forces that the novel form, in Lawrence's view, is uniquely qualified to depict. The term appears variously as "trembling instability of the balance" and "trembling centre of balance" (*STH* 172, 173). Picking up on the term in his *D.H. Lawrence and the Trembling Balance*, James C. Cowan details this subtle, even paradoxical, conception and how it forms a core value in Lawrence's work: "The balance Lawrence suggests is not a static polarity of any two opposites but the delicate, dynamic equilibrium of life. His emphasis is not upon entities mechanistically associated in simple dichotomy but upon the organic relationship of those entities in all its subtle fluidity and complexity" (15).
3 With regards to the term "surety," on the first page of *The Rainbow*, for example, we read of the Brangwens' readiness and eagerness for the unknown, "a kind of surety, an expectancy, the look of an inheritor" (*R* 9) – phraseology that implies a confidence that can only come from an attachment that allows for exploration from a secure base. Diane S. Bonds suggests that there is a differentiated significance to the word "surety" in the novel based on gender: a male expectancy and a female self-assurance (55).

She sees that surety being severely qualified in the case of Tom Brangwen (69). The flower-and-root image comes from *Kangaroo* in the context of a description of marriage from the male point of view: "Like a tree that is rooted, always growing and flowering away from its root, so is a vitally active man" (*K* 164).

4 For more on Tom Brangwen's development see chapter 3.

5 Mahler also makes it clear that symbiosis, as she uses the term, "does not describe what actually happens in a mutually beneficial relationship between two *separate* individuals of different species. It describes the state of undifferentiation, of fusion with mother, in which the 'I' is not yet differentiated from the 'not-I' and in which inside and outside are only gradually coming to be sensed as different" (*Psychological Birth* 44).

6 When we first see Cyril's father, he is lying beside a fallen tree and a fallen cap (*WP* 22); in the chapter "The Father," Cyril knocks over a brass candlestick, and the old woman who has tended to his father almost falls down the stairs (*WP* 37, 39); in "The Education of George," Annable knocks both George and Cyril off their feet (*WP* 62), while the gamekeeper himself later in the novel dies in an apparent fall, as noted (*WP* 154); George is very unsteady on his feet when first visiting Meg and knocks over a glass of liquor in a later courting scene (*WP* 142–3, 203); Annable's son Sam almost falls off a roof (*WP* 181); and George's son falls off a horse when George harasses him (*WP* 317).

7 An example of this focus in the psychology works is the following from *Fantasia of the Unconscious*: "Our poor little plants of children are put into horrible forcing-beds, called schools, and the young idea is there forced to shoot. It shoots, poor thing, like a potato in a warm cellar" (*PFU* 105). *Fantasia of the Unconscious*, Lawrence claimed, was "written primarily concerning the child's consciousness" (*PFU* 160), and he considered *Child Consciousness* and *The Child and the Unconscious* as titles for the book (*PFU* 232n). The most detailed work on Lawrence and his views on and depiction of childhood has been done by Carol Sklenicka. See her article "Lawrence's Vision of the Child: Reimagining Character and Consciousness" from 1985–86 and her 1991 book *D.H. Lawrence and the Child*.

8 It should be said that Aracana's observation is in the context of her argument that criticism of *Sons and Lovers* (at the time of her article, which was published in 1989) was "embedded in the sociocultural phenomenon of mother-blaming" (137). The key question, of course, is not whether or not critics blame Lawrence's mother for his problems or his fictional mothers for the difficulties of their sons, but whether Lawrence himself did so, justifiably or not, in his fictional and non-fictional work.

9 They add: "If one thinks of attachment as an organization that exhibits some continuity even as it changes throughout the individual's life, then one

may use the criteria for infant and child attachment as a frame of reference to describe the features of normal adult attachment" (West and Sheldon-Keller 22).
10 See chapter 5 for a further analysis of this story.
11 The idea that there is a tension in Lawrence's writing between merger or fusion tendencies and a desire for autonomy or separation is hardly a new one. Daniel J. Schneider, for instance, using Lawrence's own terms from the psychology work, argues that Lawrence's characters from 1913 onward "are torn between the 'sympathetic' desire to give themselves up to other individuals ... and the opposing, the 'voluntary' desire to hold themselves intact, pure, single, unmixed with others, free and separate" ("Laws" 239–40). Judith Ruderman, in her seminal study *D.H. Lawrence and the Devouring Mother*, writes of the "pre-oedipal tension between the desires for merger and for separation" (10). What I am claiming is that there is an inner dynamic to that tension that we need to understand: certain triggers determine its oscillations. Murray M. Schwartz sees the same tension, "between the desire for oceanic merger and the desire for dominant autonomy" in Lawrence; he helpfully adds that either extreme threatens a loss of a "sense of personal existence" and that Lawrence "moves continually between the poles, and it is this movement that gives his style its distinctive rhythm" (219–20).
12 In "The Two Principles," Lawrence writes that "[t]he cosmic elements ... have a twofold direction ... they embrace and unite and the fountain of creation springs up ... But there is also the great centrifugal motion, when the two flee asunder into space, into infinitude" (*SCAL* 266).
13 Several critics in the past have touched upon the issue without delving very deeply into it. For example, Gavriel Ben-Ephraim suggests in *The Moon's Dominion: Narrative Dichotomy and Female Dominance in Lawrence's Early Novels* that when Lawrence's male characters in the early work are alone they "suffer from the sense of being incomplete. Yet when with a woman the Lawrencian male is threatened by engulfment. The imbalance is destructive, but a fact of being, beyond the will and consciousness of the characters" (20). Chong-wha Chung gives due importance to the subject of equilibrium: "Lawrence's whole life was a constant search for this impossible state of the perfect union of dual forces in the body and in the relationship of man and woman" (74). Chung persuasively argues that Lawrence's dualism is basically Heraclitean (72), carefully details the metaphors Lawrence used for the concept of balance at the various stages of his career, and ably critiques the vagueness and other weaknesses of most of those metaphors. However, Chung is never able to pin down the precise nature or genesis of Lawrentian equilibrium.
14 Lawrence seldom has anything good to say about the Great War, but on occasion he can see positive aspects to the conflict. In the context of a call for

"genuine action" to begin to ameliorate what ails his culture in his view, he writes in *Fantasia* that "[t]he war was really not a bad beginning" (*PFU* 118).

15 Compare *Mr Noon*: "The matrix of the old mother-days and mother-idea is hell beyond hell at last: that which nourished us and our race becomes the intolerable dry prison of our death … And once it has become an intolerable prison, it is no use presuming what is outside. We don't know what is outside – we can never know till we get out. We have therefore got to fight and fight and fight ourselves sick, to get out" (*MN* 290–1).

16 Schneider, also emphasizing the instability in Lawrence's concept of balance, terms it a "dynamic balance" (*Artist* 63). Herbert Spencer's ideal of a static balance may serve as an example of the kind of late-Victorian scientific understanding of balance that Lawrence adamantly opposed. In *The Principles of Sociology* (1877), Spencer wrote of the way the relationship between the "inner and outer factors" necessary for evolution continually changes until "there is reached an equilibrium between the environing actions and the actions which the aggregate opposes to them." A little surprisingly, it is likewise with a social organism, which "undergoes modifications until it comes into equilibrium with environing conditions; and thereupon continues without further change of structure" (quoted in Greene 83). Lawrence opposed such fixity in his thinking on balance but was not entirely immune to the terms of reference within which Spencer defined balance.

17 See 6L 321.

18 See the fourth chapter of *The Forked Flame*. In contrast, as the title of his third chapter indicates, Daleski called the ideal of balance in relationships that is explored particularly in *The Rainbow* and *Women in Love* "two in one," using a term from the Hardy essay.

19 The prominence of the fall motif at the end of "Snowed Up" in *Women in Love* underscores Gerald's loss of equilibrium. After knocking Loerke off his feet and forcing Gudrun to her knees, Gerald is "very afraid of falling" (*WL* 473), but finally he "slipped and fell down" (*WL* 474), never to rise again. Similarly, in *Aaron's Rod*, Aaron Sisson, the eponymous protagonist, struggles to find a balance between autonomy and attachment, but at this point in Lawrence's career the emphasis is very much on the need to loosen the constricting bonds of attachment, especially those of marriage. So Aaron simply abandons his wife and young children and discovers what is presented as a restored equilibrium. Aaron's temporary loss of that equilibrium is figured in a physical loss of balance when he actually collapses in the street and falls ill after a "relapse" into the world of heterosexual relations. That Lilly then successfully ministers to him in the manner of a mother tending her baby (*AR* 96) suggests that Lawrence is trying to have it both ways here (attachment is bad and good) and that he is experimenting with an alternative to heterosexual attachment.

20 Compare Storch's claim that in Lawrence "[t]he male aggressively asserts independence from women, and yet also feels intimately drawn into the feminine perspective and sensibility" (118). Lawrence's putative feminine sensibility led at least one reviewer of *The White Peacock* to identify the then-unknown author with the unidentifiable initials "D.H." as a woman, as Lawrence wryly noted to his sister Ada in a letter (*1L* 229). In chapter 2, I examine how gender identity and attachment interact.

Chapter One

1 John E. Stoll, for example, writes: "The death of the father, then, does not end the presence of the father figure in the work. By a process of idealization and symbolic transference, this role passes to Annable" (29).
2 An exception to the generally negative view of Cyril is Tony Pinkney's suggestion that he embodies the ideal of balance in the novel as one who is equally at home working in the fields and in artistic endeavours (19), but Pinkney recognizes that the character never really comes off and that there is something Prufrockian about him (26).
3 On the subject of the narrator's point of view blurring into Lettie's, compare Black, who refers to the scene where George appears with open shirt to Lettie as she sits at the piano: "The reader familiar with other early fictions by Lawrence may recognize that Lawrence himself quite obsessively saw what Lettie sees here" (28).
4 Proust, like Lawrence, abnormally close to his mother, fuses images of landscape and mother in explaining that his desire to revisit the Guermantes way could never be satisfied by a similar, even a more beautiful, landscape elsewhere, any more than he could be satisfied with a woman more beautiful and intelligent than his mother taking her place in saying good night to him (201–2). Apart from the breast image, Lawrence's "the blue eyes of the waters" may also be a maternal reference. The colour blue, particularly blue eyes, in Lawrence is sometimes associated with his mother. See chapter 5 for a more detailed argument of this point.
5 Similarly, in a later work, the novella *The Fox*, Lawrence depicts a predatory young man, Henry Grenfel, attempting (without actually realizing the implications of what he is doing) to exorcize his predatory nature by killing a marauding fox, thereby civilizing himself enough to marry his attachment object, Nellie March. For a full analysis of the novella, see my *D.H. Lawrence and Survival: Darwinism in the Fiction of the Transitional Period*, 49–60.
6 As Schneider puts it: "Somehow the sensual man must emerge from unconsciousness – the dark waters in which the gray fish glide [in the book's first paragraph] – and must connect himself with the 'light' of consciousness and of spiritual development" (*Artist* 116). Jack Stewart

suggests that "George's tragedy is that he is only half awakened, not initiated into new being" ("Landscape" 7). However, other critics agree with George's own view that his collapse is somehow caused by his being awakened to consciousness by Lettie and Cyril. Herzinger argues that "George begins the novel as its most stable representative of man and nature in equilibrium … but his awkward pursuit of Lettie and his 'education' through Cyril push him irrevocably away from his nature instincts and toward a total dissolution" (83). Pinkney speaks glowingly of the not-yet-dissociated sensibility of the Saxton family on their farm (15). While George's conflict between unconsciousness and awareness undoubtedly has some emotional connection to Lawrence's own youthful dilemma and sexual crisis, such views, I think, simplify the complex interrogation of selfhood that Lawrence undertakes in *The White Peacock*.

7   Lawrence later wrote a short story entitled "Samson and Delilah" and one called "Delilah and Mr Bircumshaw." And he took a line from Handel's oratorio "Samson" for the initial title of his short story "The Prussian Officer," which was "Honour and Arms" (Cushman, *D.H. Lawrence at Work* 209). There is also a reference to Samson at the beginning of the essay "The Reality of Peace": "If we cannot cast off the old habitual life, then we bring it down over our heads in a blind frenzy. Once the temple becomes our prison, we drag at the pillars till the roof falls crashing down on top of us and we are obliterated" (*RDP* 27). It may be that the stark reality of Lawrence's mining district with its constant danger of cave-ins crashing down on the strong men below, including Lawrence's father, made references to Samson a natural mental habit.

8   Neil Roberts argues that the "rather affected literary style" of the novel, its "stifling preciocity, in which the natural world is filtered through high culture" ("Writing" 17, 32), was in part due to Helen Corke's view of what constituted an appropriate literary style influencing Lawrence's writing. Although he "removed some of [the] worst excesses" while using Corke's writing as his source material, much of it survives in the novel and, indeed, corresponds to the kind of literariness he himself aspired to at the time ("Writing" 29–30).

9   The 1981 Cambridge University Press edition of the novel features three appendices containing Helen Corke's relevant writings or extracts from them, "The Letter," "The Freshwater Diary," and "The Cornwall Writing." A.R. Atkins argues in a 1992 article that two other pieces of Corke's writing (held at the University of Texas at Austin) are also relevant: "To Siegmund's Violin" and "Aftermath" (2). Atkins also claims that Lawrence's only sources as he wrote the "Saga of Siegmund," the first version, were "To Siegmund's Violin," "The Freshwater Diary," and "Aftermath" (14).

10 The reference to Cythera here comes from one of Lawrence's title suggestions to Edward Garnett, "Trespassers in Cythera" (*T* 20). Holly Laird's interesting

article "Configurations of Trespass in the Works of D.H. Lawrence" details Lawrence's changing use of the terms "trespass" and "trespasser." Laird finds that "trespass" "acquires associations chiefly with property and class" as well as sexuality (73). I suggest that a significant added association is the psychological, something Laird only just touches upon in the sense that I argue is crucial in this novel: "'Trespass' also develops a distinctly new set of associations with threats to a man's deepest self – and to a woman's" (83).

11 This is a dig at John Middleton Murry (who is the model for the character Philip), but there is more than a little of Lawrence's own attitude and fear here as well. In fact, in a well-known letter from December 1918 to Katherine Mansfield, in which Lawrence discusses the "Mother-incest idea" and the male desire to "return unto the woman," he equates his own such tendency with Murry's: "It seems to me it is what Jack does to you ... I have done it, and now struggle [with] all my might to get out" (3L 301–2).

12 It appears that Helen Corke was worried about pregnancy during the affair with Macartney (T 19) and, in retrospect years later, came to recognize that hers was "a Lesbian temperament." The title of her book *Neutral Ground* was "intended to indicate a point in sexuality between committed homosexuality and committed heterosexuality" (T 18).

13 The one passage that shows Helena as a child and Siegmund as a mother figure occurs as they contemplate their return from the Isle of Wight: "Helena yielded herself like a forlorn child to his arms ... She shook with dry, withered sobs, as a child does when it snatches itself away from the lancet of the doctor, and hides in the mother's bosom, refusing to be touched" (T 132).

14 The identification was first made in Murry's 1935 autobiography *Between Two Worlds*. Murry claims there that Frieda told him that he was Gerald, and Murry adds that "I was not Gerald Crich, but it probably is true that Lawrence found the germ of Gerald in me" (411).

15 The Cambridge University Press edition of *Women in Love* also tells us of a connection here to Lady Ottoline Morrell, the model for Hermione. The notes cite a reference to the Book of Ruth in Lady Ottoline's 1963 memoir and quote her statement that as a young girl "[a]ll I desired was never to leave my mother" (WL 541).

16 By "selfobject needs," Cowan, following Heinz Kohut, is referring to the need for "sustaining relationships with significant others, who serve as 'selfobjects,' objects that help one to maintain self-cohesion and strengthen harmonious functioning among the constituents of the self" (*Self and Sexuality* 7). It is not entirely clear how Cowan thinks mirroring can be "excessive," but the salient point is that Lawrence's mother's caregiving was unreliable and largely served her own needs rather than being responsive to his. His growing realization of this reality is reflected in the portrayal of Mrs Crich.

17 Shakespeare's character, in Act 1, scene 7 of *Macbeth*, in exhorting her husband to carry out their planned scheme of regicide and the usurpation of the throne, infamously declares that if she had so sworn to do, she would be prepared to dash out the brains of the very infant sucking at her breast (ll. 54–9).

18 The term "devouring mother" derives from that same letter to Katherine Mansfield in which Lawrence discusses the "Mother-incest idea" (see note 11 above). He writes, "In a way, Frieda is the devouring mother" (*3L* 302). Judith Ruderman took Lawrence's descriptor for the title of her influential 1984 work *D.H. Lawrence and the Devouring Mother: The Search for a Patriarchal Ideal of Leadership*. She traces the idea in Lawrence to his reading of Jung's *Psychology of the Unconscious* (1912; in English 1916) (*Devouring* 10–11). Although Ruderman concentrates on Lawrence's leadership period in her book, the idea of the devouring mother is consistent with the attachment fear of maternal reincorporation that is present from Lawrence's earliest work.

19 Compare this description of Gerald at the death of his father noted earlier: "Something must come with him into the hollow void of death in his soul, fill it up, and so equalise the pressure within to the pressure without" (*WL* 322). We may also compare this description to the following statement in "The Reality of Peace": "I am like one of the cells in any organism, the pressure from within and the resistance from without keep me as I am" (*RDP* 49).

20 See chapter 3 for an analysis of this story.

21 In a letter to J.B. Pinker, Lawrence mentions an epilogue to the novel as a projected last chapter he has yet to write (*2L* 669) and never did write or certainly never published. There are differences in detail between the last chapter of *The First "Women in Love,"* finished in 1916, and the finale of the text published in 1920 (privately in the United States) and 1921 (in England), but the concluding Birkin-Ursula dialogue of the later work, as John Worthen has argued, is unlikely to have been based on that planned epilogue. Worthen thinks it much more likely that Lawrence intended the epilogue to incorporate a deleted fragment found in a surviving notebook that projects events a year after the finale of *Women in Love* and mentions the birth of Gerald's son in a letter from Gudrun ("The First Women in Love" 54, and see *FWL* xxxii–xxxiii). In any case, Lawrence may have felt he was not done with the novel's characters when he wrote the play.

22 The unusual, triple-barrelled name might suggest a conflation of the sufferings of the biblical Job when abandoned by God, the father figure Arthur John Lawrence, and the aspiration to be freed from attachment complications.

23 Strictly speaking, the novel, like *The Trespasser*, is a collaboration with a female author – in this case Mollie Skinner, whose manuscript "The House of Ellis" (now lost) formed the basis of the story. However, as Paul Eggert concludes in his Introduction to the definitive Cambridge University Press edition, the novel is "a complete imaginative appropriation" (*BB* lii) on Lawrence's part

of Skinner's material, and a thorough examination of all extant and relevant material "leads inevitably to one conclusion: that *The Boy in the Bush* merits the description, a 'Lawrence novel'" (*BB* xxv). Lawrence's claim to authorship is even stronger when we concentrate on the psychology of the main character, Jack Grant, for that is one aspect of the work Lawrence made wholly his own.

24 Judith Ruderman makes the Cain connection between Gerald and Jack, but she suggests that the two characters are very unalike (*Devouring* 119). I argue that there are more significant links between the two characters. Ruderman also has a briefer discussion of *The Boy in the Bush* in her 2014 study *Race and Identity in D.H. Lawrence*, where she rightly points out the biblical parallels in the novel, as detailed especially in T.R. Wright's *D.H. Lawrence and the Bible* (2000). She suggests that for Jack, who is "a budding patriarch" like Moses, looking for a kind of Promised Land in the Australia of the nineteenth century centrally means "cutting loose from England and English values" (*Race* 83–4). That rebellion against English values very much includes Jack's desire to emulate the Old Testament prophets and engage in polygamy.

25 In chapter 5, I examine Lawrence's stories of homecoming. In one of them, the never-completed "The Woman Who Wanted to Disappear," the eponymous woman's journey is initially to "her mother's country, that she had known by heart as a child" (*VG* 252).

26 Game does not sugar-coat Lawrence's racial attitude, nor, for that matter, that of European-descended Australians up to Lawrence's time, but he does suggest that there may be a critique of colonization where Lawrence "acknowledges the predatory and exploitative sexual practices of British frontier colonialism in Australia" (*Australia* 183). He has also published a later study that compares *The Boy in the Bush* to the work of Zane Grey, but adds little there that is relevant to the current argument.

27 Admittedly, there is some textual evidence suggesting Jack's maturation after his second major illness and wandering in the bush: "The boy Jack never rose from that fever. It was a man who got up again" (*BB* 295). However, I would argue that the narrator's claim here is undermined by a deeper realization of Jack's weakness and failure to outgrow his deficits.

28 While Jack's rant here might seem to be another indication of authorial or narratorial distancing, that is not necessarily the case. David Ellis cites a letter from the Dane Kai Gøtzsche to his countryman Knud Merrild about Gøtzsche's travels with Lawrence while he was separated from Frieda. Gøtzsche writes that "considering all things, he is really insane when he is as he is now" (quoted in *DG* 136). Ellis suggests that, in describing these feelings in Jack, Lawrence fails to create any distance between himself and his character (*DG* 138). In my view, Ellis fails to give sufficient weight to Lawrence's suggestion that Jack is suffering from a family madness, but, again, the evidence is inconclusive regarding the degree of distance.

29 The volcano image and the rage itself seem to be carried over from *Kangaroo*, where, in a chapter entitled "Volcanic Evidence," we read that Somers often "found himself in a seethe of steady fury, general rage" (*K* 163). Similarly, in the chapter following the description of Somers's/Lawrence's wartime "nightmare" in Cornwall and evidently as a direct consequence of the nightmare, Somers's anger is described as a volcanic rage that might erupt at any time (*K* 260–2). The similarity between the two novels on this point reinforces the link between Jack and Lawrence to some degree, especially the suggestion that the anger originates in childhood. Cowan writes of Lawrence's "sudden eruptions of narcissistic rage" in adulthood that derive from childhood attachment problems (*Self and Sexuality* 44).

Chapter Two

1 "John Thomas" is slang for penis and "coddy" for testicles (*EME* 238n).
2 See chapter 5 for a further analysis of this tale as a story of homecoming.
3 Jan Good quotes Nin as suggesting that Lawrence "had a complete realization of the feelings of women. In fact, very often he wrote as a woman would write" (quoted in Good 226n). In the same note, Good also points to Anne Smith's exploration of Lawrence's gender identification in her essay "A New Adam and a New Eve – Lawrence and Women: A Biographical Overview." Smith writes of "[t]he picture that emerges of [Lawrence] in these days [his youth] is of a 'mother's boy,' a boy who was constantly with women" (Smith 13).
4 In the Prologue, printed as Appendix II in the Cambridge University Press edition of *Women in Love*, Lawrence delves into Birkin's relationships with Hermione and Gerald and writes that Birkin "was always drawn to women, feeling more at home with a woman than with a man, yet it was for men that he felt the hot, flushing, roused attraction which a man is supposed to feel for the other sex" (*WL* 501).
5 The Cambridge University Press edition of the story records the composition date as June 1913 (*PO* xxxviii).
6 Studies that cite the letter in discussions of "The Prussian Officer" include R.E. Pritchard's *D.H. Lawrence: Body of Darkness*, 78n8; Janice Hubbard Harris's *The Short Fiction of D.H. Lawrence*, 119; Mark Kinkead-Weekes's Cambridge Biography, 77; Hugh Stevens, "Sex and the Nation: 'The Prussian Officer' and *Women in Love*," 54–5.
7 Miller also delves into Adolf Hitler's childhood as a case study of how hatred originates in the brutal treatment of a child by the father. She quotes John Toland (*Adolf Hitler*, 1976) regarding corporal punishment: "in the Austria of those days severe beatings of children were not uncommon, being considered good for the soul" (152), and suggests that the command to the

child to respect and love the very person inflicting hurt and humiliation on him or her is absurd and would "scarcely be expected of an adult (except in pronouncedly sadomasochistic relationships)" (145).

8 See Kevin McAleer's in-depth study of German duelling practices among students and the military in *Dueling: The Cult of Honor in Fin-De-Siècle Germany*, especially chapter 4, "Graduation with Honor" (119–58), and the section in that chapter on the *mensur*. James F. Scott remarks, with regard to a different Lawrence short story set in Germany, that the military both in "The Thorn in the Flesh" and in "The Prussian Officer" has the function of "proposing tests of courage and stamina, which have become the measure of manhood in a Germany dominated by the northern spirit" (148).

9 See Keith Cushman's detailed recounting in his article "Domestic Life in the Suburbs" of the biographical background to the story in Lawrence's lodging with the Jones family over several years.

10 One of the very few times Paul's struggle against his mother is explicitly expressed occurs late in the novel when he and Baxter Dawes almost come to blows in a pub and he thinks of what his mother's reaction to hearing about it would be: "He felt condemned by her. Then sometimes he hated her, and pulled at her bondage. His life wanted to free itself of her. It was like a circle where life turned back on itself" (*SL* 389). Paul generally represses his anger at his mother, conditioned as he is from childhood to identify with her and her struggles, and he dares not show any hostility to her lest he come to resemble his father. But it may be that one of the things that attracts Paul about both Clara and Baxter is their anger, an attribute connected to his father.

11 In a letter to Barbara Low of September 1916, Lawrence objected to Alfred Kuttner's newly published Freudian review of his novel: "My poor book: it was, as art, a fairly complete truth: so they carve a half lie out of it, and say 'Voilà! Swine!'" (*2L* 655). One notable exception to the critical consensus is John Turner's recent *D.H. Lawrence and Psychoanalysis* (2020).

12 The idea that Walter Morel comes across to the reader as more sympathetic than Lawrence intended or realized had its genesis in a 1948 article by Mark Schorer, and, with a few exceptions, this is now the critical consensus. Daleski's formulation may be taken as typical: "The weight of the hostile comments which Lawrence directs against Morel is balanced by the unconscious sympathy with which he is presented dramatically, while the overt celebration of Mrs Morel is challenged by the harshness of the character in action. The artist, it would seem, penetrated to the truth which the son subsequently thought he had not seen" (43). Compare Sklenicka: "Such contradictions between what is shown and what is told about Walter Morel are multiplied by the ambiguities that are embedded in many of the narrative declarations about Gertrude and Walter Morel" (*D.H. Lawrence and the Child* 46).

13 Walter's "dirtiness" is primarily related to the coal dust that is a function of his and every miner's employment in Lawrence's home district. In the later *Women in Love*, Lawrence returns to much the same psychological territory and imagery in the chapter entitled "Coal Dust." The central scene of the chapter has nothing to do with dust, however: Gerald brutally controlling his rearing mare at a railway crossing as Ursula and Gudrun look on. The chapter was actually entitled "Collieries" in draft (*WL* 544n). The published title seems to refer much more directly to a later description in the chapter when Gudrun and Ursula are walking through Beldover after their encounter at the crossing, and the black coal dust creates a kind of visual magic that also seems to emanate from the half-naked miners washing themselves. Gudrun feels "a glamorous thickness of labour and maleness surcharged in the air" (*WL* 115). The emotional significance of the coal dust from *Sons and Lovers* makes its presence felt here as well, but at a stage where Lawrence is much more determined than he had been earlier to restore a measure of identification with masculinity. In effect, the relatively insignificant butty Walter Morel is now the colliery master Gerald Crich, and the impotent and self-destructive lashing out at Gertrude has become male mastery of a more tractable equine female creature.

14 Similarly, Walter's drinking is an imbibing of sustenance that he absorbs outside of the home and can take place only if he selfishly deprives the rest of the family of their means of sustenance or greatly reduces it. The drinking/imbibing motif in the novel is a central one and includes the nourishing mother-child dyad, of course. When Paul hurls a glass of beer in the face of Baxter Dawes it is a symbolic commentary on his father's drinking (even though he himself is in a pub drinking). The motif culminates in Paul feeding his mother poisoned milk and later accepting a glass of milk from his father.

15 All three principal Morel characters, Gertrude, Walter, and Paul, it may be argued, suffer from parenting deficiencies that create emotional vulnerabilities which become projected: through resentment in Gertrude's case, rage in Walter's, and sadism in Paul's treatment of women other than his mother. Much has been made of Gertrude's puritanical father (Paul is named for his favourite writer, the Apostle Paul), but Walter's rage, like his wife's resentment, seems to stem partly from a wounded narcissism that can be traced back to a parent. To judge by the little we see of her, the elder Mrs Morel is a withholding mother. Gertrude discovers to her chagrin that Walter's mother charges her son rent – and an outrageously high rent as far as Gertrude is concerned – for the house she and her husband live in. When Gertrude denies Walter food in one vivid scene, he reacts in a savage way that may owe something to the frustrations and lack of nurturing in his childhood. She says of the piece of pork pie Walter is holding, "'Nor was

that bought for you. If you can give me no more than twenty five shillings, I'm sure I'm not going to buy you pork-pie to stuff, after you've swilled a belly-ful of beer'" (*SL* 252–3). In response, Walter throws the food into the fire "in a vicious spurt of temper" (*SL* 253). Paul's anger is manifested less straightforwardly but often in his sadistic treatment of Miriam, as Williamson has suggested: "When Paul wishes to avoid saying something hurtful to Miriam, he instead digs a sharp stick into the ground ... In the algebra quarrel, he actually flings a pencil in her face, as his father had flung a table drawer at his mother, years before" (62).

16 Douglas believes that attitudes to pollution and dirt are universal and cut across cultures and historical time periods. She argues that to understand the human attitude to dirt, including the often-discussed prohibitions on "unclean" animals in Leviticus, we must disassociate the concept from its modern connections with hygiene and pathogenicity (35) and focus on order and completeness. Dirt, then, is "matter out of place" and "that which must not be included if a pattern is to be maintained" (40). What I am suggesting is that Gertrude Morel defines dirt in a way that suits her psychological need for reinforcing a sense of separate selfhood.

17 For example, Berman observes that Paul's studied intimacy with Baxter serves the dual purpose of a way to distance himself from Clara and "as an atonement for the ill treatment of his broken-spirited father" (220). Cowan describes a "reparation by proxy" in the relationship (*Self and Sexuality* 15). When Paul has a physical fight with Dawes over Clara, the scene is a realization in a sense of the fight he and his father almost engaged in earlier but broke off when Gertrude became faint and distressed (*SL* 253). The aggression, of course, does not suggest sympathy with Dawes, but the identification of Dawes with Walter Morel is underscored.

18 The evidence for that regret comes from Frieda's "*Not I, But the Wind...*" wherein she cites Lawrence as having told her "in after years" that he would have written a different *Sons and Lovers* if he had to do it again: "'my mother was wrong, and I thought she was absolutely right'" (56).

19 See the Conclusion for a discussion of these two poems in the context of Lawrence's concept of otherness.

20 Lawrence himself called the second part of the novella "the phallic second half" in a letter of 15 March 1928 to Curtis Brown (*6L* 326).

21 In his poem "My Naughty Book," Lawrence sarcastically apologizes for having "loaded the camel's back before / with dirt" (*Poems* 426, ll. 7–8).

22 We can compare Benjamin's observation to David Cavitch's statement: "The unsatisfied need for masculine identification enters all of Lawrence's works, in which he pursues an ideal maleness that he could never recognize in the circumstantial world and that his own divided nature could never wholly accept" (*New World* 30).

23 See Neil Roberts (*Travel* 72). Roberts compares the almost word-for-word similarity between Gerald's refusal of the proffered *Blutbrüderschaft* in *Women in Love* with Somers's rejection of Jack's offer of mateship (176n). Izabel F.O. Brandão also points out the similarity (18).

Chapter Three

1 See chapter 4 for a further analysis of this tale from the perspective of class and attachment. Lawrence's implicit critique of the novel of manners' portrayal of marriage is, arguably, no more stringent than, say, Jane Austen's own satire on her age's excesses, but the point here is that Lawrence's interest lies in a much different area of human interaction.
2 See Worthen (*EY* 300–1) for a brief discussion of Lawrence's evolving views on marriage and his fictional depictions of various marriages. Worthen discusses 1911 as a pivotal year in this regard, with respect specifically to the various versions of "Paul Morel" and the short stories Lawrence was working on at the time: "the stories of 1911 allow us to trace his loyalties to different ideas of marriage ... And in particular it was significant that ideas of fulfilment should at last be supplanting moralistic analysis in Lawrence's fictional accounts of marriage" (*EY* 301).
3 The early play *The Married Man* (written in April 1912 [*Plays* cxiv]), based on the escapades of Lawrence's friend George Neville, might be seen as an anomaly within the otherwise serious view of marriage in Lawrence's writing. Lawrence wrote very few silly things, but this play may well be one of them. The Lawrence figure, William Brentnall, does try intermittently to get the Neville character, Dr George Grainger, to take his own marriage more seriously than Grainger is inclined to do and warns off the single women whom Grainger has neglected to inform of his marital status. For the most part, however, the attitude in the play is flippant despite the fact that the institution of marriage at this time was becoming a serious hindrance to Lawrence's plans with the married Frieda Weekley, whom he had recently met and with whom he was about to travel to Germany (*Plays* xxxi). Arguably, the flippancy evident in the play is a reflection of Grainger's character rather than the author's attitude. Turner situates the play in "a tradition of witty comedy going back to Congreve and Shakespeare" and as a serious attempt to "find a sexual ethic to reconcile 'goodness' and 'life'" (*Psychoanalysis* 46, 47).
4 Rudolph Glitz quotes this passage in his book *Writing the Victorians: The Early Twentieth-Century Family Chronicle* (110), in which he places Lawrence's work, particularly *The Rainbow*, in the context of early-twentieth-century family chronicles by Arnold Bennett, John Galsworthy, and Virginia Woolf (*The Years*). It is telling to note how anomalous Lawrence's inclusion seems

to be in Glitz's study and how he is often the exception to the various rules that Glitz theorizes, among other things precisely because Lawrence's interest in marriage is so different from that of the so-called materialists and even of Woolf.

5 Compare Peter Balbert's take on Lawrentian marriage and landscape, for example, what he calls the "interplay between panophilia and phallophobia" in *St Mawr* and in the famous pine tree painted by Georgia O'Keefe as "The Lawrence Tree" and celebrated in Lawrence's essay "Pan in America": "Is this pattern not a transparent version of the primal ego-support Lawrence once enjoyed with Frieda that was annealed in their sexual appetite for each other?" (*Marriage* 170; see also 161, 193). The Pan interest, which the editor of *St Mawr and Other Stories* suggests also pervades "The Overtone," may be behind the story's stilted and abstract dialogue – a rare instance of tone-deafness in Lawrence – that seems to belong more to expository writing than fiction and is the kind of conversation no real people would ever engage in.

6 For a concise but thorough summary of Lawrence's engagement with the topic of marriage, see the first paragraph of chapter 9 in David Game's *D.H. Lawrence's Australia* (195). Game writes: "All [Lawrence's] novels explore in some way the problems of marriage, or relations between couples, in the face of what he saw as the degenerative forces emanating from modern, industrial, democratic society" (195).

7 John Worthen suggests that, for Lawrence, "[l]oving Lydia Lawrence meant not only remaining a responsible son and becoming a salary earner; it meant inhibiting his own carelessness, impulsiveness, anger and (in particular) sensuality." But Worthen also qualifies Lydia Lawrence's influence on Lawrence's love life by adding that his "inability to fall in love … seems to have been conditioned as much by his habitual self-awareness and detachment as by the love for his mother which he (and Jessie) would later use to explain it" (*EY* 156). One might, of course, wonder about Lydia Lawrence's role in precisely such early conditioning into self-awareness.

8 The impulsive proposal of marriage occurred on 3 December 1910 (Worthen, *EY* 288) as Lawrence's mother neared death. She passed away six days later.

9 The mother's influence is also felt in the elaborate and plentiful repast she sends out to the field for the harvesting men's dinner: "When the load was teemed, they gathered round the white cloth, which was spread under a tree between the hedge and the stack, and, sitting on the ground, ate their meal. Mrs Wookey sent always a clean cloth, and knives and forks and plates for everybody. Mr Wookey was always rather proud of this spread, everything was so proper" (*LAH* 98). The provision of food becomes an important, recurring motif when the group generously shares its meal with a tramp and his wife and she later becomes attached to Geoffrey, who provides her with

food, shelter, and warmth when he finds her in the Wookey shed seeking respite from the rain. The last mention of the mother comes in Geoffrey's imagination after he has pushed Maurice over the side of the haystack, and, with Maurice's fate still in doubt, he pictures to himself "seeing his mother pass to the sick-room" to attend to a stricken Maurice (*LAH* 94), a subtle indication of sibling jealousy going back many years.

10 A note of abandonment and betrayal is introduced earlier in the tale in the story of the tramp Bredon and Lydia, his wife. They have been forced to abandon their home by an employer who has also perpetrated some complicated betrayal, or so Bredon says (*LAH* 101).

11 T.R. Wright argues that Lawrence's "reworking of biblical elements" in *The Rainbow* retains "a respect for the biblical original," a tendency that disappears in later work, where his "profound religious impulse" turns "increasingly bitter" (108–9).

12 Mark Kinkead-Weekes points out that, in historical actuality, "1840 was nearer the end of the canal-building age than the beginning; the Nottingham Canal had opened in 1796, and, with the Camford and the Erewash canals, had opened up markets that gave the Erewash Valley coal-owners a competitive edge" ("Sense" 125). Of course, Lawrence is more concerned here with human adaptation to change than with absolute historical accuracy and probably chose his date in part by backtracking from the contemporary endpoint he had in mind for his New Woman, Ursula Brangwen.

13 For Freud, the uncanny "is actually nothing new or strange, but something that was long familiar to the psyche and was estranged from it only through being repressed" (148). As Petra Eckhard has observed, the repression involved in the *unheimlich* is embedded in the very "un" of the word, "a lexical indicator of the act of repression" for Freud (28). While Freud also emphasizes the discomfort and spookiness of the uncanny in his essay and uses the stories of E.T.A. Hoffmann ("The Sandman" in particular) to illustrate the concept, I am appropriating the term here to denote only the simultaneously familiar and unfamiliar.

14 For a detailed analysis of Lawrence's complicated relationship both to Freudian thought and to individual members of the psychoanalytic community in England, see John Turner's *D.H. Lawrence and Psychoanalysis*, and for a good overview, see Bruce Steele's Introduction in *Psychoanalysis and the Unconscious and Fantasia of the Unconscious* (*PFU* xxiv–xxxiv). W.S. Marks III argued some time ago that Lawrence seems to have read and made use of Freud's essay on the uncanny in his story "The Rocking-Horse Winner" (381–2, 384). That story was written years after *The Rainbow*, but the later insights might suggest the existence of early concepts in Lawrence's mind that found subsequent confirmation in Freud, whether directly or indirectly.

15 We can compare this failure of maternal attunement to the similar absence of sensitivity in a wife in *Sons and Lovers* that we examined at the end of the last chapter: Mrs Morel "could not be content with the little [Walter] might be, she would have him the much that he ought to be. So, in seeking to make him nobler than he could be, she destroyed him" (*SL* 25).

16 Kinkead-Weekes writes that the choice of the name Lydia signals the fact that the Tom-Lydia relationship is to be a "re-imagining of the first part of *Sons and Lovers*," which, of course, fictionally recast Lawrence's parents' marriage (*TE* 174).

17 Robert Langbaum suggests something similar when he argues that Lydia embodies for Tom "an ideal already fabricated in his head" so that his seeing her for the first time is a kind of recognition (307).

18 Lydia's motherhood and the fact that she is six years older than Tom (as Frieda was almost exactly six years older than Lawrence) add significantly to the attraction. Apart from the biographical fact of Frieda's children, little Anna's presence may be explained as a narrative strategy. It is Lawrence's attempt to portray Tom and Lydia as equally adult as the writer squirms away from the quasi-incestuous, oedipal implications of his own fantasy even as he indulges in them. Lydia has a child already, so surely Tom cannot be that child. There is a telling description at one point in the courting stage of the relationship where the passive voice cunningly hides crucial information: "He would have liked to think of her as of something given into his protection, like a child without parents. But it was forbidden him" (*R* 39). Why forbidden him? Who forbids it? It is "forbidden him" because emotionally he is the child, not the parent, and the fantasy inversion of the dependency bespeaks an unconscious compensation for his own neediness.

19 The male feeling of non-existence in the absence of the support of a mother/wife figure is a fairly common one in Lawrence. Apart from Geoffrey Wookey and Tom Brangwen, we have, for example, the character Whiston in the early short story "The White Stocking," who, when his wife, Elsie, is out, feels that "all his light and warmth were taken away," and he is "all the while anxious for her, yearning for surety, and kept tense by not getting it" (*PO* 143, 149). The uncertainty is understandable given Elsie's ongoing flirtation with her former employer, Sam Adams, but it is only Whiston's marriage to Elsie that "gave him a permanent surety and sense of realness in himself" to begin with (*PO* 158). As mentioned in chapter 1, in the later story "The Border-Line," Philip says wistfully to Katherine, "'A man without a woman *can't* be real'" (*WWRA* 92).

20 Even before they enter the cathedral, it is clear that the building in some way represents the maternal bond for Will: "'There she is,' he said. The 'she' irritated her. Why 'she'? It was 'it'" (*R* 186). But of course for Will it can only be "she," and "[h]e was to pass within to the perfect womb" (*R* 186).

Tony Pinkney has pointed out in a more general way how in *The Rainbow* "the Gothic Cathedral ... is a body, and more specifically a female body, a womb" and how the rainbow and arch images partake of this association (185, 186). In *Sons and Lovers*, it is Paul and his mother who visit Lincoln Cathedral, so the substitution, so to speak, of wife for mother in the later novel seems significant. Paul, like Will, calls the cathedral "she" – "'There she is, mother!' he cried" (*SL* 280) – but in that case there is no resistance from his companion: Mrs Morel also refers to the cathedral using the feminine pronoun.

21 In the Hardy essay, Lawrence writes of "the little figures, the gargoyles, the imps, the human faces" in medieval cathedrals that "jeered their mockery of the Absolute" (*STH* 66).

22 Carl Krockel describes Skrebensky's sense of self as a "self-assured individuality" that "is a product of his career in the army" (31), but this is surely a misinterpretation of his character.

23 Ursula's two significant relational experiences during Anton's years-long absence prime her for the final crisis when he returns. She painfully rejects both her high school teacher Winifred Inger, with whom she is infatuated for a time, and Anthony Schofield (another "Tony"), brother to a fellow teacher at Brinsley Street School, where Ursula works. These are, in effect, proxies and rehearsals for the further development in her complicated and doomed connection with Skrebensky. In addition, Ursula's teaching experience while Skrebensky is absent, difficult as it is, is a further step in attaining her autonomy. It is also in one sense a trying-out of Skrebensky's life philosophy that an individual is only a small cog in the great machine of society. Even early on, she dissents from such a philosophy.

24 Nixon helpfully divides the critics who had written on the scene up to the time of her 1982 article into two groups: one, including H.M. Daleski, F.B. Pinion, and Scott Sanders, that sees the horses as representing "something to be transcended and kept under control" (124), and a second, including Mary Freeman, Graham Hough, Mark Kinkead-Weekes, and Julian Moynahan, that views the horses as representing "the vitality of nature ... which surges up in Ursula to keep her from betraying her quest for fulfillment by marrying Skrebensky" (124). More recently, Schapiro's view nicely reconciles the two by invoking the Lawrentian paradox, which I would argue is inseparable from attachment issues: the horses "represent an externalization of that sensual bodily expressiveness that is always both desired and dreaded in Lawrence's world" so that "the self fears it will be ... overpowered and enslaved by the very wildness it craves" (99).

25 It is noteworthy, however, that the beginning of Genesis is all about separation: on the first few days of Creation, God separates light from darkness so that there is night and day; water is separated from water so

that there is sky above and water below; and then water is disconnected from ground so that there is sea and land. Divisions between seasons, days, and years continue the process. Given the prominent place of Genesis in the structure of the novel, how crucial separation is to biblical creation, and how estrangement – a form of separation – between God and fallen humanity leads to the Flood, it is significant and appropriate that Ursula's journey toward individuation ends in a vision that is suggestive of both autonomy and attachment. The fact that the rainbow is an optical illusion might suggest that Ursula's final vision is far too optimistic, but Turner, for one, sees the positive side of illusion in the symbol: "it celebrates – and embodies – the capacity to generate illusion, to renew desire and wonder in pursuit of psychic balance" (*Psychoanalysis* 104).

26 For Lawrence's knowledge of Wordsworth's work, see, for example, *The Prussian Officer and Other Stories* (261n) and Burwell (214, 286). Michael Ross calls *The Rainbow*'s title Wordsworthian and explores the affinities between Lawrence and his romantic predecessors, specifically Wordsworth. He views the affinities as both profound and problematic (41).

Chapter Four

1 In the restored Foreword to *Fantasia of the Unconscious*, a piece intended by Lawrence to be an answer to his critics' comments on his earlier *Psychoanalysis and the Unconscious* but which was drastically cut by his publisher Thomas Seltzer for the original publication (*PFU* xliv), Lawrence sarcastically mocks in capital letters one critic's view of him as "THE SEX-OBSESSED MR D.H. LAWRENCE" (*PFU* 55).

2 The two areas of interest, sexuality and class, are not necessarily mutually exclusive in Lawrence, of course. Richard Wasson, in fact, claims that they are related: "Lawrence's sense of the male body, of phallic sexuality, is related to his perception of and identification with the dangers brought to the male body by industrial working conditions" (289–90). Wasson also credits Scott Sanders with a critical breakthrough in Lawrence studies with his articulation of "important interstices between the writer's working-class background and some of the sexual themes and categories which pervade his novels" (289).

3 Compare Janice Hubbard Harris's remark in reference to "Daughters of the Vicar": "Lawrence tends eventually to dismiss class as the central concern, focusing instead on conflicts more deeply embedded in his characters' psyches" (55). There is certainly no dismissal of class as a concern, but there is often a deep relationship in Lawrence between class and his complex attitude to attachment that does tend to displace the focus onto psychological considerations. Similarly, Andrew Harrison's comment

(in a summary of Scott Sanders's view in *D.H. Lawrence: The World of the Major Novels*) that "Lawrence is said to have escaped from historical reality into a psychological drama that locates power in the self, not in the class system" (*Casebook* 18) should be augmented with a realization of the role of attachment in Lawrence's portrayal of class and the powerful link between attachment and selfhood.

4 If we take *Sons and Lovers* to be a strongly autobiographical novel, then Terry Eagleton's suggestion about Paul in the novel reinforces the point about the young Lawrence: "his emotional turning to [his mother] from the father is, inseparably, a turning from the impoverished, exploitative world of the colliery towards the life of emancipated consciousness" (176).

5 Fox has only two very brief references to Lawrence in her book, whereas Wilson names him and Robert Tressell as the two writers who had "a profound impact on the subsequent character, development and reception of working-class fiction" (37).

6 See chapter 2, note 12.

7 John Goode sees "a threefold antithesis, industrial and rural, community and social aspiration, convention and idealism" that creates the tension in Lawrence's work "between a powerful need for human relationship and an intense dynamic of self-realization" (109).

8 To name some of them: we have Muriel in "A Modern Lover" caught between her old boyfriend, the intellectual Cyril, and her new one, Tom Vickers; the unnamed woman in "The Shadow in the Rose Garden" torn between the memory of her love for her old flame Archie, the rector's son, and her working-class husband, Frank; Louisa in "Daughters of the Vicar" eschewing class respectability and choosing the collier Alfred Durant; Hilda in "The Shades of Spring" courted by the gamekeeper Arthur Pilbeam while the returning narrator, John Adderley Syson, flirts with her; Clara in *Sons and Lovers* caught between Paul Morel and her estranged husband, Baxter; Barbara in the play *The Fight for Barbara* living with Jimmy Wesson, a decided inferior in class terms, and her desperate husband Frederick; Fanny in "The Last Straw" settling for the foundry worker Harry after a futile play for her prosperous cousin; Mrs Pinnegar in "Jimmy and the Desperate Woman" choosing the prominent editor Jimmy over her rather indifferent collier husband Pinnegar; and Yvette in *The Virgin and the Gipsy* rejecting Leo Wetherell's offhand proposal that they get engaged while dealing with her attraction to the magnetic gipsy man. Further examples appear later in this chapter, while some of these stories are discussed in the next chapter as stories of homecoming.

9 In a letter to Ernest Collings of 17 January 1913, Lawrence wrote: "I conceive of a man's body as a kind of flame, like a candle flame forever upright and yet flowing: and the intellect is just the light that is shed onto the things around."

The preference is for the flame over the light, but arguably only because of an existing gross imbalance: "We have got so ridiculously mindful, that we never know that we ourselves are anything" (*1L* 503). Paul Delany has suggested that the Lawrentian idea of the flame of life comes from the contrast brought about by technological change: "The image derives from the replacement, during the nineteenth century, of candlelight by gaslight" (157).

10 See chapter 5 for further discussion of *The Virgin and the Gipsy*.
11 Leavis suggests that "the relations between [Alfred] and his mother resemble those between Lawrence and his" (110).
12 In the "Anna Victrix" chapter of *The Rainbow*, among several metaphors describing Will's stifling dependence on Anna and her reaction to it, there is this flood metaphor: "She was as the rock on which he stood, with deep, heaving water all round, and he unable to swim. He *must* take his stand on her, he must depend on her. What had he in life, save her? Nothing. The rest was a great, heaving flood. The terror of the night of heaving, overwhelming flood, which was his vision of life without her, was too much for him. He clung to her fiercely and abjectly" (*R* 173).
13 See the extended discussion of the identification of both Bertie and Maurice in my book *D.H. Lawrence and Survival: Darwinism in the Fiction of the Transitional Period*, 145–50.
14 Lawrence's disparagement of Jane Austen is evident in *A Propos of "Lady Chatterley's Lover"*: "Already this old maid typifies 'personality' instead of character, the sharp knowing in apartness instead of knowing in togetherness, and she is, to my feeling, thoroughly unpleasant, English in the bad, mean, snobbish sense of the word" (*LCL* 333).
15 Compare Sandra M. Gilbert's comment that Lawrence "inscribed himself as both the voyeuristic but paralysed non-participant Clifford Chatterley and the revisionary father-cum-nurturer of baby birds whose name, 'Mellors,' dramatically revises the name of that primordial father 'Morel'" ("Apocalypse" 245).

Chapter Five

1 These are the opening words of the untitled essay that has been dubbed "[Autobiographical Fragment]" by various editors. James T. Boulton, the editor of the Cambridge edition of *Late Essays and Articles* in which it is found, has dated the composition of the piece as "*c*. 26–30 October 1927" (*LEA* 49).
2 In his Introduction to the Cambridge edition of *St Mawr and Other Stories*, Brian Finney identifies the source of this reported comment as the book by Lawrence's friends, the Brewsters: Earl Brewster and Achsah Brewster, *D.H. Lawrence: Reminiscences and Correspondence* (1934), 288 (*SM* xxxv).

3 Parmenter also speculates that the reissue around this time of Lawrence's first novel, *The White Peacock*, may have "intensified his homesickness while simultaneously inspiring him to return to a nearby setting" for "The Flying-Fish" (339, 340).
4 Wexler is discussing magic realism and modernism.
5 This wording appears in "The Harassed Angel," an early version of "The Shades of Spring," and is somewhat altered in the final version of the story.
6 David Ellis nicely details the biographical background to the story in the third volume of the Cambridge biography of Lawrence, *Dying Game 1922–1930* (*DG* 165–7). Balbert remarks that the three Murry stories, "The Last Laugh," "The Border-Line," and "Jimmy and the Desperate Woman," grew out of Lawrence's "developing perception of Murry as a sexual rival and narcissistic manipulator, and Frieda as a potential or actual adulterer" and that they "make an ideological virtue out of a psychosexual necessity" (*Marriage* 154–5). I am suggesting that there is a rather covert extra dimension, at least in this one story, that harkens back to much older emotions; indeed, given Lawrence's perception of Frieda's betrayal at this point, an embedded, imaginative return to a more positive view of his mother is plausible.
7 Ellis also shrewdly comments that Mr Pinnegar, the collier, is "the kind of figure Lawrence is obviously imagining he might have been had he followed his father's line of work" (*DG* 166). No doubt hearing of Murry's escapade in the coal mining district of Lawrence's childhood would have awakened memories of his early life and his mother's struggles, and although, as Ellis claims, Pinnegar is more a modified Bert than Arthur Lawrence, when Jimmy and Pinnegar first meet, Pinnegar's "'My hand's not fit to shake hands'" (*WWRA* 109) is strongly reminiscent of Walter Morel's "'Tha niver wants ter shake hands wi' a hand like that, does ter?'" to the visiting clergyman Mr Heaton in *Sons and Lovers* (*SL* 46).
8 There are a number of portrayals of defeated women during this period of writing, most notoriously the female protagonist of "None of That!" who is gang raped, that of "The Princess," who is sexually forced, and that of the story "The Woman Who Rode Away," who is about to become the victim of a ritual human sacrifice when the story abruptly ends. Less brutal but also featuring the defeat of a self-confident woman is "Monkey Nuts," which, for Kinkead-Weekes, along with the contemporaneous "The Last Straw," is an "imaginative taking down of female self-importance and presumption" (*TE* 504). In "Monkey Nuts," the land girl Miss Stokes engages in a battle of wills for the affection and loyalty of Joe with his older friend and military superior, Albert. Because of Albert's age and Miss Stokes's authoritative manner, they might be seen as representative father and mother figures struggling over their son. Miss Stokes's penetrating gaze, emphasized

throughout the story, bespeaks a self-confident woman, as does her ability to do the work of a man. But the female gaze often betokens more than that in Lawrence. Schapiro suggests that in many Lawrence works it "draws its emotional and psychological force from the eye contact, the subtle but profound attunement play of early mother-child interactions" (58). However, in this case, the oedipal struggle is inverted and the mother figure thoroughly defeated.

9 The significant exceptions to this tendency to move on are "The Primrose Path," from 1913, and "Samson and Delilah," written in 1916, where there seems to be no prospect of going forward. In the former tale, the homecoming of Daniel Sutton from Australia seems to end in failure as witnessed by his namesake nephew, Daniel Berry. The crucial scene of Sutton's horror at the deathbed of his estranged wife may be a displaced working-through of Lawrence's own attendance at his mother's slow and painful death, which involved a wrenching homecoming from his school duties in Croydon. Bruce Steele points out in the Cambridge University Press edition of *England, My England* that "Daniel Sutton is closely based on DHL's maternal uncle, Herbert Beardsall (b. 1871)." Many of the details of Sutton's life are drawn from Beardsall's, and, as Steele also reminds us, "DHL shared his uncle's name (Herbert). In MS, Berry was at first called David (DHL's first name)" (*EME* 246n). In "Samson and Delilah," Willie Nankervis returns to his Cornish tin-mining town after fifteen years abroad (in America), and the purpose of the homecoming in this case is not at all to prepare to forge ahead in life. In fact, once back home, he means to stay. He seems to be defeated when his wife has him bound and ejected from her pub, but in the end she seems to have accepted his return.

10 Some of the opposition to looking back and the association with Lot's wife come from an earlier phase in Lawrence's life that may have played into his own sense of maternal attachment: the time when he and Frieda were first living together on the continent and she longed for her children back in England. In the poem "She Looks Back," composed in June–July 1912 (*Poems* 947), Lawrence writes of his bitterness when Frieda's mother-love draws her away to thoughts of her children: "Lot's Wife! – Not Wife, but Mother. / I have learned to curse your motherhood, / You pillar of salt accursed" (*Poems* 168, ll. 60–2). Compare *Fantasia of the Unconscious*: "Because if Lot's wife, looking back, was turned to a pillar of salt, these miserable men, forever looking back to their wives for guidance, they are miserable pillars of half-rotten tears" (*PFU* 198).

11 See chapter 1 for more on the Lawrence-Helen Corke relationship and how it influenced the writing of *The Trespasser*.

12 Lawrence seems to have been fascinated by the colour blue, as evidenced in much of his writing. In *The Captain's Doll*, for example, the colour is

prominent in the symbolically significant glacier excursion of Captain Hepburn and Countess Hannele, and its significance seems to culminate in a description of monkshood (also known as "women's bane"): "That dark-blue, black-blue, terrible colour of the strange rich monkshood made Hepburn look and look and look again. How did the ice come by the lustrous blue-purple intense darkness?" (*Fox* 133). The rather vague poem "Blueness" mentions "manifold blue, amazing eyes" (*Poems* 98, l. 10), while "Bavarian Gentians" compares the titular flowers to "the smoking blueness of Pluto's gloom," and the speaker imagines being guided by such a flower "down the darker and darker stairs, where blue is darkened on blueness" (*Poems* 611, ll. 4,13). Picking up on Pritchard's point in a note, Schapiro remarks that blue is also important in "The Woman Who Rode Away," where, for the Indians (quoting from the story), it is "the colour of what goes away and is never coming back, but which is always here, waiting like death among us" (*WWRA* 64). Schapiro comments that "the description here ... suggests the experience of the mother as distant, withholding and withdrawn" (137n), and "dead," one might add. As we will see later in this chapter, blue eyes are also significant in the late story "The Blue Moccasins."

13   For example, in the chapter "Parent Love": "The cervical plexuses and the cervical ganglia, which should only begin to awake after adolescence, these centres of the higher dynamic sympathy and cognition are both artificially stimulated, by the adult personal love-emotion and love-will into response, in a quite young child, sometimes even in an infant. This is a holy obscenity" (*PFU* 143).

14   The device Lawrence uses here is a drainpipe. Pauline sunbathes just where the pipe terminates among the obscuring leaves of a creeper in such a way that the pipe functions as a speaking tube so that Ciss, sunbathing herself on a roof overlooking Pauline's spot, can hear everything when Pauline talks to herself. Ciss then ingeniously reverses the flow of talk, pretending to be the spirit of the dead Henry telling his mother how wicked she is.

15   In the early version, Lina allows Percy to reclaim the moccasins for the rest of the play. Alice thanks Lina for the footwear and then asks Percy what he really thinks of his wife. He replies: "'What she is, she's perfect, perfect. She really puts the final touch to life, if you know what I mean'" (*VG* 250).

16   In the *Prussian Officer* version, he says, "'I should ha' thought you'd rather go to a fresh place'" (*PO* 123).

17   The look in the mirror as well as other aspects of the story may owe something to James Joyce's story "The Dead," as others have observed. Brenda Maddox, for one, suggests that the similarities between the two stories "defy coincidence" (167) and, in a five-page bibliographical note at the end of her book, details the case for Joyce's work influencing Lawrence (511–15).

18 A succinct explanation of the mirroring function in parent-child attachment can be found in Winnicott's chapter in *Playing and Reality* (1971) entitled "Mirror-Role of Mother and Family in Child Development."
19 In *Sons and Lovers*, Gertrude Morel is shown pining for a lost love, John Field, "the son of a well-to-do tradesman," whose gift of a Bible she still retains (*SL* 16).
20 Paxton associates Mrs Fawcett with the pioneer of women's suffrage in Great Britain, Millicent Fawcett (67). Given the importance of water in the story, the name may also punningly suggest that she is one water tap that helps to open the floodgates of Yvette's desire.
21 Joseph Allen Boone in his *Libidinal Currents* argues: "just as the erasure of one parent, the Pater, has facilitated the incestuous bonding of mother and son in the first [generation], so the absence of another parent, Cynthia, opens the way to the incestuous intensity of Yvette's struggle with her father in the second" (quoted in Paxton 66).
22 As a Jewess, Mrs Eastwood is an outsider like the gipsy man. Older than her new husband and with two children from her dissolving marriage, she has some affinities with Frieda, while Lawrence splits himself into two characters as he often does: the upper-middle-class Major Eastwood whose "athletic, prominent chest" (*VG* 48) might be seen as a compensatory fantasy for the weak-chested Lawrence, and the lower-class, charismatic gipsy who nearly died of pneumonia during the war (*VG* 58). It is no mere coincidence that Lawrence uses Eastwood, the name of his home town, for the major's surname.
23 Ellis references Barbara Weekley as the source for Lawrence's motive not to publish *The Virgin and the Gipsy*. She was told by her mother that the reason was the portrayal of the nominal head of the family, Saywell, who was modelled on Ernest Weekley, Barbara's father, but it is quite conceivable that the Mater's depiction was also a factor in the voluntary suppression of the story. Paxton explains the decision a little more generally: Lawrence's "sympathy for Barby later compelled him to suppress the publication" (58).
24 Saywell is mentioned by Christian as the father of Talkative. He says the right things but fails to make his deeds match his words – a kind of hypocrite, then.
25 Before the Mater is washed away by the flood, the story destroys her symbolically when the rector's working-class gardener kills a bloated old toad, who, in Yvette's eyes, resembles the Mater "with her insatiable greed for life, other people's life" (*VG* 16). The old toad, a zoomorphic devouring mother, as it were, would sit in front of the rectory's beehive and swallow the bees as they emerged. The gardener crushes it while exclaiming, "'Appen thou *art* good for th' snails ... But tha'rt none goin' ter emp'y th' bee-'ive into thy guts'" (*VG* 17). It is suggestive that the symbol of the devouring mother figure is crushed by a working-class man whose north-England dialect is similar to Walter Morel's.

26 The gipsy's life-affirming, warming embrace of Yvette might be compared to the situation, on the one hand, of Alvina in *The Lost Girl* in the ice-cold home of Pancrazio seeking out Ciccio for warmth, and, on the other hand, of Dollie in "The Princess" in the frigid mountain shack with Romero. In the former, Alvina is "stunned with cold" at night and has fantasies of escape while lying awake in her horribly cold bed. But then she goes across the room to Ciccio's bed: "She felt his power and his warmth invade her and extinguish her" (*LG* 313). In the latter, in a scene that has some parallels to the one in *The Lost Girl*, a frigid Dolly, lying in bed at night in the shack, "wanted warmth, protection," and calls to Romero to make her warm. He does so but proceeds to "annihilate her," to force her sexually, and subsequently to keep her prisoner. All three scenes, incidentally, involve an ascent: to the upper floor of the house in *The Virgin and the Gipsy*, in the Italian mountain country in *The Lost Girl*, and in the Rockies in "The Princess."
27 The editors of the Cambridge University Press edition of *The Virgin and the Gipsy and Other Stories*, in which the fragment appears as Appendix V, have dated the writing of "The Woman Who Wanted to Disappear" as no earlier than January 1929 (*VG* xliii).
28 Compare this paradox from the Hardy essay: "He who would save his life must lose it" (*STH* 19).
29 As a point of comparison, one might view the early tale "Odour of Chrysanthemums" (its origin is as early as 1909), where wife and mother both minister to the corpse of a man killed in a mining accident, as a return through death: a homecoming to two mother figures where it takes death to restore a recognition of the man's authentic self.

Conclusion

1 We may compare this from *Fantasia*: "the very sacredness of my own individuality prevents my pronouncing about [other individuals], lest I, in attributing qualities to them, transgress against the pure individuality which is theirs, beyond me" (*PFU* 176).
2 James T. Boulton, the editor of the Cambridge *Late Essays and Articles*, names Cézanne's *Le Compotier* as a possible inspiration for Lawrence's reflections on apples because that work was discussed in Roger Fry's 1927 book about the painter (*LEA* 362n). Lawrence does not specify which painting or paintings he is referring to. Cézanne is also known for his *Still Life with Apples*.
3 Brault-Dreux is approvingly quoting from Pollnitz's lengthy study of the poem "Fish" in his article "'I Didn't Know His God': The Epistemology of 'Fish,'" 13. Pollnitz's study is more about the concept of blood consciousness than about otherness per se, but there is some obvious overlap between the

two ideas. In the same article, Pollnitz describes otherness as the realization that "[a] subject's furthest knowledge of another is that its knowledge is incomplete" and posits the difficulty of maintaining an equilibrium between self and other in the contest between "encroachment and reverence, attraction and repulsion" (27).

4 See chapter 2 for further discussion of "Man and Bat" and "Snake" in relation to Lawrence's feelings about his father.

WORKS CITED

Note: There are numerous entries from the periodical *D.H. Lawrence Review* in this Works Cited list. Originally called *The D.H. Lawrence Review*, the journal dropped the definite article from the title after volume 24, when Charles R. Rossman assumed the editorship. For simplicity's sake and to avoid the impression that two different but similarly named periodicals are involved, I have chosen to apply the newer iteration to all of the volumes cited.

Adamowski, T.H. "*The Rainbow* and 'Otherness.'" *D.H. Lawrence Review* 7, no. 1 (1974): 58–77.

Arcana, Judith. "I Remember Mama: Mother-Blaming in *Sons and Lovers* Criticism." *D.H. Lawrence Review* 21, no. 2 (1989): 137–51.

Atkins, A.R. "Textual Influences on D.H. Lawrence's 'The Saga of Siegmund.'" *D.H. Lawrence Review* 24, no. 1 (1992): 7–26.

Austen, Jane. *Pride and Prejudice*. [1813.] Harmondsworth, UK: Penguin, 1985.

Balbert, Peter. *D.H. Lawrence and the Marriage Matrix: Intertextual Adventures in Conflict, Renewal, and Transcendence*. Newcastle upon Tyne, UK: Cambridge Scholars Publishing, 2016.

– *D.H. Lawrence and the Phallic Imagination: Essays on Sexual Identity and Feminist Misreading*. Basingstoke, UK: Macmillan, 1989.

Baldick, Chris. "Post-Mortem: Lawrence's Critical and Cultural Legacy." In *The Cambridge Companion to D.H. Lawrence*, edited by Anne Fernihough, 253–69. Cambridge: Cambridge University Press, 2001.

Becket, Fiona. "Being There: Nostalgia and the Masculine Maternal in D.H. Lawrence." *D.H. Lawrence Review* 27, no. 2–3 (1997–98): 255–68.

Ben-Ephraim, Gavriel. *The Moon's Dominion: Narrative Dichotomy and Female Dominance in Lawrence's Early Novels*. Rutherford, NJ: Fairleigh Dickinson University Press, 1981.

Benjamin, Jessica. *The Bonds of Love: Psychoanalysis, Feminism, and the Problem of Domination*. New York: Pantheon, 1988.

Berman, Jeffrey. *Narcissism and the Novel*. New York: New York University Press, 1990.

Black, Michael. *D.H. Lawrence: The Early Philosophical Works: A Commentary*. Cambridge: Cambridge University Press, 1992.

Bonds, Diane S. *Language and the Self in D.H. Lawrence*. Ann Arbor, MI: UMI Research Press, 1987.

Booth, Howard J. "'Give me *differences*': Lawrence, Psychoanalysis, and Race." *D.H. Lawrence Review* 27, no. 2-3 (1997-98): 171-96.

– "'They had met in a naked extremity of hate, and it was a bond': The Later Chapters of *Sons and Lovers*, Psychoanalysis, and Male-Male Intimacy." *D.H. Lawrence Review* 39, no. 2 (2014): 59-76.

Bowlby, John. *Attachment and Loss, Volume I: Attachment*. New York: Basic Books, 1969.

– *Attachment and Loss, Volume II: Separation, Anxiety and Anger*. New York: Basic Books, 1973.

Brandão, Izabel F.O. "*Kangaroo*: Lawrence's Homeless Hero in Search of a Place." *D.H. Lawrence Review* 36, no. 1 (2011): 14-30.

Brault-Dreux, Elise. "Responding to Non-Human Otherness: Poems by D.H. Lawrence and Katherine Mansfield." *D.H. Lawrence Review* 37, no. 2 (2012): 22-43.

Bretherton, Inge, and Kristine A. Munholland. "Internal Working Models in Attachment Relationships: A Construct Revisited." In *Handbook of Attachment: Theory, Research, and Clinical Applications*, edited by Jude Cassidy and Phillip R. Shaver, 89-111. New York and London: The Guilford Press, 1999.

Brewster, Scott. "Jumping Continents: Abjection, *Kangaroo*, and the Celtic Uncanny." *D.H. Lawrence Review* 27, no. 2-3 (1997-98): 217-32.

Burwell, Rose Marie. "A Catalogue of D.H. Lawrence's Reading from Early Childhood." *D.H. Lawrence Review* 3, no. 3 (1970): 193-324.

Cassidy, Jude. "The Nature of the Child's Ties." In *Handbook of Attachment: Theory, Research, and Clinical Applications*, edited by Jude Cassidy and Phillip R. Shaver, 3-20. New York and London: The Guilford Press, 1999.

Cavitch, David. *D.H. Lawrence and the New World*. New York: Oxford University Press, 1969.

– "Merging – with Fish and Others." *D.H. Lawrence Review* 7, no. 2 (1974): 172-8.

Chambers, Jessie. *D.H. Lawrence: A Personal Record* by E.T. [1935.] Cambridge: Cambridge University Press, 1980.
Chung, Chong-wha. "In Search of the Dark God: Lawrence's Dualism." In *D.H. Lawrence in the Modern World*, edited by Peter Preston and Peter Hoare, 69–89. London: Macmillan, 1989.
Connell, Christine M. "Inheritance from the Earth and Generational Passages in D.H. Lawrence's *The Rainbow*." *D.H. Lawrence Review* 36, no. 1 (2011): 72–91.
Conrad, Joseph. *Heart of Darkness*. [1899.] Edited by Robert Kimbrough. New York: Norton, 1988.
Corke, Helen. "The Writing of *The Trespasser*." *D.H. Lawrence Review* 7, no. 3 (1974): 227–39.
Cowan, James C. *D.H. Lawrence and the Trembling Balance*. University Park, PA: Pennsylvania State University Press, 1990.
– *D.H. Lawrence: Self and Sexuality*. Columbus: Ohio State University Press, 2002.
Cushman, Keith. *D.H. Lawrence at Work: The Emergence of "The Prussian Officer" Stories*. Charlottesville, VA: University Press of Virginia, 1978.
– "Domestic Life in the Suburbs: Lawrence, the Joneses, and 'The Old Adam.'" *D.H. Lawrence Review* 16, no. 3 (1983): 221–34.
Daleski, H.M. *The Forked Flame: A Study of D.H. Lawrence*. London: Faber, 1965.
Davies, Rosemary Reeves. "The Mother as Destroyer: Psychic Division in the Writings of D.H. Lawrence." *D.H. Lawrence Review* 13, no. 3 (1980): 220–38.
Delany, Paul. "*Sons and Lovers*: The Morel Marriage as a War of Position." *D.H. Lawrence Review* 21, no. 2 (1989): 153–65.
DeLia, Demetria. "Bridled Rage: Preoedipal Theory and 'The Rocking-Horse Winner.'" *D.H. Lawrence Review* 41, no. 2 (2016): 128–44.
Dervin, Daniel. "Play, Creativity and Matricide: The Implications of Lawrence's 'Smashed Doll' Episode." *Mosaic: A Journal for the Interdisciplinary Study of Literature* 14, no. 3 (1981): 81–94.
– *A "Strange Sapience": The Creative Imagination of D.H. Lawrence*. Amherst, MA: University of Massachusetts Press, 1984.
Doherty, Gerald. "*Ars Erotica* or *Scientia Sexualis*?: Narrative Vicissitudes in D.H. Lawrence's *Women in Love*." In *D.H. Lawrence's* Women in Love: *A Casebook*, edited by David Ellis, 135–57. Oxford, UK: Oxford University Press, 2006.
– "A Question of Gravity: The Erotics of Identification in *Women in Love*." *D.H. Lawrence Review* 29, no. 2 (2000): 25–41.
Douglas, Mary. *Purity and Danger: An Analysis of Concepts of Pollution and Taboo*. [1966.] London: Routledge, 1978.
Eagleton, Terry. *Literary Theory: An Introduction*. Oxford, UK: Basil Blackwell, 1983.

Eckhard, Petra. *Chronotopes of the Uncanny: Time and Space in Postmodern New York Novels. Paul Auster's "City of Glass" and Tony Morrison's "Jazz."* Bielefeld, Germany: Transcript Verlag, 2011.

Eggert, Paul. "The Biographical Issue: Lives of Lawrence." In *The Cambridge Companion to D.H. Lawrence*, edited by Anne Fernihough, 157–77. Cambridge: Cambridge University Press, 2001.

Ellis, David. *D.H. Lawrence: Dying Game 1922–1930*. Cambridge: Cambridge University Press, 1998.

– *Love and Sex in D.H. Lawrence*. Clemson, SC: Clemson University Press, 2015.

Fairbairn, W.R.D. "The Repression and the Return of Bad Objects (with Special Reference to the 'War Neuroses')." [1941.] In *Essential Papers on Object Relations*, edited by Peter Buckley, 102–26. New York and London: New York University Press, 1986.

Feeney, Judith A. "Adult Romantic Attachment and Couple Relationships." In *Handbook of Attachment: Theory, Research, and Clinical Applications*, edited by Jude Cassidy and Phillip R. Shaver, 355–77. New York and London: The Guilford Press, 1999.

Fernihough, Anne. *D.H. Lawrence: Aesthetics and Ideology*. Oxford, UK: Oxford University Press, 1993.

Fox, Elizabeth M. "A Brief History of Psychoanalytic Criticism of D.H. Lawrence." *D.H. Lawrence Studies* (Korea) 12, no. 2 (2004): 177–93.

Fox, Pamela. *Class Fictions: Shame and Resistance in the British Working-Class Novel, 1890–1945*. Durham, NC: Duke University Press, 1994.

Freud, Sigmund. "The Uncanny." [1919.] In *The Uncanny*, translated by David McLintock, 121–62. London: Penguin, 2003.

Game, David. *D.H. Lawrence's Australia: Anxiety at the Edge of Empire*. Farnham, UK, and Burlington, VT: Ashgate, 2015.

– "D.H. Lawrence and Zane Grey: The Idea of North-Western Australia." *D.H. Lawrence Review* 42, no. 1–2 (2017): 29–51.

Gilbert, Sandra M. *Acts of Attention: The Poems of D.H. Lawrence*. Ithaca, NY: Cornell University Press, 1972.

– "Apocalypse Now (and Then). Or, D.H. Lawrence and the Swan in the Electron." In *The Cambridge Companion to D.H. Lawrence*, edited by Anne Fernihough, 235–52. Cambridge: Cambridge University Press, 2001.

Glitz, Rudolph. *Writing the Victorians: The Early Twentieth-Century Family Chronicle*. Heidelberg, Germany: Universitätsverlag Winter, 2009.

Good, Jan. "Toward a Resolution of Gender Identity Confusion: The Relationship of Henry and March in *The Fox*." *D.H. Lawrence Review* 18, no. 2–3 (1985–86): 217–27.

Goode, John. "D.H. Lawrence." In *Sphere History of Literature, vol. 7: The Twentieth Century*, edited by Bernard Bergonzi, 106–52. London: Sphere, 1970.

Granofsky, Ronald. *D.H. Lawrence and Survival: Darwinism in the Fiction of the Transitional Period*. Montreal, QC, and Kingston, ON: McGill-Queen's University Press, 2003.

Greene, John C. *Science, Ideology, and World View: Essays in the History of Evolutionary Ideas*. Berkeley, CA: University of California Press, 1981.

Gunn, David M. "Joshua and Judges." In *The Literary Guide to the Bible*, edited by Robert Alter and Frank Kermode, 102–21. Cambridge, MA: Belknap-Harvard University Press, 1987.

Harris, Janice Hubbard. *The Short Fiction of D.H. Lawrence*. New Brunswick, NJ: Rutgers University Press, 1984.

Harrison, Andrew. "Introduction." In *D.H. Lawrence's* Sons and Lovers: *A Casebook*, edited by John Worthen and Andrew Harrison, 3–26. Oxford, UK: Oxford University Press, 2005.

– *The Life of D.H. Lawrence: A Critical Biography*. Chichester, UK: Wiley-Blackwell, 2016.

Haughton, Hugh. "Introduction." In Sigmund Freud, *The Uncanny*, translated by David McLintock, vii–lx. London: Penguin, 2003.

Hayles, N. Katherine. *The Cosmic Web: Scientific Field Models and Literary Strategies in the Twentieth Century*. Ithaca, NY: Cornell University Press, 1984.

Hazan, Cindy, and Debra Zeifman. "Pair Bonds as Attachments: Evaluating the Evidence." In *Handbook of Attachment: Theory, Research, and Clinical Applications*, edited by Jude Cassidy and Phillip R. Shaver, 336–54. New York and London: The Guilford Press, 1999.

Herzinger, Kim A. *D.H. Lawrence in His Time: 1908–1915*. Lewisburg, PA: Bucknell University Press, 1982.

Huxley, Aldous. *Point Counter Point*. [1928.] London: Flamingo-HarperCollins, 1994.

Ingersoll, Earl G. *D.H. Lawrence: Desire and Narrative*. Gainesville, FL: University Press of Florida, 2001.

Jackson, Dennis. "'The Stormy Petrel of Literature Is Dead': The World Press Reports D.H. Lawrence's Death." *D.H. Lawrence Review* 14, no. 1 (Spring 1981): 33–72.

Kim, Sungho. "The Representation of Class and the Politics of Erotic Discourse in *Lady Chatterley's Lover*." *D.H. Lawrence Studies* (Korea) 12, no. 2 (2004): 135–58.

Kinkead-Weekes, Mark. *D.H. Lawrence: Triumph to Exile, 1912–1922*. Cambridge: Cambridge University Press, 1996.

- "The Sense of History in *The Rainbow*." In *D.H. Lawrence in the Modern World*, edited by Peter Preston and Peter Hoare, 121–38. Cambridge: Cambridge University Press, 1989.
- "Violence in *Women in Love*." In *D.H. Lawrence's* Women in Love: *A Casebook*, edited by David Ellis, 221–44. Oxford, UK: Oxford University Press, 2006.

Kirkpatrick, Lee A. "Attachment and Religious Representations and Behavior." In *Handbook of Attachment: Theory, Research, and Clinical Applications*, edited by Jude Cassidy and Phillip R. Shaver, 803–22. New York: Guilford, 1999.

Kochis, Matthew J. "Lawrence's *Kangaroo*: De-establishing the Double-Bind of Masculinity." *D.H. Lawrence Review* 36, no. 1 (2011): 1–13.

Krockel, Carl. *D.H. Lawrence and Germany: The Politics of Influence*. Amsterdam and New York: Rodopi, 2007.

Kuttner, Alfred Booth. "*Sons and Lovers*: A Freudian Appreciation." [1916.] In *D.H. Lawrence's* Sons and Lovers: *A Casebook*, edited by John Worthen and Andrew Harrison, 263–89. New York: Oxford University Press, 2005.

Laird, Holly. "Configurations of Trespass in the Works of D.H. Lawrence." *Journal of D.H. Lawrence Studies* 4, no. 3 (2017): 71–89.

Langbaum, Robert. *The Mysteries of Identity: A Theme in Modern Literature*. Chicago, IL: University of Chicago Press, 1982.

Lawrence, D.H. *Aaron's Rod*. Edited by Mara Kalnins. Cambridge: Cambridge University Press, 1988.
- *The Boy in the Bush*. With M.L. Skinner. Edited by Paul Eggert. Cambridge: Cambridge University Press, 1990.
- *England, My England and Other Stories*. Edited by Bruce Steele. Cambridge: Cambridge University Press, 1990.
- *The First and Second Lady Chatterley Novels*. Edited by Dieter Mehl and Christa Jansohn. Cambridge: Cambridge University Press, 1999.
- *The First "Women in Love."* Edited by John Worthen and Lindeth Vasey. Cambridge: Cambridge University Press, 1998.
- *The Fox, The Captain's Doll, The Ladybird*. Edited by Dieter Mehl. Cambridge: Cambridge University Press, 1992.
- *Kangaroo*. Edited by Bruce Steele. Cambridge: Cambridge University Press, 1994.
- *The Letters of D.H. Lawrence: Volume I, September 1901–May 1913*. Edited by James T. Boulton. Cambridge: Cambridge University Press, 1979.
- *The Letters of D.H. Lawrence: Volume II, June 1913–October 1916*. Edited by George J. Zytaruk and James T. Boulton. Cambridge: Cambridge University Press, 1981.
- *The Letters of D.H. Lawrence: Volume III, October 1916–June 1921*. Edited by James T. Boulton and Andrew Robertson. Cambridge: Cambridge University Press, 1984.

- *The Letters of D.H. Lawrence: Volume IV, June 1921–March 1924*. Edited by Warren Roberts, James T. Boulton, and Elizabeth Mansfield. Cambridge: Cambridge University Press, 1984.
- *The Letters of D.H. Lawrence: Volume VI, March 1927–November 1928*. Edited by James T. Boulton and Margaret H. Boulton with Gerald M. Lacy. Cambridge: Cambridge University Press, 1991.
- *The Letters of D.H. Lawrence: Volume VIII, Previously Uncollected Letters and General Index*. Edited by James T. Boulton. Cambridge: Cambridge University Press, 2000.
- *Lady Chatterley's Lover and A Propos of "Lady Chatterley's Lover."* Edited by Michael Squires. Cambridge: Cambridge University Press, 1993.
- *Late Essays and Articles*. Edited by James T. Boulton. Cambridge: Cambridge University Press, 2004.
- *The Lost Girl*. Edited by John Worthen. Cambridge: Cambridge University Press, 1981.
- *Love Among the Haystacks and Other Stories*. Edited by John Worthen. Cambridge: Cambridge University Press, 1987.
- *Movements in European History*. Edited by Philip Crumpton. Cambridge: Cambridge University Press, 1989.
- *Mr Noon*. Edited by Lindeth Vasey. Cambridge: Cambridge University Press, 1984.
- *The Plays*. Edited by Hans-Wilhelm Schwarze and John Worthen. Cambridge: Cambridge University Press, 1999.
- *The Poems*. 3 vols. Edited by Christopher Pollnitz. Cambridge: Cambridge University Press, 2013–18.
- *The Prussian Officer and Other Stories*. Edited by John Worthen. Cambridge: Cambridge University Press, 1983.
- *Psychoanalysis and the Unconscious and Fantasia of the Unconscious*. Edited by Bruce Steele. Cambridge: Cambridge University Press, 2004.
- *The Rainbow*. Edited by Mark Kinkead-Weekes. Cambridge: Cambridge University Press, 1989.
- *Reflections on the Death of a Porcupine and Other Essays*. Edited by Michael Herbert. Cambridge: Cambridge University Press, 1988.
- *Sons and Lovers*. Edited by Helen Baron and Carl Baron. Cambridge: Cambridge University Press, 1992.
- *St Mawr and Other Stories*. Edited by Brian Finney. Cambridge: Cambridge University Press, 1983.
- *Studies in Classic American Literature*. Edited by Ezra Greenspan, Lindeth Vasey, and John Worthen. Cambridge: Cambridge University Press, 2003.
- *Study of Thomas Hardy and Other Essays*. Edited by Bruce Steele. Cambridge: Cambridge University Press, 1985.
- *The Trespasser*. Edited by Elizabeth Mansfield. Cambridge: Cambridge University Press, 1981.

– *The Vicar's Garden and Other Stories*. Edited by N.H. Reeve. Cambridge: Cambridge University Press, 2009.
– *The Virgin and the Gipsy and Other Stories*. Edited by Michael Herbert, Bethan Jones, and Lindeth Vasey. Cambridge: Cambridge University Press, 2006.
– *The White Peacock*. Edited by Andrew Robertson. Cambridge: Cambridge University Press, 1983.
– *The Woman Who Rode Away and Other Stories*. Edited by Dieter Mehl and Christa Jansohn. Cambridge: Cambridge University Press, 1995.
– *Women in Love*. Edited by David Farmer, Lindeth Vasey, and John Worthen. Cambridge: Cambridge University Press, 1987
Lawrence, Frieda. *"Not I, But the Wind…."* New York: Viking, 1934.
Leavis, F.R. *D.H. Lawrence: Novelist*. 1955. Middlesex, UK: Penguin, 1973.
Levy, Eric P. "Lawrence's Psychology of Void and Center in *Women in Love*." *D.H. Lawrence Review* 23, no. 1 (1991): 5–19.
Lyons-Ruth, Karlen, and Deborah Jacobvitz. "Attachment Disorganization: Unresolved Loss, Relational Violence, and Lapses in Behavioral and Attentional Strategies." In *Handbook of Attachment: Theory, Research, and Clinical Applications*, edited by Jude Cassidy and Phillip R. Shaver, 520–54. New York and London: The Guilford Press, 1999.
Maddox, Brenda. *D.H. Lawrence: The Story of a Marriage*. New York: Simon & Schuster, 1994.
Mahler, Margaret S. *The Memoirs of Margaret S. Mahler*. Compiled and edited by Paul E. Stepansky. New York: The Free Press, 1988.
Mahler, Margaret S., Fred Pine, and Anni Bergman. *The Psychological Birth of the Human Infant: Symbiosis and Individuation*. New York: Basic Books, 1975.
Mailer, Norman. *The Prisoner of Sex*. Boston: Little Brown, 1971.
Marks, W.D., III. "The Psychology of the Uncanny in Lawrence's 'The Rocking-Horse Winner.'" *Modern Fiction Studies* 11, no. 4 (1965): 381–92.
Martin, Graham. "D.H. Lawrence and Class." In *D.H. Lawrence*, edited by Peter Widdowson, 35–61. London: Longman, 1992.
McAleer, Kevin. *Dueling: The Cult of Honor in Fin-de-Siècle Germany*. Princeton, NJ: Princeton University Press, 1994.
McCabe, T.H. "The Otherness of D.H. Lawrence's 'Odour of Chrysanthemums.'" *D.H. Lawrence Review* 19, no. 2 (1987): 149–56.
Meyers, Jeffrey. *D.H. Lawrence: A Biography*. New York: Vintage-Random House, 1992.
Miller, Alice. *For Your Own Good: Hidden Cruelty in Child-Rearing and the Roots of Violence*. [1980.] Translated by Hildegarde Hannum and Hunter Hannum. New York: Farrar, Straus, Giroux, 1984.
Milne, Drew. "Lawrence and the Politics of Sexual Politics." In *The Cambridge Companion to D.H. Lawrence*, edited by Anne Fernihough, 197–215. Cambridge: Cambridge University Press, 2001.

Moynahan, Julian. *The Deed of Life: The Novels and Tales of D.H. Lawrence*. Princeton, NJ: Princeton University Press, 1963.

Murry, John Middleton. *The Autobiography of John Middleton Murry: Between Two Worlds*. New York: Julian Messner, 1936.

Nehls, Edward, ed. *D.H. Lawrence: A Composite Biography*. 3 vols. Gathered, arranged, and edited by Edward Nehls. Madison: Wisconsin University Press, 1957–59.

Nixon, Cornelia. "To Procreate Oneself: Ursula's Horses in *The Rainbow*." ELH 49 (1982): 123–42.

Parmenter, Ross. *Lawrence in Oaxaca: A Quest for the Novelist in Mexico*. Salt Lake City: Peregrine Smith Books, 1984.

Paxton, Nancy. "Reimagining Melodrama: *The Virgin and the Gipsy* and the Consequences of Mourning." *D.H. Lawrence Review* 38, no. 2 (2013): 58–76.

Pinkney, Tony. *D.H. Lawrence and Modernism*. Iowa City: University of Iowa Press, 1990.

Pollnitz, Christopher. "'I Didn't Know His God': The Epistemology of 'Fish.'" *D.H. Lawrence Review* 15, no. 1–2 (1982): 1–50.

Pritchard, R.E. *D.H. Lawrence: Body of Darkness*. London: Hutchinson University Library, 1971.

Proust, Marcel. *Remembrance of Things Past, vol. 1: Swann's Way; Within a Budding Grove*. Translated by C.K. Scott Moncrieff and Terence Kilmartin. New York: Vintage-Random House, 1981.

Roberts, Neil. *D.H. Lawrence, Travel and Cultural Difference*. Houndmills, UK: Palgrave Macmillan, 2004.

– "Writing with Women: Lawrence, Helen Corke and *The Trespasser*." *Journal of D.H. Lawrence Studies* 3, no. 2 (2013): 13–34.

Ross, Michael. "Transcendental Climbing: Lawrence, Wordsworth, and Romantic Uplift." *D.H. Lawrence Review* 34–5 (2010): 41–54.

Ruderman, Judith. *D.H. Lawrence and the Devouring Mother: The Search for a Patriarchal Ideal of Leadership*. Durham, NC: Duke University Press, 1984.

– *Race and Identity in D.H. Lawrence: Indians, Gypsies, and Jews*. Houndmills, UK: Palgrave Macmillan, 2014.

Sagar, Keith. *The Art of D.H. Lawrence*. Cambridge: Cambridge University Press, 1966.

Salgādo, Gāmini. *A Preface to Lawrence*. London: Longman, 1982.

Sanders, Scott. *D.H. Lawrence: The World of the Major Novels*. London: Vision Press, 1973.

Sargent, M. Elizabeth, and Garry Watson. "D.H. Lawrence and the Dialogical Principle: 'The Strange Reality of Otherness.'" *College English* 63, no. 4 (2001): 409–36.

Schapiro, Barbara Ann. *D.H. Lawrence and the Paradoxes of Psychic Life*. Albany: State University of New York Press, 1999.

Scheckner, Peter. *Class, Politics, and the Individual: A Study of the Major Works of D.H. Lawrence*. Rutherford, NJ: Fairleigh Dickinson University Press, 1985.

Schneider, Daniel J. *D.H. Lawrence: The Artist as Psychologist*. Lawrence, KS: University of Kansas Press, 1984.

– "The Laws of Action and Reaction in *Women in Love*." *D.H. Lawrence Review* 14, no. 3 (1981): 238–62.

Schorer, Mark. "Technique as Discovery." *Hudson Review* 1 (1948): 67–87.

Schwartz, Murray M. "D.H. Lawrence and Psychoanalysis: An Introduction." *D.H. Lawrence Review* 10, no. 3 (1977): 215–22.

Schwarz, Daniel R. "Speaking of Paul Morel: Voice, Unity, and Meaning in *Sons and Lovers*." *Studies in the Novel* 8 (1976): 255–77.

Scott, James F. "D.H. Lawrence's *Germania*: Ethnic Psychology and Cultural Crisis in the Shorter Fiction." *D.H. Lawrence Review* 10, no. 2 (1977): 142–64.

Siegel, Carol. *Lawrence among the Women: Wavering Boundaries in Women's Literary Traditions*. Charlottesville, VA: University of Virginia Press, 1991.

Sklenicka, Carol. *D.H. Lawrence and the Child*. Columbia, MO: University of Missouri Press, 1991.

– "Lawrence's Vision of the Child: Reimagining Character and Consciousness." *D.H. Lawrence Review* 18, no. 2–3 (1985–86): 151–68.

Smith, Anne. "A New Adam and New Eve – Lawrence and Women: A Biographical Overview." In *Lawrence and Women*, edited by Anne Smith, 9–48. London: Vision Press, 1978.

Squires, Michael. *D.H. Lawrence and Frieda: A Portrait of Love and Loyalty*. London: Andre Deutsch, 2008.

Stepansky, Paul E. "Introduction." In Margaret S. Mahler, *The Memoirs of Margaret S. Mahler*, xiii–xl. Compiled and edited by Paul E. Stepansky. New York: The Free Press, 1988.

Stevens, Hugh. "Sex and the Nation: 'The Prussian Officer' and *Women in Love*." In *The Cambridge Companion to D.H. Lawrence*, edited by Anne Fernihough, 49–65. Cambridge: Cambridge University Press, 2001.

Stewart, Jack. "Expressionism in 'The Prussian Officer.'" *D.H. Lawrence Review* 10, no. 2–3 (1985–86): 275–89.

– "Landscape Painting and Pre-Raphaelitism in *The White Peacock*." *D.H. Lawrence Review* 27, no. 1 (1997–98): 3–25.

Stoll, John E. *The Novels of D.H. Lawrence: A Search for Integration*. Columbia, MO: University of Missouri Press, 1971.

Storch, Margaret. "The Lacerated Male: Ambivalent Images of Women in *The White Peacock*." *D.H. Lawrence Review* 21, no. 2 (1989): 117–36.

Thompson, Ross A. "Early Attachment and Later Development." In *Handbook of Attachment: Theory, Research, and Clinical Applications*, edited by Jude Cassidy and Phillip R. Shaver, 265–86. New York and London: The Guilford Press, 1999.

Thornton, Weldon. "A Trio from Lawrence's *England, My England and Other Stories*: Readings of 'Monkey Nuts', 'The Primrose Path', and 'Fanny and Annie'." *D.H. Lawrence Review* 28, no. 3 (1999): 5–29.

Turner, John F. "The Capacity to Be Alone and Its Failure in D.H. Lawrence's 'The Man Who Loved Islands'." *D.H. Lawrence Review* 16, no. 3 (1983): 259–89.

– *D.H. Lawrence and Psychoanalysis*. New York: Routledge, 2020.

Wasson, Richard. "Class and the Vicissitudes of the Male Body in Works by D.H. Lawrence." *D.H. Lawrence Review* 14, no. 3 (1981): 289–305.

Weiss, Daniel. *Oedipus in Nottingham: D.H. Lawrence*. Seattle, WA: University of Washington Press, 1962.

West, Malcolm L., and Adrienne E. Sheldon-Keller. *Patterns of Relating: An Adult Attachment Perspective*. New York and London: The Guilford Press, 1994.

Wexler, Joyce. "Beyond the Body in *The Rainbow* and *One Hundred Years of Solitude*." *D.H. Lawrence Review* 31, no. 2 (2003): 25–41.

Williamson, Alan. *Almost a Girl: Male Writers and Female Identification*. Charlottesville, VA, and London: University Press of Virginia, 2001.

Wilson, Nicola. *Home in British Working-Class Fiction*. Farnham, UK: Ashgate, 2015.

Winnicott, D.W. *Playing and Reality*. [1971.] London and New York: Routledge, 2005.

– "The Theory of the Parent-Infant Relationship." *The International Journal of Psycho-Analysis* 41 (1 January 1960): 585–95.

Wood, James. "Introduction." In D.H. Lawrence, *The Rainbow* [1915], xi–xxviii. London: Penguin, 1995.

Wood, Paul. "The True Cause of Dollie Urquhart's Fall: Complementary Psychological Interpretations of Lawrence's 'The Princess'." *The Journal of the D.H. Lawrence Society* 1996: 18–26.

Wordsworth, William. *Selected Poems and Prefaces*. Edited by Jack Stillinger. Boston: Houghton Mifflin, 1965.

Worthen, John. *D.H. Lawrence: The Early Years, 1885–1912*. Cambridge: Cambridge University Press, 1992.

– *D.H. Lawrence: The Life of an Outsider*. London: Allen Lane, 2005.

– "The First '*Women in Love*'." In *D.H. Lawrence's Women in Love: A Casebook*, edited by David Ellis, 51–77. Oxford, UK: Oxford University Press, 2006.

Wright, T.R. *D.H. Lawrence and the Bible*. Cambridge: Cambridge University Press, 2000.

Wyndham, John. *The Chrysalids*. [1955.] Harmondsworth, UK: Penguin, 1968.

Yeats, W.B. *A Vision*. London: Papermac-Macmillan, 1981.

INDEX

Aaron (biblical figure), 99

abandonment, 5, 6, 11, 16, 36–71, 79, 80, 86, 87, 88, 99, 101, 116, 119, 120, 122, 129, 131, 149, 150–1, 166, 177, 180, 198n19, 202n22, 210n10. *See also* isolation

abandonment anxiety, 32, 34, 36, 37, 49, 53, 54, 55, 62, 71, 79, 80, 85, 150, 161

Adamowski, T.H., 190

Ainsworth, Mary, 16, 38

androgyny, 103

Arcana, Judith, 8, 84

Atkins, A.R., 200n9

attachment: secure, 5, 6, 7, 12, 17, 28, 36, 38, 44, 101, 109, 118, 122, 129, 133, 159, 161, 177, 195n3; insecure, 28, 33, 36, 37, 114, 118, 150, 159

Austen, Jane, 106–7, 109, 145, 147, 152, 208n1, 215n14; *Pride and Prejudice*, 107, 109; *Sense and Sensibility*, 109

Australia, 34–5, 61, 62, 63, 65, 66, 69, 70, 100–1, 103, 104–5, 152, 203n24, 203n26, 217n9

autonomy, 8, 15, 16, 27, 30, 32, 34, 39, 40, 42, 43, 49, 50, 52, 54, 68, 69, 88, 96, 99, 119, 120, 121, 122, 123, 128, 129, 130, 133, 159, 189, 190, 197n11, 198n19, 212n23, 212–13n25; and merger, 4, 7, 16, 20, 22, 24, 26, 35, 37, 38, 39, 42, 49, 96, 102, 140, 190, 193, 194

Bakhtin, Mikhail, 187

balance, 4, 6, 7, 8, 15, 16, 17, 18, 19–28, 32, 33, 35, 37, 38, 39, 41, 42, 45, 57, 75, 76, 79, 81, 85, 96, 133, 149, 161, 190, 192, 194, 197n13, 198n16, 198n18, 198n19, 199n2, 212–13n25; imbalance, 17, 23, 38, 42, 75, 85, 190, 197n13, 214–15n9. *See also* equilibrium; trembling balance

Balbert, Peter, 91, 166, 183, 209n5, 216n6

INDEX

Baldick, Chris, 31

Beardsall, Herbert, 217n9

Becket, Fiona, 103

Ben-Ephraim, Gavriel, 197n13

Benjamin, Jessica, 6–7, 27, 72, 75, 86, 100, 140, 186, 189, 207n22

Bennett, Arnold, 208n4

Berman, Jeffrey, 87, 207n17

biblical allusions and episodes, 11, 44, 45–6, 55, 61–2, 99, 102, 123, 167, 185, 202n22, 203n24, 210n11, 212–13n25

Black, Michael, 38, 199n3

Boer War, 130

Bonds, Diane S., 31, 195–6n3

Boone, Joseph Allen, 219n21

Booth, Howard J., 76, 189

Boulton, James T., 215n1, 220n2

boundaries, 6, 11, 29, 30, 49, 80, 89, 90, 97, 124, 178, 181. *See also* selfhood boundaries

Bowlby, John, 4, 8, 9, 10, 12, 16, 17, 39, 56, 69, 107

Brandão, Izabel F.O., 208n23

Brault-Dreux, Elise, 189, 192, 220n3

Bretherton, Inge, 9

Brett, Dorothy, 68

Brewster, Achsah, 215n2

Brewster, Earl, 215n2

Brewster, Scott, 100

Brontë, Emily: *Wuthering Heights*, 12

Buber, Martin, 187

Bunyan, John: *The Pilgrim's Progress*, 183

Burgess, Anthony, 142

Burrows, Louie, 37, 48, 113, 170

Bynner, Witter, 23

Canada, 146, 147, 148, 150, 158, 164

Cain (biblical figure), 59, 61, 62, 63, 203n24

Carswell, Catherine, 101

Cavitch, David, 189, 207n22

Cézanne, Paul, 188; *Le Compotier*, 220n2; *Still Life with Apples*, 220n2

Chambers, David, 168

Chambers, Jessie, 3, 10, 18, 19, 38, 48, 156, 157, 163, 167, 168, 170, 176, 178, 179

Chambers, Sarah Ann, 164

child and children, 4, 6, 8, 9, 12, 15, 16, 20, 25, 28, 33, 42, 47, 52, 53, 55–8, 61, 65, 66, 69, 70, 73, 75, 78, 79, 80, 83, 86, 87, 88, 89–90, 91, 92, 93, 94, 95, 99, 101, 103, 104, 108, 109, 112, 114, 126–7, 128, 130, 131–2, 137, 140, 145, 148, 149, 151, 155, 158, 159, 165, 167, 174, 177, 180, 182, 184, 196n7, 196–7n9, 198n19, 201n13, 204–5n7, 211n18, 218n13. *See also* maternal bonds

childhood, 4, 8, 9, 10, 14, 16, 33, 40, 50, 54, 55, 56, 59, 66, 67, 69, 70, 85, 107, 113, 114, 118, 122, 123, 125, 131, 133, 136, 145, 149, 151, 159, 183, 184, 196n7, 204–5n7, 205n10, 206n15

Chung, Chong-wha, 197n13

class, 30, 35, 46, 77, 80, 81, 88, 89, 91, 95, 100, 106, 107, 134–58, 166, 175, 181, 185, 201, 208n1, 213n2, 213–14n3, 214n8, 219n22, 219n25 colliers. *See* mining and miners

Collings, Ernest, 214n9

Congreve, William, 208n3

Connell, Christine M., 123

Conrad, Joseph: *Heart of Darkness*, 25; *Nostromo*, 58

Corke, Helen, 47–8, 51, 156, 170, 200n8, 201n12; "Aftermath," 200n9; "The Cornwall Writing," 200n9; "The Freshwater Diary," 200n9; "The Letter, 200n9; "To Siegmund's Violin," 200n9

Cornwall, 63, 100, 104, 161, 204n29

corporal punishment, 55, 78–9, 204–5n7

Cowan, James C., 11, 19, 22, 35, 54, 55, 76, 83, 84, 85, 86, 99, 167, 195, 201n16, 204n29, 207n17

Crèvecoeur, J. Hector St. John de, 192

Croydon, 82, 139, 168, 170, 171, 217

Cushman, Keith, 81, 139, 205n9

Daleski, H.M., 19, 23, 142, 198n18, 205n12, 212n24

Dante and Beatrice, 10, 102, 178

Darwin, Charles, 19

David and Jonathan (biblical figures), 102

Davies, Rosemary Reeves, 19

Defoe, Daniel, 12, 13

Delany, Paul, 88, 90, 214–15n9

DeLia, Demetria, 78

Dervin, Daniel, 93, 94

detachment (Bowlby), 39–40, 69

devouring mother, 56, 65–6, 90, 91, 104, 117, 185, 202n18, 219n25; meaning of, 91

Dickens, Charles: *Dombey and Son*, 3; *Oliver Twist*, 143

dirt, 30, 86, 87–92, 93, 95, 96, 99, 206n13, 207n16, 207n21; Douglas's explanation of, 89

Doherty, Gerald, 33, 57

Douglas, Mary, 89, 207n16

dualism, 19, 197n13

Eagleton, Terry, 214n4

Eckhard, Petra, 117, 210n13

Eggert, Paul, 138, 202–3n23

Eliot, George, 3; *Adam Bede*, 155

Eliot, T.S., 135

Ellis, David, 64, 134, 155, 157, 174–5, 203n28, 216n6, 216n7, 219n23

engulfing mother, 72, 75, 86, 118, 140, 161, 162, 167

engulfment, 4, 5, 6, 13, 16, 22, 37, 43, 52, 197n13; fear of, 22, 27, 33, 38, 39, 40, 41, 42, 45, 49, 51, 102, 171, 172, 193

equilibrium and disequilibrium, 3–35, 38, 39, 41–2, 43, 44, 45, 46, 63, 79, 84, 105, 117, 121, 161, 193–4, 195n2, 197n13, 198n16, 198n19, 199–200n6, 220–1n3. *See also* balance; trembling balance

estrangement, 27, 39, 55, 62, 86, 117, 118, 119, 120, 122, 124, 125, 126, 132, 141, 164, 165, 167, 168, 169, 176, 177, 178, 193, 212–13n25

Esau (biblical figure), 62

Fairbairn, W.R.D., 4, 79

father figure, 38, 42, 75, 79, 82, 83, 90, 103, 104, 109, 174, 184, 185, 199n1, 202n22. *See also* mother figure

father-daughter relationship, 3, 108–9

father-son relationship, 12, 33, 43, 78, 79, 83, 84, 85, 86–7, 89, 92, 94, 96, 100, 143

Fawcett, Millicent, 219n20

female identification, 33, 73, 74, 75, 76, 83, 84, 94, 96. *See also* masculine identification

Fielding, Henry: *Tom Jones*, 143

Finney, Brian, 215n2

First World War, the. *See* Great War

flood, 122–3, 124, 127, 133, 146, 182, 183, 212–13n25, 215n12, 219n25

Ford, Ford Madox (né Hueffer), 134–5, 137–8

Fox, Elizabeth M., 4

Fox, Pamela, 138, 214n5

Frazer, James George: *Totemism and Exogamy*, 67

Freeman, Mary, 212n24

Freud, Sigmund, 4, 85, 87, 117, 132, 205n11, 210n13, 210n14; "The Uncanny," 117

Fry, Roger, 220n2

fusion, 6, 12, 13, 24, 26, 30, 43, 49, 50, 85, 102, 111, 124, 125, 129, 159, 160, 161, 192, 196n5, 197n11. *See also* merger

Galsworthy, John, 208n4

Game, David, 63, 64, 65, 66, 67, 68, 203n26, 209n6

gamekeepers, 14, 19, 49, 141, 155, 156, 157, 176, 196n6, 214n8

Garnett, David, 18

Garnett, Edward, 47, 77, 95, 112, 143, 200n10

Gaskell, Elizabeth: *North and South*, 158

gender fluidity, 72–4, 84, 103, 140–1

gender identification, 34, 35, 72–105, 162, 204n3. *See also* female identification; masculine identification

gender roles, 64, 91, 140, 148

Germany and German culture, 49, 77, 78, 81, 111, 114, 126, 129, 153, 155, 167, 205n8, 208n3

Gilbert, Sandra M., 135, 143, 189, 215n15

Glitz, Rudolph, 208–9n4

Good, Jan, 76, 204n3

Goode, John, 141, 214n7

Gøtzsche, Kai, 203n28

Great War, the, 61, 166, 197–8n14

Greiffenhagen, Maurice: "An Idyll," 37

Grey, Zane, 203n26

Haeckel, Ernst, 19

Haggs Farm, 157, 167, 168, 176

Handel, George Frideric: "Samson," 81, 200n7

Hardy, Thomas: *Jude the Obscure*, 21; *Tess of the d'Urbervilles*, 155

Harris, Janice Hubbard, 74, 213n3

Harrison, Andrew, 19, 37, 168, 213–14n3

Haughton, Hugh, 117
Hauptmann, Gerhart, 49
Hawthorne, Nathaniel: *The Scarlet Letter*, 19
Hayles, N. Katherine, 22, 31, 32, 110
Hazan, Cindy, 107, 112
heimlich, 117, 132. See also *unheimlich*

Herzinger, Kim A., 199–200n6
Hitler, Adolf, 204n7
Hobson, Harold, 18, 162
Hocking, William Henry, 76
Hoffmann, E.T.A.: "The Sandman," 210n13
Holt, Agnes, 168
homecoming, 35, 157, 159–85, 203n25, 217n9, 220n29
homoeroticism, 75, 76, 77, 103
homosexuality, 76, 77, 201n12
Hough, Graham, 212n24
Huxley, Aldous: *Point Counter Point*, 20, 22, 26
Huxley, Thomas Henry, 19

incest and incestuous desire, 57, 151, 175, 182, 184, 192, 201n11, 202n18, 211n18, 219n21
individuation, 4, 5, 6, 7, 8, 15, 16, 17, 30, 38, 40, 95, 109, 115, 117, 125, 132, 140, 147, 149, 154, 159, 178, 212–13n25. See also separation-individuation
Ingersoll, Earl G., 124
insecure attachments, 28, 33, 37, 114, 127, 131, 159

internal working model (Bowlby), 9, 10, 11, 52, 120, 178, 190
isolation, 3, 12, 13, 14, 15, 27, 34, 37, 39, 42, 43, 44, 45, 47, 50, 52, 53, 54, 60, 63, 79, 80, 87, 88, 89, 125, 129, 131, 144, 189, 193. See also abandonment
Italy, 18, 141, 153, 155, 220n26

Jackson, Dennis, 134
Jacob (biblical figure), 62
Jacobvitz, Deborah, 33, 55
James, Henry, 63
Jesus, 11, 185
Jones family, 82, 139, 205n9
Joyce, James: "The Dead," 218n17
Judas (biblical figure), 11
Jung, Carl Gustav: *Psychology of the Unconscious*, 202n18

Keller, Evelyn, 110
Kim, Sungho, 158
Kinkead-Weekes, Mark, 18, 61, 76, 77, 146, 204n6, 210n12, 211n16, 212n24, 216n8
Kirkpatrick, Lee, 125–6
Klein, Melanie, 4
Kochis, Matthew J., 100
Kohut, Heinz, 201n16
Krockel, Carl, 49, 212n22
Kuttner, Alfred, 86, 87, 205n11

Laing, R.D., 17
Laird, Holly, 200–1n10

landscape, 40, 42, 44, 100, 110–1, 164, 177, 199n4, 209n5

Langbaum, Robert, 211n17

Lawrence, Ada, 170

Lawrence, Arthur, 11, 98, 104, 113, 143, 170, 181, 185, 216n7

Lawrence, D.H.: and equilibrium, 22–3, 26–28; and his father, 11, 17, 72, 80, 93, 98, 99, 104, 136–7, 139, 143; and his mother, 11, 12, 13, 29–30, 34, 37, 48, 73–4, 85, 92, 112–13, 136–7, 143, 163, 172, 173, 175; and his parents, 9, 11–12, 136, 139–41, 174, 181; and paradox, 31–2; and symbolic boundaries of the self, 30–1; and the desirability of balance, 21–2; as a psychological writer, 8, 16–17, 19, 20, 34, 74, 186; attachment tendencies of, 54; childhood and upbringing of, 10, 11, 12, 13, 15, 28, 71, 72, 75, 84, 136–7, 139, 140, 167, 175, 182, 185, 191, 204n29, 216n7; evolving attitude to class of, 137–42; evolving attitude to marriage of, 108–13; self-sabotaging behaviour of, 11, 29; slippery focalization in the fiction of, 63–4

Lawrence, D.H., works:

fiction:

Aaron's Rod, 8, 10, 14, 15, 30, 73, 75, 99, 110, 155, 167, 198n19

"The Blind Man," 144, 148, 150

"The Blue Moccasins," 108, 173, 175–6, 217–18n12

"The Border-Line," 49, 211n19, 216n6

The Boy in the Bush, 12, 34, 61–71, 72, 162, 202–3n23, 203n24, 203n26

"Burns Novel," 111

The Captain's Doll, 134, 143, 153, 166, 217n12

"Daughters of the Vicar," 35, 106–7, 135, 145–7, 149, 152, 153, 163, 213n3, 214n8

"Delilah and Mr Bircumshaw," 200n7

"Elsa Culverwell" (early version of *The Lost Girl*), 154

England, My England and Other Stories, 217n9

The Escaped Cock, 99, 185

The First "Women in Love," 202n21

"The Flying-Fish," 160–1, 162, 184, 216n3

The Fox, 41, 77, 148, 151, 164, 174, 175, 199n5

"Glad Ghosts," 108, 141, 159

"Goose Fair," 108

"Hadrian" (also known as "You Touched Me"), 35, 150–1, 164, 175

"The Harassed Angel" (early version of "The Shades of Spring"), 216n5

"The Horse-Dealer's Daughter," 91, 163, 185

"In Love," 109

"Intimacy" (early version of "The Witch à la Mode"), 170, 172

"Jimmy and the Desperate Woman," 163, 214n8, 216n6

INDEX

Kangaroo, 14, 15, 35, 63, 64, 67, 100–5, 110, 133, 134, 138–9, 161, 162, 195n3, 204n29

The Ladybird, 112, 144

Lady Chatterley's Lover, 14, 35, 74, 99, 100, 112, 134, 148, 155–8

Lady Chatterley's Lover, Version 2, 155

"The Last Straw" (also known as "Fannie and Annie"), 165–6, 214n8, 216n8

The Lost Girl, 35, 73, 74, 107, 141, 144, 152–4, 155, 162, 184, 220n26

"Love Among the Haystacks," 35, 59, 112, 113–16, 121, 160

"The Lovely Lady," 173, 174–5

"The Man Who Loved Islands," 14–15, 25, 112, 180, 190

"The Man Who Was Through with the World," 15

"A Modern Lover," 75, 168–70, 177, 179, 214n8

"Monkey Nuts," 216–17n8

"Mother and Daughter," 173–4

Mr Noon, 18, 36, 37, 106, 108, 111, 162, 198n15

"New Eve and Old Adam," 13, 23

"None of That!" 216n8

"Odour of Chrysanthemums," 191, 220n29

"The Old Adam," 35, 82–3, 85

"The Overtone," 35, 111–112, 209n5

"Paul Morel" (early version of *Sons and Lovers*), 208n2

The Plumed Serpent, 74, 99

"A Prelude," 164–5

"The Primrose Path," 217n9

"The Princess," 17, 109, 144–5, 216n8, 220n26

"The Prussian Officer," 35, 76–81, 83, 200n7, 204n6, 205n8

The Prussian Officer and Other Stories, 179, 181, 213n26

"A Pure Witch," 74

The Rainbow, 5, 12, 25, 27, 28, 30, 31, 32, 35, 54, 56, 74, 106, 108, 109–10, 112, 113, 116–33, 146, 160, 190, 193, 195–6n3, 198n18, 208n4, 210n11, 210n14, 211–12n20, 213n26, 215n12

"Rawdon's Roof," 30–1, 110

"The Rocking-Horse Winner," 78, 167, 210n14

"The Saga of Siegmund" (early version of *The Trespasser*), 200n9

"Samson and Delilah," 200n7, 217n9

"Second-Best," 141, 181

"The Shades of Spring," 10, 157, 176–8, 214n8, 216n5

"The Shadow in the Rose Garden," 176, 179–81, 184, 214n8

Sons and Lovers, 10, 16, 30, 32, 35, 47, 48, 56, 73, 76, 81, 82, 83–97, 98, 99, 100, 107–8, 112, 135, 137, 139–40, 144, 148, 156, 158, 160, 163, 167, 172, 174, 175, 185, 196n8, 206n13, 207n18, 211n15, 211n16, 211–12n20, 214n4, 216n7, 219n19

St Mawr, 24, 110, 162, 173, 209n5

St Mawr and Other Stories, 209n5, 215n2

"Sun," 141

"The Thorn in the Flesh," 29, 205n8

"Tickets Please," 72, 91

The Trespasser, 23, 34, 47–53, 202n23

"Two Blue Birds," 106, 108

"Two Marriages" (early version of "Daughters of the Vicar"), 106, 145, 146, 147

"The Vicar's Garden," (early version of "The Shadow in the Rose Garden"), 179, 180

The Virgin and the Gipsy, 80, 109, 144, 182–4, 214n8, 215n10, 219n23, 220n26

The White Peacock, 3, 7, 13, 18–19, 23, 24, 25, 34, 37–46, 50, 52, 53, 63, 69, 76, 103, 107, 110, 139, 141, 164, 168, 199–200n6, 199n20, 216n3

"The White Stocking," 211n19

"The Witch à la Mode," 51, 168, 170–2

"The Woman Who Rode Away," 17, 109, 216n8, 217–18n12

The Woman Who Rode Away and Other Stories, 74

"The Woman Who Wanted to Disappear," 184–5, 203n25, 220n27

Women in Love, 3, 8, 13, 23–4, 25–6, 31, 33, 34, 52, 53–9, 60, 61, 66, 70, 76, 77, 83, 86, 91, 102, 107, 108, 109, 111, 113, 159, 167, 177, 180, 184, 193, 198n18, 198n19, 201n15, 202n21, 204n4, 206n13, 208n23

non-fiction:

A Propos of "Lady Chatterley's Lover," 215n14

"Aristocracy," 189

"[Autobiographical Fragment]," 137, 215n1

The Crown, 21–2, 24, 26, 45

"Democracy," 192, 193

"Education of the People," 173

Fantasia of the Unconscious, 8, 12, 20, 73, 75, 113, 161, 173, 187, 196n7, 197–8n14, 217n10, 220n1

Foreword to *Fantasia of the Unconscious*, 213n1

Foreword to *Women in Love*, 61

"Getting On," 137

"Introduction to These Paintings," 188

Late Essays and Articles, 215n1, 202n2

"Love," 22, 192

"Morality and the Novel," 188, 195n2

Movements in European History, 81

"Myself Revealed," 137

"Nottingham and the Mining Countryside," 143

"Pan in America," 209n5

Prologue to *Women in Love*, 76, 204n4

Psychoanalysis and the Unconscious, 3, 8, 19, 112–13, 213n1
"The Reality of Peace," 16, 22, 98, 200n7, 202n19
"Reflections on the Death of a Porcupine," 41
"[Return to Bestwood]," 137
"The State of Funk," 136, 158
Studies in Classic American Literature, 19, 136, 159, 186, 192–3
Study of Thomas Hardy, 21, 73, 114, 126, 127, 187, 198n18, 212n21, 220n28
"The Two Principles," 19, 197n12
"We Need One Another," 134, 194
"Which Class I Belong To," 136, 137, 141
"Whitman," 14

plays:
A Collier's Friday Night, 94–5, 137, 156
The Daughter-in-Law, 9, 35, 148
The Fight for Barbara, 143, 214
The Married Man, 208n3
Touch and Go, 34, 59–61, 80, 138, 158

poetry:
"Bavarian Gentians," 217–18n12
"Bereavement," 175
Birds, Beasts and Flowers, 191
"Blueness," 217–18n12
"Climbing Up," 138
"Figs," 54
"Finding Your Level," 138
"Fish," 189, 191, 220n3
"Humiliation," 36
Look! We Have Come Through! 191
"Man and Bat," 97–8, 191, 192, 221n4
"Manifesto," 191–2
"Monologue of a Mother," 74
"Mosquito," 191, 192
"My Naughty Book," 207n21
"New Heaven and Earth," 191
"Prestige," 138
"Red-herring," 137, 156
"The Saddest Day," 138
"She Looks Back," 217n10
"Snake," 97, 98–9, 191, 192, 221n4
"Up He Goes!–" 134, 138, 153
"Wedlock," 36, 191

Lawrence, Emily, 170
Lawrence, Ernest, 175
Lawrence, Frieda (née Weekley), 10, 18, 29, 64, 74, 80, 81, 85, 100, 110, 111, 112, 113, 143, 157, 163, 182, 201n14, 202n18, 203n28, 208n3, 209n5, 216n6, 217n10, 219n22; infidelity of, 18; "*Not I, But the Wind...*" 207n18
Lawrence, Lydia, 37, 48, 83, 113, 114, 137, 141, 147, 160, 163, 167, 168, 172, 173, 175, 209n7
leadership, 23, 65, 67, 153, 202n18
Leavis, F.R., 135–6, 146, 215n11
Levinas, Emmanuel, 187
Levy, Eric P., 31, 107
Lot's wife (biblical figure), 167, 217n10

Low, Barbara, 205n11
Lyons-Ruth, Karlen, 33, 55

Macartney, H.B., 47, 48, 201n12
Mackenzie, Compton, 108
Maddox, Brenda, 218n17
Mahler, Margaret S., 4–8, 24, 32, 39, 42, 50, 69, 117, 159, 160, 161, 162, 176, 196n5; *The Psychological Birth of the Human Infant*, 3, 5
Mailer, Norman, 74, 75
manhood, 60, 62, 65, 81, 91, 112, 156, 205n8. *See also* masculinity
Mansfield, Elizabeth, 48, 51
Mansfield, Katherine, 189, 201n11, 202n18
Marks III, W.S., 210n14
marriage, 13, 21, 23, 32, 35, 40, 41, 42, 49, 62, 64, 84, 86, 89, 92, 96, 98, 104, 106–33, 137, 142, 144, 145, 146, 148, 150, 151, 152, 154, 155, 163, 164, 165, 166, 175, 179, 181, 184, 193, 195–6n3, 198n19, 208n1–3, 208–9n4, 209n5, 209n6, 209n8, 211n16, 211n19, 219n22
Martin, Graham, 135, 147
masculine identification, 74, 76, 81, 82, 83, 84, 90, 100, 103, 104, 105, 167, 169, 178, 207n22. *See also* female identification
masculine maternal, 75, 103
masculinity, 29, 72, 79, 80, 86, 99, 100–1, 102, 147, 206n13. *See also* manhood
maternal bonds, 5, 13, 14, 15, 18, 32, 33, 37, 39–40, 48, 50–1, 57, 60, 66, 65, 95, 96, 107, 113, 118–19, 122, 125, 173, 180, 206n14, 211n20, 216–17n8
maternal security, 58, 103, 159, 161
McAleer, Kevin, 205n8
McCabe, T.H., 191
McLeod, Arthur, 11
merger, 4, 5, 7, 11, 22, 27, 29, 30, 32, 37, 39, 42, 49, 52, 86, 100, 105, 121, 122, 125, 126, 128, 129, 140, 149, 150, 154, 190, 191, 192, 197n11; desire for, 12–13, 28, 40, 45, 50, 112, 123, 171; and autonomy, 4, 7, 16, 20, 22, 24, 26, 35, 37, 38, 39, 42, 49, 96, 102, 140, 190, 193, 194. *See also* fusion
Merrild, Knud, 203n28
Meyers, Jeffrey, 75, 76, 137
Miliaris, Barbara S., 142
Miller, Alice, 78–9, 204–5n7
Millett, Kate, 135
mining and miners, 59–60, 68, 85, 87, 88, 89, 90, 94, 97–8, 117, 137, 143, 146, 147, 148, 152, 154, 155, 156, 163, 200n7, 206n13, 214n4, 214n8, 216n7, 217n9, 220n29
mirroring (Winnicott), 55, 61, 91, 110, 179–80, 185, 201n16, 219n18
Morrell, Lady Ottoline, 201n15
mother. *See* devouring mother; proxy mother; unreliable mother
mother figure, 35, 66, 90, 148, 151, 161, 164, 165, 166, 173, 175, 179, 181, 182, 183, 201n13, 216–17n8, 219n25, 220n29. *See also* father figure
motherhood and mothering, 4, 18, 42, 51, 58, 59, 71, 78, 153, 211n18, 217n10

mother-son attachment, 83–4, 92, 94, 96, 97, 147, 148, 151, 219n21

Mountsier, Robert, 104

Moynahan, Julian, 53, 174, 212n24

Munholland, Kristine A., 9

Murry, John Middleton, 54, 163, 201n11, 216n6, 216n7; *Between Two Worlds*, 201n14

Neville, George, 208n3

Nietzsche, Friedrich, 49

Nin, Anaïs, 75, 204n3

Nixon, Cornelia, 132, 212n24

narcissism, 6, 17, 34, 56, 57, 67, 78, 88, 91, 92, 96, 109, 122, 123, 126, 140, 144, 148, 179, 180, 181, 185, 204n29, 206n15, 216n6

Noah (biblical figure), 123, 127

nostalgia, 122, 149, 159–60, 161, 167, 168, 169, 176, 177, 178

novel of manners, 106, 208n1

object relations, 79

oedipal issues, 57, 72, 79, 80, 82, 83–5, 95, 117, 149, 211n18, 216–17n8. *See also* pre-oedipal issues

O'Keefe, Georgia, "The Lawrence Tree," 209n5

otherness, 29, 35, 91, 93, 186–94, 220–1n3; defined, 187

Panken, Shirley, 86

paradox, 22, 26, 28, 29, 30, 31–5, 38, 39, 41, 50, 84, 87, 100, 102, 116, 118, 127, 128, 133, 140, 152, 161, 162, 184, 187, 190, 192, 193, 195n2, 212n24, 220n28; and balance, 22, 27; and equilibrium, 16, 19, 26, 27, 28, 117; of attachment, 3–35, 59, 75, 118, 121, 131, 189, 194

Parmenter, Ross, 160, 216n3

Paxton, Nancy, 182, 219nn20&23

phallicism and phallic symbolism, 93, 99–100, 207n20, 209n5, 213n2

Pinion, F.B., 212n24

Pinker, J.B., 202n21

Pinkney, Tony, 199n2, 199–200n6, 211–12n20

Poe, Edgar Allan, 192; "The Fall of the House of Usher," 31

Poland and Polish descent, 110, 114, 116, 120, 121, 128, 129

Pollnitz, Christopher, 189, 220–21n3

pre-oedipal issues, 4, 35, 80, 84, 85, 186, 197n11. *See also* oedipal issues

Pritchard, R.E., 172, 204n6, 217–18n12

projection, 51, 52, 54, 65, 67, 70, 80, 101, 129, 132, 155, 160, 190

Proust, Marcel, 199n4; *Swann's Way*, 9, 40

proxy mother and motherhood, 18, 33, 39, 49, 57, 58, 115, 120, 128, 146, 153, 164, 165, 167

psychological hollowness, 15, 25–6, 56, 61, 70, 78, 80, 91, 101, 102, 190, 202n19

Radford, Dollie, 104

Rananim, 64, 140

rapprochement (Mahler), 5, 6, 24, 39, 84, 159, 160, 161, 162, 166, 171, 172, 176, 177, 178, 179 reliability and unreliability, 6, 18, 33, 37, 53, 55, 56, 58, 59, 60, 61, 65, 66, 69, 71, 104, 114, 167, 174, 177, 180, 182, 185, 190, 201n16

Rhys, Jean: *Wide Sargasso Sea*, 12

Richardson, Samuel: *Pamela*, 143

Richtofen, Baroness von, 143

Roberts, Neil, 48, 103, 135, 158, 186, 189, 190, 200n8, 208n23

Ross, Michael, 213n26

Ruderman, Judith, 8, 35, 62, 65, 66, 67, 68–9, 104, 197n11, 202n18, 203n24

Russell, Ken, 54

Ruth (biblical figure), 55

Sagar, Keith, 133

Salgādo, Gāmini, 31, 85, 118

Samson (biblical figure), 44, 45–6, 200n7

Sanders, Scott, 139, 147, 148, 155, 212n24, 213n2, 213–14n3

Sargent, M. Elizabeth, 186, 187

Savage, Henry, 76

Schapiro, Barbara Ann, 32, 35, 73, 80, 86, 87, 90–1, 91–2, 93–4, 96, 121, 122, 123, 130, 180, 189, 212n24, 216–17n8, 217–18n12

Scheckner, Peter, 138

Schneider, Daniel J., 16, 19–20, 197n11, 198n16, 199n6

Schopenhauer, Arthur, 49

Schorer, Mark, 205n12

Schwartz, Murray M., 197n11

Schwarz, Daniel R., 84

Scott, James F., 205n8

Second World War, the, 79

security and insecurity, 5, 12, 16, 18, 31, 33, 36, 38, 58, 68, 76, 84, 85, 103, 114, 115, 116, 117, 123, 124, 125, 128, 144, 145, 150, 154, 159, 160, 162, 166, 171, 172, 177, 192. *See also* maternal security

selfhood, 4, 6, 16, 27, 29, 30, 31, 36, 39, 49, 56, 62, 89, 90, 91, 96, 97, 99, 121, 122, 130, 131, 133, 161, 183, 189, 193, 199–200n6, 207n16, 213–14n3

selfhood boundaries, 3, 30, 49, 50, 97, 112, 121

self-sufficiency, 12, 14, 16, 17, 49, 50, 54, 69, 70, 71

Seltzer, Thomas, 213n1

separation, 3, 4–8, 11–12, 14, 15, 23, 32–3, 39, 40, 45, 46, 50, 54, 63, 64, 69, 74, 86, 90, 92, 94, 125, 133, 140, 159, 160, 171, 187, 191, 192, 197n11, 212n25; healthy separation, 85, 87, 132

separation-individuation (Mahler), 4, 6, 8, 11, 178. *See also* individuation; separation

sex and sexuality, 17, 23, 24, 48, 51, 73, 74, 75–7, 83, 91, 94, 99, 112, 134, 135, 144, 155, 158, 165, 168, 175, 198n19, 199–200n6, 200–1n10, 201n12, 203n26, 204n4, 208n3, 209n5, 213n1, 213n2, 216n6, 216n8, 220n26. *See also* homoeroticism; homosexuality; phallicism

Shakespeare, William, 208n3; *Macbeth*, 202n17

Sheldon-Keller, Adrienne E., 9, 36
Siegel, Carol, 75
Skinner, John Russell, 66
Skinner, Mollie, 34, 63, 64; "The House of Ellis," 66, 202–3n23
Sklenicka, Carol, 196n7, 205n12
Sleeping Beauty, 150
Smith, Anne, 204n3
social class. *See* class
solipsism, 73, 191, 192
Spencer, Herbert, 19; *The Principles of Sociology*, 198n16
Squires, Michael, 106, 167
Steele, Bruce, 103, 210n14, 217n9
Stepansky, Paul E., 4
Stevens, Hugh, 77–8, 204n6
Stewart, Jack, 80, 199–200n6
Stoll, John E., 199n1
Storch, Margaret, 38, 42, 43, 85, 94, 96, 199n20
suicide and attempted suicide, 41, 47, 48, 49, 53, 129, 163, 184
surety, 5, 178, 195–6n3, 211n19
symbiosis (Mahler), 5, 6, 7, 12, 16, 24, 40, 42, 117, 196n5

Taylor, Rachel Annand, 72, 84
Thornton, Weldon, 160, 165, 166
Toland, John, 204n7
trauma, 48, 79
trembling balance, 5, 22, 26, 195n2. *See also* balance; equilibrium
trespass and trespassers, 29, 49, 117, 121, 176, 177, 187, 200–1n10

Tressell, Robert, 214n5
trust and distrust, 29, 56, 60, 61, 66, 70, 104, 123, 156
Turner, John, 25, 31, 86, 140, 190–1, 205n11, 208n3, 210n14, 212–13n25

unheimlich, 117, 119, 210n13. *See also heimlich*
unreliable mother, 56, 59, 66, 71, 174, 180, 182
Urang, Sarah, 142

Van Gogh, Vincent, 188
violence, 53, 54, 55, 60–1, 62, 70, 77, 79, 80, 83, 92, 93, 94, 98, 99, 103, 104, 112, 136, 175

Wagner, Richard, 49
Wasson, Richard, 139, 158, 213n2
Watson, Garry, 186, 187
Weekley, Agnes, 183
Weekley, Barbara (Barby), 182, 219n23
Weekley, Ernest, 219n23
Weiss, Daniel, 85, 96
West, Malcolm L., 9, 36
Wexler, Joyce, 161, 216n4
Williams, Linda Ruth, 31
Williams, Tennessee: *I Rise in Flame, Cried the Phoenix*, 142
Williamson, Alan, 32, 72, 75, 83, 86, 95, 206–7n15
Wilson, Nicola, 138, 214n5

Winnicott, D.W., 4, 15, 28, 93, 219n18

Wood, James, 27, 31, 108

Wood, Paul, 17

Woolf, Virginia, 135; *The Years*, 208n4

Wordsworth, William, 213n26; "My Heart Leaps Up," 133

World War One. *See* Great War.

World War Two. *See* Second World War.

Worthen, John, 9, 113, 137, 141, 152, 186, 202n21, 208n2, 209n7

Wright, T.R., 203n24, 210n11

Wyndham, John: *The Chrysalids*, 12

Yeats, W.B.: *A Vision*, 26–7

Zeifman, Debra, 107, 112